Songs of Life and Grace

Songs of Life and Grace

Linda Scott DeRosier

THE UNIVERSITY PRESS OF KENTUCKY

Publication of this volume was made possible in part by a grant
from the National Endowment for the Humanities.

Scholarly publisher for the Commonwealth,
serving Bellarmine College, Berea College, Centre
College of Kentucky, Eastern Kentucky University,
The Filson Historical Society, Georgetown College,
Kentucky Historical Society, Kentucky State University,
Morehead State University, Murray State University,
Northern Kentucky University, Transylvania University,
University of Kentucky, University of Louisville,
and Western Kentucky University.
All rights reserved.

Editorial and Sales Offices: The University Press of Kentucky
663 South Limestone Street, Lexington, Kentucky 40508–4008

07 06 05 04 03   5 4 3 2 1

Frontispiece: Life and Grace Preston, 1936.

Library of Congress Cataloging-in-Publication Data

DeRosier, Linda Scott, 1941–
    Songs of Life and Grace / Linda Scott DeRosier.
      p. cm.
    ISBN 0-8131-2276-7 (hardcover : alk. paper)
    1. Preston, Lifie Jay, 1917–1994. 2. Preston, Grace, 1915–1994.
3. DeRosier, Linda Scott, 1941– 4. Appalachians (People)—
Kentucky—Social life and customs. 5. Kentucky—Biography.
6. Appalachian Region, Southern—Biography. 7. Appalachian
Region, Southern—Social life and customs. I. Title.
    CT275.P84233D47 2003
    976.9'1043'092—dc21

                                                        2003007975

This book is printed on acid-free recycled paper meeting
the requirements of the American National Standard
for Permanence in Paper for Printed Library Materials.

Manufactured in the United States of America.

For Life and Grace, who sang without training or trial, but sang nonetheless.

For Brett Preston Scott, Patricia Preston Greer, Ryen Preston Greer, and Amanda McKinley Greer, whose legacy is to sing . . . sing . . . then keep on singing.

For Arthur DeRosier and Michael Greer, who have added the score to our Sweet Songster.

CONTENTS

To many, maybe most, of my people, the force that draws us ever home to eastern Kentucky is like the pull of the moon on the tide. Most of us who leave look to the day when circumstance will allow us to return. However long we may stay away, we never see ourselves as out for good, and that was truer of each generation preceding my own.

I left the hills of Appalachia many years ago, but the language, the lore, and the life lessons I learned in those hills never left me. When Momma and Daddy died within three weeks of each other, breaking my closest blood tie with eastern Kentucky, my attempt to deal with the emotional remains of their deaths resulted in *Creeker: A Woman's Journey*. Writing that memoir enabled me to return to the home place and revisit my parents and grandparents. Indeed, it allowed me to look in on them at a time in their lives when they were still young and vital and shaping their world and mine. It brought back to me a young Life and Grace Preston, far more vivid and powerful than the ever-fading old folks they had become in their last years. After that book was published, I received a number of letters from folks who read and related to my *Creeker* experiences and sent along stories of their own histories. More than a few of those who wrote suggested that I tell more about my mother, father, and the other folks they'd come to know in Creeker Country. Others—especially family members—asked me to write a more comprehensive and historical view of our people. They shared genealogical records with me, proposing that I look back to the first decade of the nineteenth century, when our forebears marched up the creeks and into the narrow valleys of what would become eastern Kentucky. Their idea was for me to look back a couple of generations, maybe more, to see what the folks who preceded us were really like, how they lived, especially how they made a living off those hogback ridges and uncertain seasons—that sort of thing.

I began this project excited by the prospect of putting my academic skills to work researching family history, thereby putting some distance between my personal life and my writing. I loved the idea of tracing my extended family through public records, then putting flesh on those bones through informal interviews with distant cousins who remembered scraps of information their mammaw or pappaw had passed along. Such a project promised the passion of personal inquiry while providing the safety of academic distance. Sure, I could do that.

Between bouts of genealogical research on the Internet, I spent time with some of the folks who had known one set or another of my grandparents or great-grandparents. I also contacted cousins who remembered Momma and Daddy when they were not yet my parents, when they were Lifie Jay and Gracie (a nickname my mother hated, by the way), yet to meet and know each other. As I met with folks, I found that those people did indeed have stories of my family. Those reports, however, were intertwined with anecdotes of their own—tales of going on a drunk with my infamous uncle Burns or of going with their mother to stay all day with Grandma Emmy, descriptions of passing around hand-me-downs from family to family. Even when the visits did not glean stories germane to the project I envisioned working on, the visiting itself became part of the story. I often found myself yearning to stay longer, to sit and savor time that could only be termed unproductive if I were to stay on task.

It was as if the past forty-some years fell away and I was once again swapping stories out on the porch, or in the kitchen, or most times right in the living room. These people had changed—as had I—but together as we reminisced, the past came alive for us through bringing back the family members, most long dead, and comparing our stories, letting each other in on long-held secrets. Bear in mind that many of these secrets were widely known in the community though unacknowledged family to family. Sometimes somebody would say, "Now don't you write this down . . . or if you do, make sure you don't say I said it."

So many sentences began, "I remember the first time I ever saw your mother," or "I'll never forget what Lifie Jay said about . . ." While I enjoyed these intensely personal stories, they had little place in the sweeping historical work I envisioned. Still, I drew such comfort from the visits that I began rationalizing why I should squander my time just visiting.

Another part of my journey involved tracking down the remaining contents of my maternal grandmother's trunk. While Momma was pretty good at keeping records, we lost our recorded history, along with everything else we owned, when our house burned in December 1955, so all our letters, pictures, deeds, and such date from that time. When Momma and Daddy died, Sister and I could not deal with closing their home and carting away all vestige of their existence. That house was sitting just as they'd left it for more than a year when Sister and I packed up the contents of Daddy's desk and my son, Brett, pulled several boxes of old papers—most predating the '55 fire—from their attic. Those papers, many from my grandmother's trunk—letters to Grandma Emmy from three of her sons, four of her daughters, two sons-in-law, and various others—changed the course and character of this project.

Included in this packet, along with many postcards, letters, deeds, and pictures, was an envelope, posted October 4, 1941, that contained three folded, yellowed tablet sheets. And there, scrawled in pencil, was probably the only letter my daddy ever wrote to my mother. It was written when Daddy was staying in Aunt Polly Blevins's boardinghouse and working the mines in Hemphill, West Virginia. At the time, Momma and I were staying with Grandma Emmy at Three Forks of Greasy in the house where both of us were born. As I read Daddy's letter, I knew that eventually I wanted to write a more personal book about our World War II years, the time spent shuttling back and forth by train, bus, and car between the coal camp and home. But initially I put this away, filing it in that to-write-someday folder located somewhere behind the present historical work, and then soldiered on.

As part of my research project, I was committed to looking up genealogical records of my family, and I extended my Internet search with a visit to the Kentucky History Center, in Frankfort. The place is a treasury of information on American, Kentucky, and individual family history, all accessible to the general public. This was my first exploration into the world of genealogical research, so armed with laptop computer—pencil and tablet at the ready—I found three files and began to read and copy information. Within the first forty-five minutes, I discovered a family member named "Peker." As I came upon this record, I shifted my eyes to either side of me to see if any of these serious researchers could look on my paper. Then my irreverent daddy spoke to me from beyond the grave: "What'd you think you were going to find, girl? You knew you'd not have to look back very far to find a peckerwood in our family. I'd say our history's full of 'em." As I sat there grinning, this work took a turn toward the personal, as I thought, *I can't do this. I am not yet ready to follow the trail of serious historians, the checking of records, or even the reading of oral histories. I'm going to have to leave the critical research, the history—oral and otherwise—to those who have the desire, the will, and the seriousness of purpose to do such things. I have served my academic time, and I am through with that.*

That decision jerked me right back into my own little four-person nuclear family, and to tell you the Lord's own truth, I'd be a lot more comfortable writing about almost anything else. From the minute I began working on *Creeker*, it was clear to me that I was somehow going to have to come to terms with stories that did not always put me—or the folks I loved—in the very best light. Surprisingly, writing about my own missteps was not as difficult as I had expected it to be. I already knew pretty-well where the snakes were hiding, so I didn't have to turn over a one of those rocks without preparing myself first. Even then, I knew I was a match for any reptile under there; I'd wrestled with that scaly sucker before. I was not prepared, however, for the complexities and outright contradictions I discovered as I sorted through long-unquestioned memories about Momma and Daddy, their brothers and sisters, and back of them, Grandma Emmy and Pop Pop's generation. As more stories came, I grew ever less comfortable with their content.

One of the first results of peering into the recent past is that I soon came to understand just how many versions exist of the truth I thought was my very own. From the time I began researching my historical work, every time I went back home, somebody—often several somebodies—would come up to talk to me about some story in *Creeker*. After telling their favorite piece, they would follow with "but why didn't you tell about . . . ?" Often, but not always, the stories were about Momma or Daddy or some member of their extended family. Sometimes they were tales I had already heard in some form or another; sometimes they were a correction of an occurrence I had written in my own version. While this kind of correction made me want to run back to the safety of my original project, it was too late. Daddy had already told me how to go—right into the middle of it. That meant there was no way to get around focusing on those folks I knew best, family and friends—just like I had done with *Creeker*, but backing up a bit.

I think most of us do little interpretation of our experiences as we are having them. We make our way into and through situations, all the while assuming those circumstances are normal or common and our next step is somehow already programmed, lying dormant in the step we just took. We get so busy taking those steps—just living our lives—that we have no time to reflect on them. While I was doing my own brand of stepping, I never took a lot of time to think about whether each footfall was a move forward or backward on the path to where I thought I might be headed. Just like nearly everybody else, I was trying hard to keep it rational and get on down life's road. Once I began to look back on my experiences, however, it became clear that a number of particulars I had been certain were true or false were only true or false by me. The most unpalatable truth I uncovered was that my life has been so everlasting easy—and okay, happy, even—while my mother's life . . . well, it was much too full of hard work and illness, real or imagined, and worst of all, the pains of *might-have-been*.

Since I was privileged to go school on Momma's life, I doubt I've had a might-have-been hanging over my head in the last forty years. If something looked as if it could perchance become a might-have-been, I just flat figured out a way to allow myself do it. This is not necessarily a good thing. I'm not saying here that the decision to turn every might-have-been into a *was* made me a clever chooser. I'm not even suggesting that most of those moves were wise ones. What I am saying is that just knowing I was the one doing the choosing has made living with the results of each choice easier for me. I've never questioned who is rowing this old boat—even when she's going over the falls. But Momma? Well, that's a different story—a story I've been tracing for the past quarter century.

I would love to tell the stories of Momma's vivacity, hard work, perseverance, and humor, and leave stories of her tendency toward hypochondria and exaggeration to those of us who knew her. At first I tried to write it that way, but I found the results to be sterile and not at all reflective of the mother who created me just about as close to her image as possible. So I suppose when I began writing this book, I was hoping that going back and exploring more of our history would in some way absolve me of any responsibility for Momma's fulfillment deficit. I should note here that redemption is big among those of us who grew up keeping close to the Cross, as it were.

From its beginning this book has been more difficult to write than *Creeker*, because I have had to work harder to get it right. *Creeker* was easy to get right, because it was *my* story, *my* memories, thus it was always right—by me. I lived through all the things I told about and simply recounted what I recalled, precisely as I remembered it. It was also easier for me to set to paper, because I really never expected much of anybody to read it—beyond my immediate family and close friends, that is. Less than a month after it was published, I received the first letter from a third cousin once removed, informing me that I had transposed two great-uncles, an error that could have been avoided "if you had only checked with . . ." Well, since this effort was to be less about me and more about family, less about the times I lived through and more about the period before I was born, I vowed to do more "checking with." In nine months I put more than seventeen thousand miles on my Jeep—considerably more on my body—in a valiant attempt at "checking with." I have concluded, however, that trying to get consensus between and among folks who recall a number of versions of the same story—not to mention those who are intent on suppressing a version of said story—is a job for somebody better trained in mediation than I am. I'd have a better chance of getting Israelis and Palestinians to agree on the occupation of the West Bank.

Over the past couple of years, I have talked with a whole host of folks, done a modicum of genealogical research, and read a lot of history, all of which has informed this effort. I have tried to correct the facts I got wrong last time—the transposing of great-uncles, for example—but some things I am flat not going to change. That means I continue to talk about people and events that some folks would just as soon not remember. If that gives some of my second, or third, or fifteenth cousins a permanent case of the sour turn . . . well, so be it. *Creeker* was pure recollection, based on my recall—my memory—and I told my version of the truth. As for this book, I have tried to get it straight, based on the memories of a whole gaggle of people and all the historical record I could uncover. Still, the stories herein are not pure truth. They are strained through my sensibilities, and perhaps my strainer is not quite so fine as the sieve of the cousin who said to me, "Linda, our family was Southern. We were not Appalachian."

For the record, some members of my family are much more refined, others far more pious, and just about to a person they're financially better off than I am. I have not chosen to write about their reconstituted remembrances, because stories of fancy folks who won't admit to knowing a "slop bucket" from a "slop jar" require repressing or revising the very experiences that remain a source of strength for me. These are my people I'm writing about—folks bound to me by blood or history—and my generation built our lives on their bones. I owe it to them to document as truthfully as possible what they went through. Far as I can tell, not one of them is pure saint or sinner, and if I am to tell their stories in any credible way, I have to tell as much of it as I know. If I do that, some of each (saint and sinner) is sure to show.

The people in this book did not have the advantage of our historical perspective; they made their decisions and lived out their consequences. Just like the rest of us, they did the best they could with all the truth they knew and understood right then. These stories are as close as I can come to bringing back that place, those times, and those people. I think we grow up and grow old certain in our minds that we know the truth of things, faith positive in our version of our own reality. Well, memory is a funny thing. That anchored image of circumstance appears to move and change on us depending upon where we happen to be standing to view it at the time. Maybe memoir is each writer's own paltry attempt to stop the evolving and re-volving apparition of his truth—hold the damn thing still so he can get a bead on it—look at it once and for all in stop time.

What has evolved here is a personal story of my mother, Grace; my daddy, Life; my sister, Pat; and me—a series of stories, really—stories about how Life and Grace got together, lived together, died together. It begins with their first meeting on a dusty road at Three Forks of Greasy Creek in August 1936 and continues through their deaths three weeks apart in the big house Daddy built on Sant Preston Branch just west of Kentucky Route 40's last blind curve before the River Narrows. But it does not end there. Though the primary focus of the work is on Life and Grace, there are segues into their respective histories from the time their forebears came to eastern Kentucky, back when it was still part of Virginia. Since surroundings shape us as we are shaping surroundings, there are stories of Momma's and Daddy's extended families and the communities where they lived and died.

Grandma Emmy's letters led me to look more closely at our years in the coal camp in West Virginia. As I became ever more involved in the world described in those letters, this project became more and more a story about coal—about the ways coal mining in eastern Kentucky shaped Momma, Daddy, Sister, and me. I suppose what drives this extended attempt at exploring one family's story of coal is that ours is a story not much told.

One remarkable difference between the home folks' response to *Creeker* and that of my colleagues in academe was in the latter's questions and discussion centering on the few pages I included on Daddy's work at the mines. At academic conferences, after I read from *Creeker*, someone—often several someones—always questioned why I had not taken a stand on the issue of coal mining in Appalachia. In every case, colleagues seemed to think there was only one stand to be taken and I had missed an opportunity to demonstrate the degree to which I was horrified by the effects of coal mining on my home country. The outcome of such conversations left me at a loss to take any sort of arguable position, much less articulate it.

As I met with people from home to gather material for this book, the coal question kept cropping up, but this time I was asking it of them. Most folks who grew up when and where I did—including some few men of my generation who worked the mines for a decade or two—share my sense of ambiguity as to what the coal mines have given eastern Kentuckians versus what those mines took away. Thus, in this effort I found myself spending considerable time and energy discussing coal camps and coal mining. Still, I have only scratched the surface here. There are no simple explanations of the positive and negative effects of coal

on my region. Each of us has a different perspective, and this work re-
flects only my thoughts. I found it impossible to look at my mother and
father's life together without delving into the effect of coal mining on
my family. My colleagues who study populations for a living don't seem
to understand why anyone might have made the choice to go into the
mines when he could have gone into a cleaner and safer occupation—or
better yet, could have made his living off the land as did his father. In
my family, the choice was simple. My people were a part of the patch-
off tradition, but the land ran out, the ground worked out, and we chose
not to starve out.

Acknowledgments

I'm owing here and I know it, since this book—like every other thing in my life—is just one more group project. Setting thoughts to paper is hard—especially for those of us who take up writing in our old age—so anybody with a lick of sense doesn't try to go it alone. While it may be true that I am sitting by myself before this computer screen, I have not been unaccompanied in putting this work together—far from it.

As I set about trying to thank the folks without whose everlasting support this song would never have been sung, I know full-well somebody will be left out and I will suck sorrow for forgetting. If I've neglected to name you, please know you're in my heart even though not in my head at the moment. In an attempt at making my own sense of the past two hundred or so years of my people's history in Kentucky's hill country, I have drawn on the collective experience of sundry folks who have segued in and out of my life over the past half-century. In no particular order, I thank the following for their most generous help:

Billie Edyth Ward taught me way back in eighth grade that the first rule on the road to learning is to show up ready to run. Now, almost fifty years later, Ms. Ward is still living by that rule, and her generosity in opening her head and home to me has been a gift that keeps on giving.

John Mitchell Preston, born a quarter mile down the road from me a couple of decades before I made the scene—and his wife, the late Ruth Preston—filled me in on the culture of early Two-Mile and environs, and their great good fellowship made the most of short but sweet visits.

In October 2001 I was reminded at the United Baptist funeral of Herman Preston (Great-Uncle Ernest's boy) that, though some things in eastern Kentucky might have changed, the church stands strong today. I'm proud to be blood kin of a man like Cousin Herman and hope his spirit and curiosity pass through his son Ron and me to both our Bret[t] Prestons.

Cousins Roby Lee and Robert Jay Potts (Aunt Irene's boys), Robert Lynn Elam and Linda Clemmons (Great-Aunt Awilda Pack's great-grand-children), Ron and Carol Preston (Great-Uncle Ernest Preston's grand-son and wife), Dick, Chad, and Judy Perry (Great-Uncle Asberry Preston's grandsons and wife) allowed me to raid their memories and/or picture collections.

Two-Mile neighbor and schoolmate Bettie Sue Williams Franklin sent me a 1934 picture of Momma.

Bob and Jane Allen (Great-Aunt Luan Cline Brown's grandson and wife) and daughter Mary Jo and Marlene Wells (Billie Edyth Ward's niece) answered my many questions and refreshed my memory with stories old and new.

Raymond Bradbury (Daddy's former boss at the David coal mines) talked with me about my daddy and remembered the very things Daddy would have wanted recalled.

Peggy Ward Crutchfield and Betty Ward Keys (nieces of Two-Mile neighbor Frank Ward and Aunt Polly Blevins, who ran the coal camp boardinghouse where Daddy, Momma, and I lived in the early forties) unearthed their own boardinghouse memories and stimulated mine.

James and Ann Tramel (owners of hometown bookstore Words & Stuff) offered frequent words of encouragement and helped me get back into my coal camp memories. Though Jim and I were in high school together, neither of us had any idea that we'd both spent some early days in Hemphill Coal Camp. That time and place marked him, as it did me, and our conversations brought back the singing tipple, black Tug River, and the grit of the bug dust.

David and Lynne Joyce and Union College (where I did my first gradu-ate work thirty-five years ago and was writer in residence the fall semes-ter of 2001) called me back to Kentucky where I could live among my people while researching this book.

The Ragdale Foundation (where the peace and beauty of the physical surroundings—coupled with lively suppers with other resident writers and artists—provide the nearest thing to an ideal writing environment) granted me a two-month residency fellowship in summer 2000.

Hindman Settlement School (where crossing Troublesome is a rite of passage for any Appalachian writer) punched my ticket to home in summer 2001.

Pikeville College, alma mater (where I served as writer in residence the spring semester of 2002) allowed me to revisit and maybe correct impressions I had made there more than forty years ago. Can, too, go home again. Everlasting thanks to Gerri, Elaine, Lucy, Stephanie, Elgin, James, Wally . . . Lord, I love you all.

Margaret Ripley Wolfe opened the door for me to write *Creeker,* and Nancy Grayson Holmes gave guidance and comfort as she midwifed that effort through writing and into publication.

Paula Call—copy editor par excellence—paid close attention to every permutation of the English sentence falling from my Appalachian tongue (pen?) and made my work comprehensible to the outside world.

Jennifer Peckinpaugh, Angelique Galskis, Leila Salisbury—indeed, every worker bee at UPK—consistently greet my me-first whines with good cheer when they could just as easily catch a bad case of the sour-turn.

More than two hundred folks have written me about *Creeker,* sending queries that formed the basis of this work. Their letters pushed me to look for answers to questions I didn't even know I had.

Barbara Jean Vail, mighty protector of flanks, during over twenty years of feat and friendship has never once flown bad on me.

Charles and Lee—fellow travelers on this narrow road—have oft been guided by the same stars. And I thank those lucky stars for bringing both of you into my life.

Pat, Mike, Brett, Sharron, Lindsay, Betsy, Nan, Connie Sue, Paula, Jeanette, Barb, Heather, Linaya, McKinley, Ryen, Sunner, Deborah, Marsha, Melissa, and the Vinsons—my roadies—are the best damn support group a girl ever had.

Brett Dorse Scott—still family after all these years—shared unique memories of Momma and Daddy that added immeasurably to this work.

Pat and Mike Greer and Gwen and Wallace Williamson nurtured and sustained me over the past year when I repeatedly showed up unexpectedly at the door long after supper had been cleared away. One crisp Tuesday evening in November last, I found myself near Ashland, Kentucky, at the intersection of I-64 East-West and KY-23 North-South. The only person who had any idea as to my whereabouts was my husband, who was two thousand miles away. When we spoke the previous evening, Arthur had been heading to a remote Montana cabin for a retreat. I had told him I planned to go to Ashland (about four hundred miles, round-trip, from my apartment in Barbourville) the next day, and since our schedules were not in synch, we agreed we'd not make contact until Wednesday. As is often the case, however, my Tuesday had not unfolded according to plan. After a 5:00 A.M. wake-up, I had driven to Ashland for a 10:00 A.M. funeral, but when it was over, I did not head back immediately. Instead, I stayed around and talked with some old friends I had not seen since high school. On my way out of town I decided to stop by and see the new offices of the Jesse Stuart Foundation, where I tarried to swap stories with old friend Jim Gifford, director of the foundation. I didn't get out of JSF until about quit time, hence the quandary at the intersection of I-64 and KY-23. As I approached the crossroads, I knew I didn't want to drive back all the way to Barbourville that evening, but I had a couple of options. Sister's bed and board lay about an hour and a half down I-64 West, and Gwen Holbrook's house was nearly an hour and a half South on KY-23. As the sun sank low in the November sky, it occurred to me that whichever road I took, I'd find myself at home, no questions asked. Gwen or Sister would hug me, scold me for not calling ahead so she could have "fixed something" and begin to pull the remains of supper out of the fridge. The fact that I can depend on that kind of reception replicated at any number of places within three hours drive of where I grew up speaks volumes about the people and the place. Though it's true that much has changed since I left eastern Kentucky, the ties that bind us to family, church, and community are as strong as ever.

And, once more, to Casey Joans—all the muse that's fit to print—thanks.

The Opening Act

Each time I stand at a microphone ready to tell a house full of folks about something or another I'm supposed to know, I am once again aware of the debt I'm owing to my parents, grandparents, indeed to all those folks who came before me. Every truth and tattle I've been able to turn up attests to how each generation of my people had life just a little bit harder than did their children. That has certainly been true of my family, all of whom labored long in field or coal mine—on the ground and under it, you might say—so that I could make a living without breaking a sweat. And so, as I stand at that lectern and sing my heart out, I am singing for my family; for Pop Pop and Grandma Emmy, Uncle Keenis and Aunt Exer, and most of all, for Daddy and Momma—Life and Grace. All I say and all I write is funded by those figures who inhabit my history, as well as my present-day reality—my people, scalawag and scholar, who passed to me both the stories I remember and the sensibility to interpret those tales.

My family's story is bound and tethered to a bunched-up mountain range in eastern Kentucky—a piece of earth not many folks would say is worth a damn. Conventional wisdom is that they've already dug out, chopped down, and hauled off just about everything any outsider ever found valuable in those hills. Still and all, we hill-country folk keep on cherishing those hollows and hillsides where we came into knowing. Some of us left for good. Some left and came back as soon as we could. Some stayed within ten or fifteen miles of home. Still others squatted right where we started, adding on to or remodeling the home place, sometimes tearing it down and replacing it. Though we may have made diverse choices, grown in different directions, our roots in those mountains are deep and not forgotten by any means.

So much of my own heritage is grounded in the very special person who was my mother and the man who was so captivated by her that he became the quintessential family man. But let's begin with Momma—Grace Jean Mollette Preston.

In 1979, as the first director of the Institute for Appalachian Studies at East Tennessee State University, I spent most of my work life writing grant proposals to fund the institute and speaking to various groups in the area to publicize it. Thus it was that I found myself, on a perfectly ordinary Knoxville autumn afternoon, speaking to a local historical society. Having just made a perfectly ordinary speech, answered perfectly ordinary questions, and thanked everyone for their time and attention, I stood saying the customary good-byes to lingerers. Eventually I was alone with a distinguished older gentleman who had hovered since the meeting adjourned.

"Miss," he inquired, "didn't you say you were from eastern Kentucky?"

When I said yes, he asked, "Did you ever know a woman named Grace Mollette?"

When I said my mother's maiden name was Grace Mollette, Dr. John DeRossett told me a forty-five-year-old story.

Dr. John was originally an orphan boy from northern Kentucky, where he had lived the early years of his life. As he moved around among the homes of one relative or another, he dropped in and out of school several times and did not finish high school until he was past twenty years old. After spending four years in the army, he returned to Kentucky and entered Morehead State Teachers College, where he put himself through school by some combination of part-time jobs during the semester and selling encyclopedias full time over the summers. In 1934, between his graduation from college and entrance into medical school, twenty-seven-year-old Johnny DeRossett sold his wares all over the Kentucky hills.

Plying his trade in the Muddy Branch coal camp one searing July afternoon, he knocked on the door of one of the camp houses and was greeted by young Grace Mollette. According to Dr. John, he became so enchanted with this beautiful young woman that he spent the entire afternoon talking with her. As the two sat on the top step of her sister Lizzie Colvin's front porch, Grace told young Johnny that she planned to be a teacher and hoped to attend Morehead someday. He spoke of having intended to teach until he was halfway through college, when an unexpected love for biology and chemistry persuaded him to change to premed. Grace and Johnny then agreed to correspond, exchanged addresses, and never saw each other again.

As the clean-up crew bussed tables all around us in the community room of that suburban Holiday Inn, seventy-two-year-old John DeRossett assured me that his one contact with my mother had been anything but ordinary. "We wrote each other," he said, "for about a year, maybe more. But then she just stopped writing and I assumed she had moved on to other interests. Some years later I married, was widowed, remarried, and only occasionally thought about Grace, but I never forgot . . . not about her or that afternoon. Tell me, is she still alive?"

When I said that she was alive, well, and married for the past forty-three years to my daddy, the older gentleman rummaged through his wallet and fished out a worn picture of my mother. "That doesn't do her justice, you know," he said of the faded image he handed to me, and indeed the likeness was not particularly stunning. "There was something dazzling about Grace. . . . You take that picture to her and see what she says. And thank you for reminding me of all this. I always knew I'd run across that girl again." The older gentleman walked away without leaving an address, and I never heard from him again, nor did Momma. I did take the picture to my mother, who claimed to have no memory of the man or the incident. I believe she was telling the truth.

Momma lived on for fifteen years after my meeting with Dr. John DeRossett, and their relationship—such as it was—was never discussed again, at least not in my presence. The story, however, was meaningful to me in that it helped me to see that I am not the only one to have perceived that quality in my mother. Yes, Momma was a beautiful woman, but her persona was more complicated than that. She seemed to have a force field around her—an inner light, if you will—and that light diminished just a little bit every year she lived. Through all her years of incessant "sick," Momma would show flashes of buoyancy and brilliance that made all of us around her feel privileged to be in her presence.

Here's the thing about my mother, though: when she was young, she shimmered. During those drab early days in the coal camp and the community of Two-Mile, Momma positively shone, and in so doing she cast off enough light to see the rest of us through a lot of darkness. The early Grace was brilliant, beautiful, high-spirited, and far too sure of herself to have grown into womanhood in the first half of the twentieth century. As a young girl, she showed more independence of spirit and a better sense of what she wanted than I ever did. What's more, as I researched this work it became clear that the biggest contrast between my mother's life and mine is that her few significant choices were all used up on the front end, while mine opened up later on. Part of that variance is a function of the quarter-century difference that divides her era from mine, along with the cultural shifts that have taken place.

Of one thing I am certain: The best and worst choice Momma ever made was to hitch her wagon to the star that was my daddy. If ever anybody deserved her very own star it was my mother, and over the years the lack of her own life's passion took the spirit right out of her. Now, it didn't happen all at once. We saw flashes of that sunshine right up till death took her in a bed five feet from Daddy's, there in the master bedroom of the columned house he'd built for her.

The ninety-pound skeleton left of my mother went to her death wearing a pale blue, spaghetti-strapped chiffon gown and matching peignoir, with her freshly set blond hair arranged just so by her caregiver. Momma used her final morning getting all fixed up, because Daddy was in the next bed and he liked for her to look nice. It mattered not that her husband of fifty-eight years was lying across the bedroom where they had spent countless hours sharing coffee, cigarettes, songs, and secrets completely unaware of where or even who he was.

I wonder sometimes which way I would choose to go out. Momma's lights were on, and she could see clearly right up to her death . . . she still had memories and dreams. Even as my mother lay dying, she knew what she had lost. Indeed, her primary loss was that strapping, curly-headed young man with the azure eyes who tried to pick her up in his fine car on a late August day almost sixty years before. The 120-pound shell of that blue-eyed boy lay five feet away, crumpled into a fetal position, carrying on his own rambling conversation with the men who'd worked with him nearly two decades before.

Dying is painful—however dreaded or desired—painful for those departing as well as for those they leave behind. The legacy left to Sister and me by Daddy and Momma is an easier life than either of them ever had a chance at. Clearly my life is better because of the past fifty years of economic prosperity in the United States and the attendant technological gifts and cultural shifts, but it's more than that. The real legacy my family left me is my memory of the life they lived—the good and bad of it so intricately intertwined that the virtuous cannot be separated from the sinful without taking energy from both.

Individual
Heritage
Chart
of

Eliphus Jay Preston
3/12/1917–12/5/1994

Paris Preston
Father
1/7/1879 – 7/8/1955

Married 3/?/1909

Alice Ward
Mother
7/12/1885 – 4/12/1947

Eliphus Preston
Paternal Grandfather
2/1/1845 – 12/6/1929

Married 5/22/1866

Elizabeth Ward
Paternal Grandmother
1/5/1851 – 6/5/1928

Asbury Ward
Maternal Grandfather
5/?/1859 – 6/14/1936

Married 3/8/1877

Laura Bell Price
Maternal Grandmother
1/8/1861 – 1946

Eliphus Preston, Sr 1795 – 3/2/1861
Great-Great-Grandfather
Married 2/10/1815
Anna Pelphrey
Great-Great-Grandmother

James Preston
Great-Grandfather
1817 – ?

Married 5/3/1835

Stephen W Wheeler 10/13/1780 – 4/6/1835
Great-Great-Grandfather
Catherine Remy 5/10/1786 – 11/27/1812
Great-Great-Grandmother

Anna Wheeler
Great-Grandmother
1814 – 2/2/1849

William Ward 1792 – 1860
Great-Great-Grandfather
Elizabeth Meck 1804 – 1875
Great-Great-Grandmother

Shadrach Ward
Great-Grandfather
ca.1829 – 1897

Isham Daniel
Great-Great-Grandfather
Polly Borders
Great-Great-Grandmother

Nancy Hettie Daniel
Great-Grandmother
ca.1830 – ?

William Ward 1792 – 1860
Great-Great-Grandfather
Elizabeth Meek 1804 – 1875
Great-Great-Grandmother

Shadrach Ward
Great-Grandfather
ca.1829 – 1897

Isham Daniel
Great-Great-Grandfather
Polly Borders
Great-Great-Grandmother

Nancy Hettie Daniel
Great-Grandmother
ca.1830 – ?

Jesse Price
Great-Great-Grandfather
Lynchie Preston
Great-Great-Grandmother

C. C. Price
Great-Grandfather
8/28/1837 – 10/5/1895

Married 7/10/1857

Sarah Meck
Great-Grandmother
3/22/1841 – 2/15/1908

Individual
Heritage
Chart
of

Grace Mollette
6/28/1915 – 11/11/1994

Elijah Mollette
Father
1/27/1872 – 5/31/1939

Married 12/3/1891

John "Big-Eye" Mollette
Paternal Grandfather
ca.1822 – 1907

Married ca.1864

Amanda Wells
Paternal Grandmother
ca.1843 – 1876

Emma Cline
Mother
5/18/1874 – 4/15/1953

Jacob William Cline
Maternal Grandfather
3/18/1849 – ca. 1937

Martha Setser
Maternal Grandmother
5/?/ 1850 – 1/?/1934

Elias Mollette
Great-Grandfather
1783 – ca. 1865

Noah Mollette
Great-Great-Grandfather

Sarah Barker
Great-Great-Grandmother

Sarah Gibson
Great-Grandmother
1795 – 1870

William Cline
Great-Grandfather
ca.1824 – ?

Jacob Cline *ca.1788 – 1858*
Great-Great-Grandfather

Nancy Fuller *ca.1810 – 1855*
Great-Great-Grandmother

Margaret McCoy
Great-Grandmother
ca.1828 – ?

John McCoy
Great-Great-Grandfather

Margaret Jackson
Great-Great-Grandmother

THE OVERTURE

On a muggy end-of-August afternoon, fragrant with wild honeysuckle, Grace Mollette—blond hair shining in the sun— headed up Greasy Creek, marching along toward home. Though it had rained that morning, it had been a droughty summer, and the rain hadn't gone a long way toward tamping down the polky dust that had turned Grace's brown shoes to a smoky tan. The new leather kitten-heeled pumps pinched both of her little toes, and she could feel a blister rising on her left heel. It didn't concern her that the shoes squeezed her feet, for Grace had never owned a pair of comfortable shoes. There wasn't a shoe made that didn't pinch somewhere, and Grace liked the way her ankles looked when she wore high heels. She had a long calf muscle, and it took some height in the heel for Grace to have the appearance of a well-turned ankle. The fact that she walked the mile or so to teach school in high heels was just one more thing her mother termed "Grace's foolishness," but then what did Mommy know about anything?

Mommy—Grace's mother, Emma—had spent her whole life on what passed for a farm at Three Forks of Greasy Creek, having babies, milking cows, and slaughtering hogs, working from before daylight until way into the night just to keep her husband and children from going hungry. Grace was the youngest of Emma and Elijah Mollette's nine children, and as far back as she could remember, her mother had worked herself right to the bone raising crops and kids and caring for her paralyzed husband. Everybody agreed that after "Lige" got down, Emma waited on him hand and foot. While Grace respected her mother, she did not have such a future in mind for herself. She wanted out of Greasy Creek, and since her high school graduation two years earlier, Grace had been accomplishing her flight, if only by degrees.

She'd spent most of the winter just past in the Muddy Branch coal camp with her sister Lizzie's family. Grace had returned to Three Forks in mid-July to teach school in Hurricane, and it didn't take but a few days for her to miss the excitement of Lizzie's big family. She loved her sister's kids—especially Lizzie's daughter Frances, who had become her closest confidante—but Grace also missed the opportunities to socialize offered by the coal camp and its proximity to Paintsville, where the real action took place. Though the public story was that Grace had returned to the Mollette home place on Greasy in order to take up the teaching job she had left the previous November, that was not precisely reflective of the situation.

She had substituted for another teacher from July into November of 1935. When the regular teacher returned and Grace was out of a job, her mother asked her third daughter, Amanda, if Grace could spend the next few months with her in Paintsville—maybe get a job over Christmas and make a little extra money. That was the way of the Mollette family, each child helping out as he or she could to launch the younger ones. Amanda had readily agreed, but within just a few weeks she'd grown disenchanted with her younger sister's behavior. According to Amanda:

> I don't know where she got the money, or how it happened, but somehow Grace got hold of a car and there was just no way of handling her. Kash [Amanda's salesman husband] was on the road and gone all the time, and I was doing clerical work over at Mayo, and I never had any notion of

where Grace was. She put in for a job at one or two places in town, but nothing came through right away and she was at loose ends.

In those days it was unusual for a woman to drive, much less have a car of her own, and it was not considered proper for a single woman to be out by herself after dark. Half the time when I got home from work at five-thirty, Grace was nowhere to be found. She'd come in at six, or eight, or even later and say she'd been down at Lizzie's helping with the kids. I tried to talk to her, but she'd just say she wasn't doing anything wrong.

Wrong was not the point. Why, I'd lived in town on my own for three years before I married Kash, and never a bad word was said about me. I tried to tell Grace she'd get herself talked about. But do you think she cared? Finally, I wrote Mommy and told her Grace was smoking cigarettes right in public. I said I wouldn't be responsible for the kind of name she was getting. By that time Grace had got Lizzie to agree to let her move in with her [Colvin] family down on Muddy Branch, and poor old Mommy didn't have any say in it.

While it's true that Lizzie more than had her hands full with those three boys, Frances was a great big girl by then and able to help out every bit as much as Grace. Grace was only a couple of years older than Frances and they looked alike enough to be twins. Everybody told them how pretty they were and they ate that up. I know in reason Grace was one more burden on Lizzie, but you know Lizzie, she just took her in and wouldn't tell Mommy a thing.

A card postmarked Thealka, Kentucky, December 13, 1935, from Lizzie to her mother, Emma Mollette, says: "Mama, Grace is going to work at Maggard's [hardware and furniture store] Saturday and through all the holidays. Manda called her yesterday and told her to be sure and come. . . . So she said she would not be home for Christmas. I'll take care of her, Mama." Amanda agreed that Grace got work at Maggard's and was kept on for a time after the holidays. But then Amanda continues:

The next thing I heard, sometime in the spring, Grace was supposedly engaged to that Johnson boy, who was connected to the biggest bootlegger in the county. Grace swore to me that she and Frances weren't drinking and I believe her, but I'll tell you the people they were fooling around with were the rakings and scrapings of the earth. I didn't write a word of this to Mommy, but she heard it from somebody. I know the whole family was relieved when Grace didn't get on at Muddy Branch School and went back to Hurricane for another year. Of course, by that time the Johnson boy had got Jim Caudill's girl in trouble and had to marry her. In my opinion, Grace is just lucky he took up with that Caudill woman.

Truth to tell, her sister Lizzie's family was not all Grace was missing on this sultry August afternoon; she was also missing Burt Johnson. She had met him when she was visiting Lizzie nearly a year earlier and Burt had walked past the Colvin house with Johnny Setser. The boys came into the yard and passed the time with Grace and Frances, and by the time they ambled off down the camp road, Grace knew she had an admirer. But then Grace had a string of admirers, so she didn't give much thought to Burt Johnson. She did notice, however, that somehow Burt always managed to come around whenever she visited Lizzie. Once Grace moved in with Amanda, she spent more time at Lizzie's and more time with Burt.

Though Lizzie had warned her about Burt's reported drinking and womanizing, he had been a perfect gentleman to Grace. She had never even seen him take a drink, much less get drunk, and he had promised her that if she would marry him he would straighten up and stop his drinking. He said she was just what he needed to settle him down. Grace was accustomed to men falling for her immediately and promising her anything if she would agree to marry them. Though she had accepted four proposals of marriage before Burt Johnson's, she had never been intrigued enough to mean it. To Grace, agreeing to marry this one or that one was a necessary step in the courting process. After all, unless the two were formally engaged, Emma wouldn't even let Grace out of sight with a boy. Grace thought Mommy hadn't been nearly that hard on the older girls, but then maybe she hadn't had to be.

Amanda, with all her dire predictions and worries about her good name, had been an old woman at fifteen, or so Grace thought. What's more, the world had changed a lot since the older girls were young and sparking. As far as Mommy was concerned, the 1920s might as well not have happened. Though Grace considered herself a thoroughly modern young woman, she had scarcely kissed Burt Johnson before he asked her to marry him. And just for the record, that proposal of marriage came a full week before she and Amanda had it out over Grace losing her good name. As far as Grace was concerned, a good name was hardly worth having if it meant settling down with the first boy who asked you to marry him.

Grace liked dressing up in pretty clothes and going out with a crowd of people to listen to music and have a good time. She was a good dancer, loved to dance, and she and Frances could do a mean Charleston together. Neither of them drank liquor, but they were often the life of the party stone sober—two beautiful blonds dancing together. For all her "fiancés," Grace had more fun with a crowd than as part of a twosome—especially if Frances happened to be part of the crowd. Grace figured there was plenty of time to settle down and get married after she had done a few of the other things she wanted to do. She had come of age during the Depression, when it had been a struggle just to get something decent to wear to school. In Grace's opinion, the Depression just meant more of the same at Three Forks of Greasy—there never had been much to go around; still wasn't.

In spite of the constant financial struggles, Grace had managed to get good grades, a high school diploma, a teaching certificate, and a job or two. Teaching at Hurricane didn't pay much, but Grace was able to live at home, help Mommy financially, and still have enough money to buy herself some good clothes and a car. The year just past had been the best time of her life. She had loved the fun, the attention, and, most of all, the freedom to make her own decisions about what she would do and where she would go.

Even though she had lost Burt Johnson, she admitted to herself that she had not been in any big hurry to marry him—especially if marrying him meant having kids and ending up tied down to one man in one place. When he and Grace had talked of the future, Burt expressed no desire to go anywhere but Muddy Branch. He had been in the service and thought Grace's longing to see more of the world was foolishness. "Travel is overrated," Burt had said. If he could get on at the mines, he was ready to settle on Muddy Branch, right there, right then. Then Janie Caudill's bit of news about being pregnant with Burt's child had jumped right smack-dab in the middle of Burt and Grace's future. Grace had to admit that Burt's scenario of the future had come true. He had been picked up at Van Lear Mines and was lucky enough to get a house in the camp. Settled down, indeed, he was.

Though Grace had cried the requisite buckets of blue tears over the Burt Johnson disappointment, on this steamy August day she was not at all sure her heart was all that shattered. Now if she could just figure out a way to get Mommy to acknowledge that she was a grown woman who could make decisions about her life on her own, Grace would really have it made. She and Mommy had already had a battle royal about Grace bringing her car home with her, with Emma insisting that she leave her car at Amanda's so Kash could sell it for her. By enlisting the help of every member of the family, Emma had won that one. By now Grace's car was just another fond memory, and she'd see them all dead and buried before admitting that she missed her car considerably more than she missed Burt Johnson. She was also bitterly disappointed not to have won the job at Muddy Branch School, though she suspected Amanda or Lizzie or maybe even Mommy might have had a hand in her being assigned to Hurricane again.

This would be her second year of teaching grades one through six at Hurricane School. The work wasn't easy, but Grace was up to it. She wasn't one bit afraid of the big old boys everybody said were impossible to keep quiet, much less to teach. They could usually be co-opted to help around the classroom, and if they got too rambunctious . . . well, she had been known to throw the paddle at one or another of them. Grace had tossed that paddle a couple of times the year before, so she already had the name of being somebody they couldn't push around. No, teaching was a piece of cake, and it sure had clerking in a store or working in the fields beat all to pieces.

Though the afternoon sun glared on her head unmercifully, Grace had taken off her hat so the sun might have its way with her hair. *The sun beats peroxide every time,* she thought as she rounded the last curve before home, walking right in the middle of the road. She was stepping carefully around the fresh and flattened horse hockey left by the usual traffic, when she saw in the distance, just past her house, an approaching car. The driver was coming along at a right good clip, raising a cloud of fine sand, just splittin' and gettin' in her direction.

In August 1936, only three people on all three forks of Greasy had access to a car, and Grace recognized every one of them. In fact, she thought she knew every car on the east side of Johnson County, but this one was not familiar. She wondered why anybody would be coming down the Left Fork of Greasy in the middle of the afternoon and what his business might have been. She knew in reason the driver was a *him,* because in those days women just did not drive. To quote sister Amanda, "It wasn't proper." That very thought brought a smile to Grace's face as she moved to the left side of the road, because she knew a woman who could drive a car—*she* could. And she would again, too, in spite of her mother, Amanda, and anybody else ignorant enough to question modern women.

Hard on the heels of that thought, the car skidded to a stop beside her. "What're you laughing about?" the driver inquired through the haze of fine yellow-brown dust rising all around his vehicle. The young man was laughing himself, and Grace could see that he was more than middling handsome, with the bluest eyes, long wavy hair, and a full mouth.

"Laughing at the same thing you are, I reckon," Grace replied, ducking her head and gazing at the fellow from beneath an abundant fringe of lashes.

"J'ont a ride?"

"Hmm-mmm. I'm about home anyway," she answered, nodding in the direction of her home place.

"Whose girl are you, anyway?" he inquired.

"I'm Grace, Lige Mollette's youngest girl. Who're you and what're you doing in our neck of the woods?"

"I'm Lifie Jay Preston," he began, but before he said another word, Grace could see her mother stand up from where she had sat stringing beans on the porch of the home place.

Emma crossed past the stand of sweet peas to the very edge of her yard. She raised her hand to her forehead to shade her eyes and looked to see what on earth was going on there in the middle of the road where anybody coming or going could see her baby girl talking to some rank stranger. And wasn't that just like Grace?

That youngest daughter of hers had always had a mind of her own, and Emma had been so busy just keeping the family fed, clothed, educated, and together that she had been more lax with Grace than she had with her older children. Though Emma's three boys had always been wild, drinking and sworping around just like their daddy, her three older girls (Lizzie, Stella, and Amanda) had been pretty good. Fourth daughter, Gladys, was as high-spirited as Grace, but Gladys was sickly and so never managed to get herself into much trouble. Everybody expected boys to get a little wild, just to get it out of their system before a wife and family settled them down. Women, however, were not given such an option, and for a girl to get herself talked about brought shame on the whole family.

Lord knows, Grace was plenty old enough to know that, but at twenty-one she seemed in no hurry to lock in her future and did not seem to care at all that people were beginning to whisper about her. Emma had warned Grace more than a few times that if she got herself talked about, that bad name would follow her the rest of her life. Everybody agreed that girls who were talked about and women with a bad name could not expect to get a good man to take care of them. Grace just laughed and said if people didn't have any more to talk about than her, then they were in bad shape. In fact, she and Emma had a knockdown, drag-out fight about this very thing less than a month before Grace met and married Lifie Jay Preston.

To hear Grace Mollette tell of her years after high school is to hear of a woman looking for anything but marriage. This is an unlikely story in that place and time, when men *made* their future while women *married* theirs. Grace never disagreed with that dictum, and she certainly expected to fulfill it by finding the right man and marrying him. Spinsterhood was the last thing she wanted, and Grace knew that someday she would marry, settle down, and have one or two children. She knew she did not want a house full of kids though, for she saw folks reproducing themselves right into poverty. While marriage was definitely Grace's goal for the future, she differed from many of her friends in that she loved being single and on her own. Grace was in no hurry to settle down. Before the future of settling and children, Grace wanted a present—a present that included pretty clothes, and parties, and the freedom to go new places and meet new people. She was certain of that, and she had no desire to hook up with someone who was serious, who would bring her good time to an end.

As for that blue-eyed young driver, in his own words, "There may not have been a young man in all of Johnson County who was looking for a good time as hard as Lifie Jay Preston." Though he had never had a girlfriend, it was more because he was afraid he would be pushed to marry than that he was immune to female charms. He liked to drink beer and play his guitar with the other wild young men—and a few young women—who frequented the sparse roadhouses in the area. Lifie Jay Preston had a car, and that car meant he had freedom. He was a hard worker, but at the end of the week he traded the fruits of his labor for fuel, gassed up his car, and took off for all parts party.

Until the August day he spied Grace Mollette walking up the middle of Greasy Creek Road, Lifie Jay had lived a charmed life. When he met Grace, he was only nineteen—maybe even eighteen, depending on whom you believe. He was born over on Bob's Branch, the third son of Paris and Alka Ward Preston, and even he had to admit that his parents— especially his daddy—spoiled him rotten. The two older boys, Mitchell and Glen, were just about grown and his sister Irene was nearly three when Lifie Jay made his appearance, and his daddy just petted him to death. His mother, Alk, lost three children in infancy—one of them be- tween Lifie Jay and Jo Imogene, which means Lifie Jay was the baby of the family until Jo was born in 1924. Though Paris worked for a living as a skilled independent carpenter, he was careful enough with his money that he had some cushion built up by the time of the Depression and was not hit that hard by it.

Paris taught all three of his boys how to do carpentry work, and all three worked in the building trades. Unlike Mitchell, who moved out at fifteen when he married, and Glen, who also left home at sixteen to find work, Lifie Jay stuck close to the home place and worked at whatever his daddy was doing. He attended school sporadically but never placed any priority on it. This meant that if he could pick up some little job that would bring in money, Lifie Jay thought nothing of missing school for it.

When Lifie Jay was sixteen or seventeen, Paris bought him one of the first cars to come into Johnson County. By his own admission, Lifie Jay hardly attended school a day after that. Instead, he took it upon himself to hire out and carry people here or there in his fine car. Since cars were a scarce commodity and public buses didn't travel up the hollows, Lifie Jay found plenty of takers for his off-the-books taxi service. One Mon- day, after an extended absence, he returned to school and was told that he needed to report to the principal's office. Lifie Jay's response to this command was to walk right out the doors of Meade Memorial High School for the last time.

A scant two years later, it was this very car Lifie Jay was driving as he came upon Grace Mollette there on Greasy Creek Road. It seems Garfield Ward had hired Lifie Jay to take him around on Spring Knob, a few miles past the Lige Mollette home place, to see old man Ward's daughter, who had just given birth. Lifie Jay was headed home with nothing much on his agenda when young Grace Mollette appeared, but by the time she sent him on his way, Lifie Jay Preston had the closest thing he'd ever had to a date. He wasn't sure just how these things were supposed to work, but best he could tell this pretty woman had just the same as asked him for a date the very next day.

Grace knew full well that any minute now her mother was going to embarrass her by calling her home, and knowing Mommy, she might just walk over and speak harshly to Grace right in front of this good-looking fellow. Thus, Grace quickly conveyed the message that she taught at Hurricane School and if Lifie Jay wanted to come by around three the next day, she might just allow him to carry her home in his fine automobile.

Two weeks later, on September 12, 1936, Grace Mollette and Elipha Jay Preston were married in the front room of the Mollette home place. Though none of Lifie Jay's people were in attendance, that was in no way indicative of any displeasure on their part. Actually, they were happy Lifie Jay had found him a wife, but they were just not the kind of people to make much over such occasions. Only Lige, Emma, and Emma's grandson, Leon—who had come to live with the family the year before—witnessed the nuptials. This was in fact the first of her children's weddings Emma herself had attended, for the older children had just gotten themselves married without Emma and Lige having anything to do with it. But their youngest always was one to make much of the least little thing, and Emma had to admit that Grace had put this wedding together without any help from anybody.

The ceremony was conducted by Freewill preacher John Hammond, who had preached the revival where Grace found the Lord and became a Freewill Baptist. That was when she was seventeen, and Preacher John had baptized her right there in Greasy Creek across from the home place.

Later, Grace had taught Preacher John's girl in school, and he thought enough of her to come around and marry her to Lifie Jay.

It must have been eighty degrees, yet Grace's bridegroom wore a charcoal gray serge suit and a navy blue tie. Emma knew he had to be uncomfortable, and she'd have bet money that suit wasn't two days old. Preacher John had sense enough to be in shirtsleeves—short shirtsleeves—but he was wearing a tie. Lord only knows what Grace had told him about dressing up for the wedding.

Despite the September heat, Grace wore a pale lavender-gray wool crepe dress she had bought ready-made over in Paintsville. The dress, with its white lace collar and cuffed long sleeves, set off the bride's blond beauty perfectly. Grace later admitted—and even laughed about—having to hold her arms away from her body during the ceremony to keep from getting sweat stains under the arms of the dress she wore as her "best" for the next two decades. Despite her mother's strong suggestion that Grace's pale blue, sleeveless dimity would have been much more appropriate for the weather, Grace had insisted that September twelfth was near enough to autumn that she was going to wear a fall dress. In Emma's view, this was just one more piece of evidence that "Grace was smart as a whip when it came to learning anything from a book, but she never had a lick of common sense."

Emma thought the smartest thing Grace had ever done was to get this boy to marry her and take her off the family's hands. As the preacher read the words, Emma felt a profound sense of relief and offered up a silent prayer that this new husband would be powerful enough to "do something" with this willful child of hers.

THE EARLY VERSES

When Lifie Jay Preston married Grace Mollette, it appeared to be a match made in heaven, and the first years of the marriage bore that out. My mother, Grace, often characterized the first ten years of her marriage to Daddy as the happiest of her life. Though they didn't have any extra money, everything seemed possible. First of all, Daddy didn't make Momma quit work immediately, which was quite a concession in a time when a woman working was thought to undermine a man's ability to support the family. Since Momma had signed a contract to teach out the year, Daddy thought it okay for her to fulfill that contract, which seemed quite liberal to all looking on.

Meanwhile, that meant the two young Prestons had a bit of a financial cushion they would not otherwise have had. To the both of them, success seemed not just latent but almost inescapable — doors opening in all directions. One of their many blessings was that from the beginning their union seems to have had the complete support of both sets of in-laws. Grandma Emmy told me many times that Daddy was the best thing ever to happen to Momma, and Momma said Grandma Alk treated her better than her own mother ever did. Over the course of their marriage, the relationships with their parents never changed, and I never heard either Momma or Daddy say a harsh word about any one of my grandparents.

During the first months of my parents' marriage, while Pop Pop and Daddy were building them a house, the newlyweds lived with his family or hers. After working all day, they would eat a supper prepared by Grandma Alk or Grandma Emmy. Then Momma would wash dishes and the whole family would retire to the front porch or fireside, where they shared jokes and stories, and Daddy often played his guitar and sang until after dark. Momma and Daddy worked hard all week, but on Friday and Saturday night they partied. Momma had never known as much freedom individually as she experienced as part of a young married couple. Prior to her marriage Momma had never been to a roadhouse, since it would have been inappropriate for a single woman. Once married, though, she and Daddy often spent Friday and Saturday evenings at such places.

During the week, when she taught school, Momma wore her yellow hair slicked back in a neat bun, clipped at the nape of her neck, but when they went out on the weekends, she allowed her hair to fall loose around her shoulders. Momma knew she got lots of sidelong looks from other men, but since she thought herself well-mated she was not at all interested. Moreover, Momma knew her young husband appreciated the way she looked, and those envious glances made him proud rather than jealous.

Now and then they would run into one or another of Momma's brothers and enjoy listening to some of the Mollette boys' big stories as one or both brothers drank the evening away. Unlike Momma's brothers, Daddy was not bad to drink, which meant the two of them could go into a place, listen to live music, and even have a beer or two. As a newlywed, Momma learned to drink beer, and since her husband was always with her, nobody but the most hidebound church people could criticize her for it. Besides, who was going to tell the church folks anyway? In those days, Momma's view was what those church folks didn't know wouldn't hurt them. Her new husband thought she was the bang-up best, and everybody else could suck sand for all she cared.

One Saturday, a couple of months after Momma and Daddy married, they drove one of Momma's cousins, Johnny Maynard, and his girlfriend, Sue Ratliff, over to Virginia to elope. When they brought the newlywed couple back to their families to tell them what they had done, Sue's folks took it just fine. That was not always the case, and sometimes the bride's father went and got his gun or at least made some attempt at grumbling about an elopement. In this case, the surprise came after Momma helped Sue pull together her personal effects and they went on to the house of the groom. It was expected that the new couple would be living with the groom's family, so Momma, Sue, and Johnny each got out of the car carrying some portion of Sue's belongings. According to Daddy, as he got out from behind the wheel, old Josh Maynard—Johnny's father— walked out the door to the edge of his porch and took a long look at the carful of young people walking into his yard. As the four of them stood at the foot of the steps, Johnny said, "Paw, I went over to the head of the river last night and got myself married." Old Man Maynard shook his head slowly and said, "Now you've played hell," turned, and walked into his house. Such response did not bode ill for the newlyweds, though. The Maynards took them in, and Sue and Johnny made a happy match as well as reliable companions for Momma and Daddy's weekend road-house tours.

Once their house across from Pop Pop's place on Two-Mile was under roof, Momma and Daddy spent most evenings working to get it into move-in condition, so they were able to spend Christmas of 1936 in their own home. The young Prestons even had their own Christmas tree, a tree that had first stood in Momma's classroom at school. Momma said most of their first decorations were pictures her students had cut from old magazines Aunt Amanda had passed on to Grandma Emmy and Momma had taken to school. These decorations were supplemented by ornaments her classes had cut, colored, and pasted to adorn the school tree. As Momma described it, the students had no construction paper, and paper for arithmetic and writing practice was so scarce they used it on both sides. They took that used paper, colored it, cut it into stars and circles, and hung those handmade ornaments with bits of twine on the little cedar tree Daddy cut and carried from the hill across from the Mollette home place.

The school did not get all that much time off for Christmas, but on the last day of school, Momma brought homemade gingerbread cookies and each child got to take home a cookie, along with the ornaments he or she had made. Most of the students gave one of their ornaments to the teacher for her tree, especially those whose families didn't keep Christmas—no tree or gifts. Momma and Daddy thought themselves lucky that both came from families where they made over Christmas at least a little bit. The newlywed Prestons bought a couple of red glass balls, a string of silvery tinsel, and a silver star for the treetop, and along with the student-made decorations, that was the extent of their Christmas trimmings.

Momma recalled the only sadness of that Christmas was that her sister Gladys could not be there to see how good they all had it. Both in age and proclivities, Aunt Gladys, who had died in the spring of '34, was the sister closest to Momma. Grandma Emmy always said that one of those girls was rambunctious enough, but together they were impossible. When it came to mischief, even the boys were no match for Gladys and Grace.

Because both families cooked special at Christmas, Momma and Daddy had to eat Christmas dinner at both sets of in-laws and felt "fat as pigs" for days afterward. As Momma said, "We felt like we were living right at the top of the stack."

Though home folks were about as well-off or as bad-off after the Depression as before it, this is not to say they had not been marked by it. According to Daddy, Pop Pop was one of the few people in the community who trusted banks with his money, and he lived to suck sorrow over it. When Daddy was around twelve years old, he was working on the home place with Pop Pop when the traveling sewing machine salesman came by for his regular monthly visit. This was in the years before mortgages and interest charges were common. In those days, when folks bought anything they had to pony up the whole price right then. It seems that since Pop Pop was a man of some substance, however, he was allowed to buy things on time. About a year before, Pop Pop had bought Grandma Alk a sewing machine, and each month the salesman came by to collect the dollar-a-month payment. Every month the salesman/bill collector would appear, Pop Pop would write him a check for a dollar, and after determining that there was nothing more he could do for or sell to the Paris Preston family, the man moved on. Apparently this was the tenth or twelfth installment check Pop Pop had written to pay for Grandma Alk's sewing machine.

On this day, however, there had been a run on the bank in town, and when Pop Pop pulled out his checkbook, the man said, "I'm sorry, Pare, but every sumbitch in this county's claiming money in that bank this morning. I'll have to have it in cash this time. Maybe by next month it'll all be cleared up and we can go back to doing business by check." Daddy said Pop Pop walked back to the house, got a hundred-dollar bill, brought it back to the salesman, and said, "Just take everything I owe you out of that." When the salesman said he just needed the regular one-dollar payment, Pop Pop replied, "No, we'll just settle up right now. Take the whole nine dollars out of that."

According to Daddy, his father never again bought anything on time, and neither man ever trusted a bank to keep all their assets. Daddy liked to have most of his money in his pocket and never put all his assets in the bank. Daddy said he never took out a note from a bank till he moved to West Virginia and needed more money than he had on hand to buy a car capable of driving back and forth home.

Though Pop Pop never again bought anything on time after the sewing machine incident, Daddy believed in buying everything on the installment plan. That way he could have whatever he wanted when he wanted it, pay for it as he was able, and not take a chance on blowing his money on foolishness. He always knew how much of his money was committed to somebody else, and he took care of those commitments before he blew any money on fun. Daddy liked to have some walking-around money in his pocket, and he was proud of never overcommitting his paycheck. When Pop Pop would caution him about buying something he didn't need, Daddy would remind his dad that he'd "never gone overdue on a bill" in his life.

Daddy was also fond of saying he "never saw anything I wanted that I didn't buy." The week after payday Momma would go to town and make cash payments for everything from the power bill to the insurance payment. If the payment had to be mailed, she got a money order from Leonie Wallen at the post office. I don't believe Daddy and Momma had either a checking or savings account with a bank until after I left home in 1958, and whenever I needed money for something at school, Momma always sent me with cash—even for some big thing like my class ring.

An expense such as the class ring, though, which was major—maybe fifty or one hundred dollars—had to come from Daddy's billfold, which he kept on his person at all times. I don't recall ever asking for so much money that Daddy was unable to come up with it, though he never showed me any money until I needed it. When Daddy told me the sewing machine story, he said that was the first time he'd ever seen a one-hundred-dollar bill. I asked if he had such a bill on him and he said, "Hell, no. Where'd I get that kind of money?"

I walked straight down to Pop Pop's, where he was sitting in his porch swing peeling apples to fry for his and Jo's supper. (Pop Pop could peel an apple without ever cutting through the skin after the initial cut; his peeling pan would be filled with little spirals of apple peel.) I repeated Daddy's sewing machine story, got Pop Pop's confirmation, and asked him if he had any more hundred-dollar bills. Pop Pop placed his paring knife in the pan, set it on the floor beside the swing, and unbuttoned the placket of his bib overalls. From this tiny pocket he extracted two crisp twice-folded bills—a fifty and a hundred. Pop Pop allowed me to hold the bills and smooth them out, and they appeared to be new, not all wrinkled and worn. I asked could I go get Gwen so she could see this money, but Pop Pop demurred. He said it was never a good idea to flash money around, and Gwen's daddy had probably already showed her such bills. He then cautioned me never to tell anybody about this, for "people who brag about money usually don't have none."

I also never saw what Daddy called his "pocketbook" outside his own hands either. Since Daddy slept with his billfold, I just figured every man did that. During the time he lived in the boardinghouse in West Virginia, Daddy developed the habit of sleeping with the waistband of his pants— including the pocket containing his billfold—under his pillow, a practice he continued until I left home in the late fifties. When I finally asked him why he slept with his pants legs hanging pressed out from under his pillow, he told me about learning the practice in the boardinghouse and continuing it out of habit. I never thought to ask about this practice until I was grown, for I simply assumed that all men, for the sake of modesty, liked to have access to their pants in case they suddenly had to get up at night. Since I don't recall ever seeing my daddy in his under-shorts, I assumed keeping his pants handy was the reason for such sleeping arrangements. People had some opinions about sleeping arrangements, and so long as those beliefs didn't bother anybody else, they generally slept ever which way they wanted to and kept it to themselves.

Our across-the-road neighbors, Aunt Exer and Uncle Keenis Holbrook, kept the headboard of their bed against the east wall of their bedroom because it looked better that way and fit in with the contours of their bedroom. Each night, though, they moved the pillows to the foot of their bed so as to sleep with their heads at the west end of the bed. Their reason for this was because Two-Mile Creek ran west to east, and the Holbrooks would not sleep with their heads pointing down the creek. The rationale was that if a person slept with his head down the creek, he'd get a headache. As close as the two families were, I didn't know about this practice until recently, nor did Gwen Holbrook know of my daddy's sleeping on his billfold.

Habits, whether they be money-related or not, are often hard to trace or to explain. Still, in 1936 people in eastern Kentucky were getting along financially just about as well as they had managed before the Depression. Truth to tell, they never really had much in the way of material goods even before the country went flat. Nobody of my parents' acquaintance even knew of anybody who might have owned stock that didn't have to be fed. To them, the stock market was where you sold your shoats or cattle. One of Daddy's favorite sayings was, "Never put money in anything you can't feed, till, or paint." Daddy never worried about money, however, because he knew there were jobs out there. Since he was never one bit particular about the kind of work he did, Daddy was not a man who could be out of work for long. He always said he'd "do anything to earn a poor man's dollar, and fifty cents if that's all they were paying. There's always a job for a man that's willing to work it, and, by God, I'm out for finding 'er." From the time he dropped out of school at sixteen or seventeen, Daddy had hardly gone one day when he wasn't earning a little money for some task nobody else wanted to do, even ferrying some passenger to the hospital or to visit. He was proud of always finding another job of pick-up work before the one he was working ended. He was also convinced that the big money was in the mines and had laid in his application at both Van Lear and Muddy Branch.

The whole family thought it was great luck that we had mines right there in Johnson County so our men didn't have to go far off to find work. Near the end of the thirties, Momma's brother Fred had got on at Van Lear, and while Daddy had not yet been hired, he figured that sooner or later an opportunity would come his way. Though friends and relatives had gone over to the mines in West Virginia, Daddy had resisted in hopes that he wouldn't have to break from home just yet. Like Momma, he wanted to get out and see some of the world, but he never wanted to live anywhere except right there on Two-Mile, in the shadow of his family.

The late thirties were uneventful for Lifie Jay and Grace Preston. After the 1936–1937 school year, Momma quit her teaching job and set to housekeeping, which left them with a little less money, but both were proud of the way Momma took to the role of wife. She kept the cleanest house around, waxing every floor in the house once a week and ironing everything but the dishrags. Much to the chagrin of both, Daddy did not get on at either Johnson County mine, but he was able to find pretty steady pick-up work. Daddy never lost hope that he might be taken on at Van Lear or Muddy Branch, while Momma politicked hard to "go over to West Virginia and try it."

When they married and moved to Two-Mile, Momma and Daddy had grown close to several of Frank Ward's kids. Frank and Edna Ward were Pop Pop and Grandma Alk's next-door neighbors, and they had two sons, Frank and Jess, and two daughters, Becky and Agnes, who were close in age to Daddy and Momma. The boys also played music and would add their voices and guitars to Daddy's as they sat in one or another's yard in the evening. The young folks all had ambition, and one by one the Ward boys left Two-Mile to go north to factory work. Then Becky and Agnes went to a cousin in Baltimore and got secretarial work there.

Meanwhile, there was much talk about the West Virginia mines and the opportunities over there. Two of Frank Ward's brothers were at mines over in Montgomery, and his sister Polly ran a boardinghouse in McDowell County, near Welch, West Virginia. The word was that they were paying even better over in West Virginia, and Momma thought it might be exciting to live over there. She had enjoyed her time living with Aunt Lizzie in the Muddy Branch coal camp, and she kept trying to convince Daddy how much better life would be if they just went on and moved. After all, Momma reasoned, there was a train running from Kermit, West Virginia, straight into Welch, which meant they could come right home any time they wanted to. Why, they could catch the bus to

Kermit right there in front of the house and ride it to the train station, get on that train, and be in Welch by the end of the day. They could even stay in Polly Ward Blevins's boardinghouse. Momma was certain that if Daddy would give it a try, he would love the freedom of being out from under his parents. Daddy, by contrast, had never felt in any way restricted by living with or near Pop Pop and Grandma Alk, so he resisted the call of West Virginia coal. By the time Grandpa Lige died in May 1939, Daddy had persuaded Momma that Grandma Emmy needed for them to stay close and help her with the Mollette home place.

By 1938 all the Mollette children were married and gone, and the only assistance Grandma Emmy had was twelve-year-old Leon. When Leon was five years old, his mother, Alma, had come down with tuberculosis and had to go to a sanitarium. Uncle Fred (Grandma Emmy's fourth child) took his baby girl, Barbara, to Alma's people (the Wells family) and brought his boy, Leon, to Grandma Emmy. Though Alma was able to return from the sanitarium a couple of times, she always relapsed and finally died in 1938, leaving Grandma Emmy with a sick husband and a little boy to raise.

Ever since 1937, the summer after they married, Momma and Daddy had helped with—and lived out of—the gardens of both sets of in-laws. Everybody was satisfied with this arrangement, though Momma brought her produce to her own house to can and preserve, preferring to help both Grandmas Alk and Emmy can their vegetables and then do hers and Daddy's separately. Grandma Emmy argued it was just as easy to add Momma's vegetables to hers or Grandma Alk's without going to all the trouble of a whole new batch of canning, which meant heating up yet another house. Momma, however, preferred her own canned stuff— done by her alone, in her own way—however labor-intensive it might be. Grandma Alk said this was fine with her, commenting, "Grace is real particular." Grandma Emmy's take on it was, "Grace is real foolish."

Life's Background Ballads

"Your Grandma Preston and your Pop Pop were first cousins—brother and sister's children. I didn't know that before I married your daddy." Momma was standing at the ironing board, doing up a batch of Daddy's mine clothes when she imparted this bit of information to me. Her tightly pin-curled hair revealed the shape of her tiny little head as she pressed the iron down one long tan sleeve. Her cigarette smoldered in the heavy, blue, crystalline ashtray balanced on the pile of damp, rolled-up khaki shirts and pants in the bushel basket at her feet. "It wouldn't have mattered though," she went on. "It's nothing to be ashamed of. A lot of people married their cousins in those days. People didn't get out much, so they tended to marry the people they met. Pop Pop grew up down on River, and he didn't meet your grandma until they were grown. Her people are all from Bob's Branch, and I think they met when he went over there to do some work on a house for a Price fellow."

So, my paternal grandparents were brother and sister's children. Shadrach Ward was my daddy's great-grandfather twice over, for he and his wife, Hettie, were parents of both Daddy's maternal grandfather as well as his paternal grandmother. That's about all the information I got from my parents about my daddy's people, because Daddy wasn't one to say and whenever Momma said, she generally talked about her own family. Pop Pop, too, was not forthcoming about family history, though occasionally he'd make some little comment in regard to the Prestons. The Wards, however—well, my childhood was fulsome with the richness of Wards. Since they were Pop Pop's first cousins, I picked up most of what I know of the Prestons through the Ward connection.

I was not embarrassed about Momma's cousin revelation when I heard it as a child, and I'm still not. For the past two decades, genetics data have shown the probability of impairment of children born to such a marriage as insignificant. Though within the family we tease each other about the cousin-marriage thing, I am not amused by outsiders' joking references to our circular Appalachian family tree. I should also point out that Sister is the Presbyterian elder, antigun member of my family and that I have taken no oath in either direction, which means an outsider might not want to make such mention in my presence.

Frankly, it has always been hard for me to believe Pop Pop and Grandma Alk were close kin, since their families seem so different in appearance and in manner. The Wards were big, strapping folks who were always gathering to go to church, or eat together, or go to funerals, or visit new babies—just about any excuse for a party and you could count on a bunch of the Ward sisters to show up. Now, they wouldn't have called it a party, but I can't think of a better name for the kind of get-together where there was a lot of eating and drinking and laughing and tale telling. That drinking was nonalcoholic, of course—all the Ward girls were religious-natured, and I doubt a one of them ever had an alcoholic drink in her life. Nobody ever needed alcohol to have a good time at a Ward gathering; you could laugh yourself sick, stone sober. Somehow the Wards mastered the knack of getting high on each other. And they all looked alike, too, though I always thought Aunt Millie Franklin was maybe the prettiest. Had a biting wit, too, Aunt Millie did, but she delivered her comments with such wit and charm you had to think twice before you noticed.

Sharp-tongued Aunt Millie and sweet Aunt Winnie were famous as the closest thing our family had to "professional mourners." They carried the Ward flag to the funeral of anyone who was even tangentially related to somebody they knew, which included just about everybody on the east side of Johnson County. In my growing-up years, I don't recall going to a single funeral where Aunt Millie and Aunt Winnie did not put in an appearance. They favored each other in that both were rather large women, with silver hair gathered in high knots at the backs of their heads, and both were quite large of butt. Aunt Winnie, especially. She had a hind end so large that if she had to haul butt, it'd take two loads—maybe three. They wore big black hats and black crepe dresses, with scented white handkerchiefs tucked into their bosoms, as they hugged and comforted everybody in sight. And that singular Ward serenity was indeed a comfort when we needed it. Those women had seen considerable struggle and hardship while shaping their families into existence, yet there they were, standing testimony to the fact that our people could endure and live to laugh again.

In 1994, the Christmas after Momma and Daddy died, Sister bought herself a big black hat reminiscent of Great-Aunts Winnie and Millie. She bought one for me, too, and gave it along with the suggestion that it was time we grew up and took up some of the mourning slack left by our great-aunts. Sister is considerably more faithful about her church and funeral responsibilities than I am, so by Christmas 2001, she'd about worn out her funeral hat. During that seven-year period, my black hat had not been out of the box, and it did not seem likely that I was going to grow into it, so I gave mine back to her with the note "Merry Christmas, Sister. With love from Peter Pan." I have no idea why I have not yet managed to grow into my funeral hat. Perhaps I'm not quite ready to take on the responsibility yet, or maybe I'd feel like an imposter trying to pass as a Ward. You see, Sister of the silver hair and Ward mouth apparently got about all those Ward genes—right down to that inner-peace essence. My physical heritage seems to be more a combination of the scrawny Mollette and wizened little Preston lines, and my neuroses reproduce with an abandon that has to be carried on a Mollette gene somewhere.

Somehow, too, Grandma Alk got way more Ward than Pop Pop, and while they may well have been first cousins, I swear you sure couldn't tell it by looking. As stocky and robust as were the Wards, so were the Prestons lank and lean. I'm not sure what most of them looked like in their youth, but best I could tell, as they aged, Wards turned to pudding, while Prestons turned to prune. In Daddy's family, Uncle Mitchell and Aunt Irene were pure Ward, while Daddy and Uncle Glen were more like the Prestons. Now Daddy did favor the Wards in the face, but his physique came courtesy of the Preston line.

Clearly, all of us are some combination of characteristics, with one or another showing itself from time to time. For example, I'd just as soon not include this little fact, but if I don't, Sister and Gwen Holbrook will never let me live it down: Truth is, though I seem to have inherited the Preston/Mollette upper-torso leanness, if I am not careful about what I eat, I could have Aunt Winnie's hind end in about fifteen minutes. There is a God and He has a sense of humor. So there.

Great-Grandma Laura Bell Ward—Grandmommy Ward—is the only member of that generation of Daddy's people that I actually met. When I was a little girl, she lived on Two-Mile with Grandma Alk and Pop Pop, and my earliest memories are of her nussing me in her lap. Grandmommy Ward was born a Price in January 1861 and married Great-Grandpa Asbury in March 1877, two months before his seventeenth birthday. During one of our spells in West Virginia, I remember Daddy coming home early from work with a telegram saying Great-Grandma Ward had died. Momma quickly got our things together, and we caught the train that evening to go home for the funeral. When we got to Kentucky, Momma took me to Grandma Emmy's, and I stayed there for most of the time Grandma Ward lay a corpse in the front room at Pop Pop's. In those days we didn't have the visitation at the funeral home. Folks brought their loved ones home and usually kept them up for three or four days to give all the family time to get home. Neighbors would bring in food and come in the evening to "set up" all night with the family.

I don't recall how many times I went around to see Great-Grandma Laura Bell during the time she lay a corpse, but I'm sure of having been there at least once—with Grandma Emmy when she went by to pay her respects. My memories are of lots of folks, lots of food, lots of flowers—most of all, lots of great-aunts from Bob's Branch who hadn't seen me since I was a baby and wanted to nuss me. "Come here, honey, and give me some sugar," they'd say, holding out their arms and inviting me to climb into their laps. Probably my most intense memory of virtually all such occasions is of how pleased the old ones always were to see and love on the children. A brief visit provided compelling evidence of the affection of my large and loving family. In retrospect, I am certain we kids must have been a bother sometimes, but I do not recall one instance where we were told to go play or to stop bothering anybody. All the adults, male and female, took time to pay attention to us kids.

If I went to the Great-Grandma Laura Bell's funeral, I don't recall it, and it may well be that my recollection of this visit is funded by memories of later visits when Grandma Alk, then Uncle Keenis, each lay a corpse in that very room. By the time Aunt Exer died in May 1975, the practice of folks laying a corpse at home had died out, and she was taken to the funeral home in Paintsville. For as long as it lasted, however, keeping the body at home seemed to follow an unvarying script.

We'd walk across the road from our house, take the path up the bank, and then step up on the wooden walk past the well box to the back porch. There'd be kids playing in the yard and assorted neighbors and family members sitting in the wooden rockers and cane-bottomed chairs, and some on the edge of the porch itself. We'd hug all around because some were sure to be in from Ohio or Michigan. We never, ever kissed anybody—not even the air around anybody, but we were big huggers.

"Well, hidie, honey," some older cousin or great-aunt would say, "Look at you."

"Lord, you look so good," we'd reply. "When'd you get in?"

"About three hours ago. Johnny made good time."

"Is that your boy? Why, he's a big boy!" (My son, Brett, gets hugged all around and perhaps pulled into a lap.)

"Have you had anything to eat? Why, there's more food than anybody can eat. I brought some of my cabbage rolls and a sour cream cake. Exer always loved my cabbage rolls."

Though such occasions were inevitably sad, they were bittersweet in that they allowed us all to come together and eat, meet, and greet. One or more of us would remain on the back porch to catch up, while after fifteen or twenty minutes of greeting, the others would continue on into the kitchen. There the conversation from the porch would be repeated, the only change being the presence of the kitchen crew and the food. When I say "kitchen crew," I don't mean these were folks who stayed in and worked in the kitchen. Most folks rotated in and out of the different rooms in the house, while some just stayed on one of the porches or in the kitchen. As you passed through the kitchen and the first food encounter, however, you had to eat something—even if it was a piece of pie or candy.

I think of all those "setting up" experiences every time someone mentions comfort food. Even today, whenever I hear of a friend's death, I set to baking. Food did indeed provide comfort, not only to the immediate family of the departed, but to the friends and extended family who could do nothing about the loss but cook and carry food and sit up all night with the deceased to show their love and respect. "Do you remember the time . . ." could be heard in different rooms throughout the house as we recalled our first taste of Aunt Exer's dumplings or how she put just a touch of a certain sweet spice in her chow chow. Or, "Uncle Pare sure loved his parched corn. He's the first person I ever saw eat black corn kernels."

"Why, what do you mean? I love parched corn. Beats popcorn by a mile."

Conversations took predictable segues, folks joining in or splitting off as we moved from room to room. Each room had its own habitués. From the back porch . . . through the kitchen . . . then the dining room—its table laden with stews, casseroles, a loaf or two of light bread, pimiento cheese salad, the inevitable "ham" salad (made from ground bologna), and all manner of dessert offerings—to the front room, where the coffin was opened for us to say our good-byes, we progressed, hugging, laughing, crying. Some people would not look at the deceased, but most of us made at least a short visit and spoke the required comments. "She looks good, doesn't she?" Or, "Law, she sure fell off a lot during this last sick spell, didn't she?" Or, "They sure did a good job" (referring to the funeral directors). Or, "Why, he looks just like himself."

Then it was on to the front porch to see who all was out there, or into the upper room, or back to the kitchen, or maybe the back porch. It was not at all unusual for somebody to come from the front porch to the kitchen for a glass of iced tea and encounter what he thought was a newcomer. "Why, when did you get in?"

"We drove straight through. Got here about two this morning. Where've you been?"

"I've been out on the porch. Where's Harry?"

"He went on to take the kids to Aunt Jock's. We came as soon as he got off. He's on the early shift now, so he hadn't had a wink of sleep. He was about to fall over by the time we got here. He'll be back around after while."

For two—sometimes three—nights, the extended open house, replete with the commingled smells of food and gladioli, went on as we took comfort in food and each other and helped the immediate family become accustomed to the loss of the loved one. In the case of the deaths of all the ones who came after my great-grandmother, I also attended their funerals, each followed by a trip to the family burial ground atop a ridge down on Bob's Branch. Though geological maps have the graveyard designated as "Preston Cemetery," it is populated primarily by the descendants—four generations strong—of Asbury and Laura Bell Ward, who started their lives together in what my cousin Kathleen Holbrook Daniel calls the "little red tin house," which sits in the head of Bob's Branch.

Every piece of research I have read traces the Ward side of my daddy's people six generations back from me to one James Ward, who showed up in Kentucky in 1803. What's more, it does not take much time or any particular expertise to ferret out this bit of information. All that's necessary is a sheet of paper, a sharp pencil, and a twenty-five-mile round-trip to three graveyards. The bloodline beyond James, however, is not quite so obvious and depends on which family member you're bent to believe.

It becomes a mite confusing because in 1803, Kentucky issued land warrants to not one, but *two* James Wards. Still, there is general agreement about which of the two Jameses my family can claim, because the property he was granted, though broken up considerably, is right near the home place of my distant cousins. Indeed I found out recently that Sister and I are heirs to some tiniest piece of the Pack-Preston cemetery—recently christened the Friendship Memorial Gardens—also close to this property.

According to Billie Edyth Ward—an up-the-creek neighbor and local historian who has looked into this matter—these two James Wards were differentiated in court records as "James Ward, Senr." and "James Ward, Junr." but were "not necessarily father and son." To which I have to respond, "Too bad!" I mean, really, too durned bad. If these two had been father and son, we'd have an easier time peering back of them with some degree of certainty into our more distant Ward family history back there in Virginia and on over in the north country of England, Scotland, and Ireland. But I don't want to lay claim to a bloodline based on pure conjecture, so I'll just tell stories about those folks anybody can find in the old burial grounds and be done with it.

For the record, I'm claiming James Senior, whose land warrant reads: "100 acres beginning 14 poles above the mouth of Greasy Creek . . . 'thence up the river to the beginning." Billie Edyth Ward notes that "this survey surrounded what is now known as Old House Branch and came back to the river opposite the mouth of Tom's Creek," which is the Levisa Fork of the Big Sandy. Don't misunderstand here; I did not simply choose James Senior capriciously. I have more of a right to lay claim to this James Senior than a simple land warrant. Most of my ancestor-searching relatives agree with Billie Edyth Ward's account that "the senior James Ward was married to Sarah 'Sally,' whose last name was likely Osborn." The rest, as they say, is history. The Ward book lists the offspring of Sally and James Senior as Solomon (1775), Shadrach (1786), Sarah "Sally" (1790), William (1792), and Mary "Polly" (1795). All of these children were born in Virginia; James and Sally had one other child, Abby, whose birth date is unknown but whose existence is documented in Floyd County, Kentucky, records of 1812, wherein she is listed as the "infirm daughter of Sarah Ward," who was allowed "$20 for her support."

The next kin I'm claiming is James and Sally's fourth child, William (1792–circa 1860), who first shows up in Kentucky records when he took out a license to marry Elizabeth Meek (1804–circa 1875) on January 11, 1816. According to the Ward book, William and Elizabeth settled on the Levisa Fork of the Big Sandy River near River or Offutt, Kentucky, and produced fifteen children, the eighth of whom was my daddy's great-grandpa Shadrach Ward (1829–circa 1897). Shadrach, who was known as "Shade" or "Shady," married Nancy "Hettie" Daniel (circa 1830–after 1910) sometime before 1850. From 1851 to 1874, this union produced nine children, two of whom figure prominently in my daddy's heritage. Shade and Hettie's oldest child, Elizabeth Ward (1851–1928), married Eliphus Preston (1845–1929) and bore him nine children. Their fourth child, Paris (1879–1955), was my daddy's father, my Pop Pop. Shade and Hettie's fourth child, Asbury Ward (1859–1936), married Laura Bell Price (1861–1946), whose second child, Alice (1885–1947), was Daddy's mother, my grandma Alk. Most of Grandma Alk's side—the Wards—can be found in the Bob's Branch graveyard, beginning with Asbury and Laura Bell Ward, Grandmommy Ward—the first one of my relatives I remember from anything other than worn pictures.

The Asbury and Laura Bell Ward family that began with the two of them in the little red tin house, still standing in the head of Bob's Branch, is now scattered like wildflower seeds across the world. The fecundity of Asbury and Laura Bell's generation—and that of their children—combined with the mobility of the last two generations suggests this family's DNA is unlikely to die out until the final accounting is called by the Lord. What's more, "when that roll is called up yonder," at least four generations of the Asbury line will be found resting on that Bob's Branch ridge within the same fence and nestled up as close as we can get to the old Patriarch himself.

That high ridge is within walking distance of the little red tin house, within walking distance of where my daddy was born—indeed, where most of Asbury and Laura Bell's children were born. At one time during his middle-aged years, old Asbury could walk from his place on the head of Bob's Branch to where he now lies at final rest and visit along the way with the families of four of his daughters. That's every one of my Ward great-aunts except Hettie, who'd moved up the river to Auxier so her husband could work in the mines. Now three of those girls—along with several grandkids and greats—cluster up there in the Ward Preston graveyard near him and Laura Bell. Those of us who are left regularly make our way through the gate, up the hill, through the cow pies, sometimes to pay our respects, but more often to take our troubles home.

First, of course, is Asbury (though his name is spelled As*berry* on the tombstone, most of the descendants agree his name was originally spelled with a *u*), whose tomb near the center of this graveyard faces the morning sun, without a sign of a shade tree to block the early light. By his death on June 14, 1936, Asbury did not have far to travel from his deathbed to his gravesite. By all reports, he breathed his last in his bed downstairs in the home of his youngest daughter, Exer, whose family lived upstairs in the only brick house on Bob's Branch (in 1936). This brick house—two stories tall—hugged the hillside barely a mile south of the little red tin house where most of Asbury and Laura Bell's younger children grew up.

As their children and grandchildren began to patch off down the branch, Asbury and Laura Bell helped their children get a start. Later their kids in turn helped them. Thus, when they were no longer able to live on their own in the tin house, Asbury and Laura Bell moved into the first floor of the brick house, where their youngest daughter, Exer, could take care of them. Exer and her husband, Keenis Holbrook, (Gwen's parents) had bought the brick house from Dan and Annalee Gambill—daughter of Asbury's oldest daughter, Ella, and her husband, Roby Johnson—when the Holbrooks grew tired of wintering over in the Estep place up nearer the head of Bob's Branch. That Ella Johnson was my great-aunt Ella, who herself created and sold hats sometime in the thirties.

When she was eight years old, one of my Ward cousins, named Jane, bought a white straw hat with pink ribbons streaming down her back from Aunt Ella. Jane recalls her mother taking her to Aunt Ella's house, where she got to choose from a selection of hats laid out on the bed. The day after purchasing the hat, Jane had to stay home because she was too sick to go to school. By noon, however, she was feeling better, and her mother let Jane wear her new hat to school. The family was living in the little red tin house then, and Jane remembers braids and ribbons flying out behind her as she skipped all the way down Bob's Branch to the school.

The first twenty-five years of the twentieth century in rural America was a hard life for anybody who tried to live off the land. Old folks would add, "The farther up the branch, the harder it got, too." Aunt Exer's older girls have fond memories of their early days on the head of Bob's Branch and of moving from the tin house, to the Estep place, to the brick house, and of families following each other one at a time in the inexorable march out of that hollow. Though they recall the hardships of those times, more powerful are memories of exultation, of skipping to school in the sunshine, ribbons streaming in the pure joy of youth. As Jane says, "People would just get tired of all the trouble—getting in and out of there, with the snow and the mud and all—and would move one or two houses down the creek."

Though most folks moved down the branch, then out altogether, it is not at all unusual to find descendants who went away to find work, then later moved back near the home place. I still have at least one cousin, however—a granddaughter of Asbury and Laura Bell—who lives with her husband in her family's home place near the head of the Left Fork of Bob's Branch. She could have moved out and away long ago, for her husband has made a good living, but they chose to stay and raise their family in the now-modernized house she was born in. Choosing to stay on or near the home place has never been uncommon among those who had that choice to make. Improved roads, electricity, and indoor plumbing have made the head of Bob's Branch a far more comfortable venue than it was a hundred years ago, when Asbury and Laura Bell were at home in the little red tin house.

Now then, to figure out the other side of Daddy's family—also descended from old Shadrach and Hettie—we need to travel approximately ten miles by highway or just across the mountain if we were inclined to walk it. I don't know where Shade and Hettie lived in their youth or even how they met, but I know they ended up on Bob's Branch in an old graveyard up on the ridge behind what's left of the little red tin house. Their oldest child, Elizabeth Ward (1851–1928), married Eliphus Preston (1845–1929) and bore him nine children. The fourth child born to this pair, Paris (1879–1955), was my daddy's father, my Pop Pop.

Any attempt to place my great-grandfather Eliphus in the context of known history raises the question of his leanings, indeed his probable conscription into one army or another during the Civil War. He would have been in his late teens when the fighting was going on and almost surely would have been needed. Apparently, however, old Life lucked out there . . . or opted out . . . or even hid out, maybe, but as far as I can determine, he—like the rest of our people—never fought on either side. Don't interpret this to mean our people were just chicken-hearted either. I think it just reveals our propensity for staying out of what's none of our business.

Great-Grandfather Eliphus, known to my daddy as Grandpa Life, married Elizabeth Ward on May 22, 1866, little more than four months past her fifteenth birthday. Their oldest child, Jesse, was born in 1869. Three girls and four boys later, in November 1896 forty-five-year-old Elizabeth gave birth to their last child, Jay. Uncle Jay was something of a dandy, and more than one person has said his wife, Gladys, was the prettiest woman in the Big Sandy Valley. The two of them seemed old when I knew them, so I cannot confirm that opinion, but they lived in a tiny house on the main street in Paintsville.

When Uncle Jay lay a corpse in that house in the summer of 1949, I recall hearing some folks talking about what killed him. I believe that's the first time I ever heard the word "cancer," but I overheard a neighbor saying that Uncle Jay could have prevented his death. According to this woman, all he had to do was eat a lot of meat and the cancer would live off the meat and not attack my great-uncle's vital organs. When we got in the car to go home, I told Momma and Daddy, who assured me that such was not the case. The woman whose conversation I had overheard seemed so much more certain of her knowledge than either of my parents that I remember thinking I'd sure try the meat-eating cure if *I* ever got cancer.

I was always given to believe that my daddy was named for his Grandpa "Life" and his Uncle "Jay." Until I began researching this work, however, I didn't know his grandfather was named "Eliphus" Preston and his uncle Jay was named "William Jennings Bryan" Preston. Daddy had no birth certificate, but nowhere does a Bible, personal correspondence, or census record report his name as Eliphus or William Jennings Bryan. Over the course of his life, however, he was addressed and recorded as everything from Life to Lifie Jay to Jay to Elipha to E. Jay.

Great-Grandpa Life Preston and Elizabeth bore and raised all nine of their children in the home place between Two-Mile and Offutt, right near the mouth of Greasy Creek. Life owned and ran a gristmill across Greasy Creek from Meade School, about three miles from where Greasy empties into the Levisa Fork of the Big Sandy down at River. I went to the home place with Daddy and Pop Pop a couple of times when I was a girl, and we took a route that cannot be traveled today. Turning off the main road (KY 40) near where Two-Mile Creek empties into Greasy there at Meade School, we headed down Offutt to Herb Pack's house. Herb is Aunt Wid (Awilda) Pack's boy, hence Pop Pop's nephew. From there we walked across a swinging bridge and walked up behind the millpond to the home place. I don't recall a house being there when we went, but I do remember Daddy saying, "Now you think about that old sumbitch raising that big family on a piece of property no better'n this." Pop Pop just shook his head. "He was a worker."

The swinging bridge is gone now, torn down, and you just can't get to the home place from that direction anymore. I understand that if you want to walk it, you can take off up the branch past the old Myrtle Ward place near the mouth of Two-Mile Creek and reach it that way. The best way, however, to find the old Life Preston home place is to go to where Life Preston rests to this day. There's a road—or something that passes for one—following the old narrow-gauge railroad track that used to let them haul coal from the head of Two-Mile down to the river. My cousin Robert Lynn Elam has the original deed giving the coal company the right to lay that track, signed by Eliphus Preston and Bartley Pack, both his great-grandfathers. The tracks and ties are gone now, but the makeshift road that took their place carries a traveler to the graves of Eliphus, Elizabeth, and a number of their heirs.

To the right of the lane, a small wooden sign bearing the name "PRESTON" is nailed to a tree at the entrance to the burial ground, which sits on a point overlooking the millpond, where Life made his living. Just before the graveyard, another lane turns off to the left at the entrance to the old Eliphus and Elizabeth Preston home place. Just like Daddy's other grandfather—Life's brother-in-law, Asbury Ward—Life, too, could walk from his home place to his grave without breaking a sweat.

Going home has always been an easy task for me, since in many ways I never left in the first place, but the trip home does not begin with Two-Mile—or even Greasy, where I was born in the same room as my momma and maybe even her daddy. The other side of my family began down at River and over on Bob's Branch with my daddy's people, several generations of which are represented in a family graveyard on the top of one of those Bob's Branch hills.

I turn my car east off the new U.S. 23 just west of Paintsville, Kentucky, drive the bypass past Johnson Central High School, built in the early sixties to consolidate Meade Memorial (my old high school) with the other county high schools, Oil Springs and Flat Gap. On the right, I pass the roads up the mountain to Kmart and Kroger as I take note of the Wal-Mart and Dollar Store, among others, perched in the bottom-land shopping center on my left. All the signs of late-twentieth-century progress convene right here on the Paintsville bypass. Some might say that not nearly enough has bypassed Paintsville, the Johnson County seat. Pizza Hut, McDonald's, and Arby's, among others, offer quick relief from hunger pangs or thirst. By the time I get to "the Stafford Bottom" (what Momma always called the Stafford addition to what was once Paintsville proper), I have passed not one entity that was in existence during the time I was growing up in the forties and fifties in Johnson County. Other than annoyance at being slowed down, I hardly notice this small-town sprawl, because I consider it none of my business. I was never really at home in this part of the county anyway, so what happens—or doesn't—over here is not my concern. Since I never claimed to have anything to do with anybody or anything within these city limits, Greater Paintsville, as it were, was never within my emotional or intellectual jurisdiction.

The bottom, however, that part of town, while not exactly my old stomping ground, does hold some fond memories. There's Doug Plummer's service station, though Doug doesn't own it anymore. Doug was married to my first cousin, Betty Ann Mollette—Uncle John's girl—and we thought of him as family. Daddy traded with Doug—and later with the next couple of owners, so I'll gas up here on my way back out of town. Old habits die hard, so I continue to express what feels like loyalty long after anybody knows about it or expects it. Indeed, since I have no idea how many times this old service station has changed hands—or whose hands, even—my "loyalty" is irrational. I know that. It's also strangely comforting.

For now, I cut through the street back of Doug's service station, pass the Paintsville High School football field—home of the Tigers—winding up at the Dairy Queen, perhaps my favorite Paintsville destination. Their footlong-sauce-and-slaw used to be about worth the eight-mile trip from Two-Mile; still is, in my opinion. But today, I just do a right at the stop sign, then a fairly quick left and, crossing Paint Creek, am soon at the stoplight, where I pick up KY 40, the highway home.

From my earliest memory, Kentucky Route 40 was known as the main road through the River Narz (Narrows), 'cross Two-Mile Hill, and on through Spicy Gap to Inez and Kermit—the only way in or out of Two-Mile. I could say that in my head it's Creeker Highway. Then again, so are U.S. 460, U.S. 23, and all roads leading in or out of the city limits of any small town in these hills.

Heading east on 40 toward home, it's hard to recognize anything much for all the development. I smile in fond remembrance as the first short straightaway reveals the site of the Cain Drive-in Theater. There, on many a summer's Saturday night, Billy Daniel and I were restrained from making a commitment neither of us was ready for by the presence of our little sisters watching both us and the movie from the back end of his 1955 green pickup truck. The drive-in, that familiar relic of the fifties—where many a family was started, I'll betcha—has given way to an extended care facility, surrounded by houses and what looks to be an apartment building or two.

But soon I'm past the King addition, the River Narz road construction, and turning left down Bob's Branch. I drive down Thelma, through the progress of the last half of the twentieth century. Though I haven't roamed down Bob's Branch more than a mile or two beyond the graveyard in maybe forty years, Gwen Holbrook is with me today and we decide to drive on a piece. We pull in and take a picture or two of Little Friendship Primitive Baptist Church, built by my Pop Pop. Next thing you know, old Gwen and I are on our way to the head of Right Fork of Bob's Branch, where both our families began—the old Asbury Ward place. Time and prosperity have wrought predictable changes on Bob's Branch, as expensive new houses now line the road up to the old Ward home place.

About twenty feet above the road, at the top of a winding path, the little house now stands alone on this damp spring morning. I would have expected the very picture of a shack, listing a little, maybe—rotted boards that had not known paint for more than half a century. But such is not the case. This small house has endured more than a hundred years of hard family living, but it's still standing strong, covered now in tan asbestos shingles and clean as a pin. With old Shadrach and Hettie buried right up on that point, the little house stands as testament to the Ward heritage. Today, all is quiet. Not a soul to be seen on the road or up the bank, no sounds of children, no animals even.

But *once* . . . once it was completely covered in red tin siding, corrugated to look like brick, and that tiny place housed a family now strewn throughout the lower forty-eight. Originally, the tin house was the home of Grandpa Asbury (1859–1936) and Grandma Laura Bell (1861–1946) Ward, whose second daughter, Alice Ward Preston (1885–1947), was my daddy's mother, whose last daughter, Exer Ward Holbrook (1899–1975), was Gwen's mother.

I stop my Jeep in the middle of the road to take a picture of the house of our common grandparents as we swap stories we have heard about that side of the family. Since both Gwen and I trace our bloodline back to that house, we wonder aloud to each other about what Asbury and Laura Bell would make of the huge brick homes now a part of that hollow. Gwen thinks I should get out of the Jeep to take my pictures, but I point out to her that we don't know any of these folks anymore.

"We may not know them, but I'll bet most of them are kin to us," she says.

"Okay, but since they don't know they're family, and this Jeep's got Montana plates, I'm not getting out."

"Linda Sue! What's wrong with you?"

"Ain't come all this way to get shot by a cousin. Besides, I got my pictures. Can't believe the little red tin house is in as good a shape as it is."

According to Gwen's sister, Kat, in the mid-thirties Grandpa Asbury and Grandma Laura Bell still lived in that little house. When any one of the Ward daughters—or granddaughters—were expecting, Grandpa Asbury would ready the sleigh two months before the due date so as to go for the doctor. The doctor would then come and stay with the family until the child was delivered. Sometimes he was there for only one night, sometimes longer. A lot of babies were born on this branch before all these fine brick houses were built. Aunt Exer had Gwen just one hundred yards down Bob's Branch, on a three-by-five-foot table in the very same house where my daddy was born. Gwen's birth on June 8, 1940, was one of the last of that particular Ward line to be born there on Bob's Branch.

Progress and prosperity of a sort came to our people along with World War II, and, for a time, the small town of Paintsville was home to three hospitals. Most births after the war would have been in the Paintsville Hospital, a two-story wooden structure in the lower end of Paintsville;

the Golden Rule Hospital, a few blocks west of the Johnson County Courthouse; and later at the Paintsville Clinic, just a half block east of Courthouse Square. Since Bob's Branch was closer to Paintsville than, say, Greasy or Two-Mile, it is likely that home births were less frequent there than in the more remote reaches of eastern Johnson County.

After about half an hour of time travel and picture taking, Gwen and I head back down Bob's Branch. We pull up to the meadow gate, get out, unchain and drag the gate, pull across the stile, and clear the gate. Then I get out, chain it up again, and head my Jeep Cherokee—with its Montana-RMC (Rocky Mountain College) plates—up the hill for another date with Momma, Daddy, Gwen's mother and daddy, and at least three generations of Ward/Preston history, going all the way back to ancestor Asbury.

I suppose this hill, like most others in the area, was once log woods, but it must have been a long time ago, because this climb has been through a cow pasture as long as either of us can recall. Though each person has a slightly different version of the history of this graveyard, Momma always said that Pop Pop bought the property and fenced it to keep the cows out. That may be just one more tidbit in the myth of my immediate family, so I cannot say for sure that it is true. One thing I can do with certainty, however, is describe what—and who of my own kin— is here at this moment. I can even trace how far they traveled to get here.

Here in the twenty-first century, the birds still sing you awake on a summer's morning at Three Forks of Greasy, and the frogs and the crickets serenade you to sleep at night. That much has not changed since young Elijah Mollette carried his bride, Emma Cline, here in December 1891. He had good intentions, Grandpa Lige. Who'd have thought he'd have to live out his last twenty years with his wife playing the roles of both man and woman on the home place? But that's the way it was, much as it plagues me to tell it.

Most of the land my family called the hillside bottom that lies to the west of Three Forks of Greasy Creek is on record as mine now—mine and Sister's. We've not sold off any of it since Daddy died, and I seriously doubt we ever will. Now, the good Lord knows we could sure use the money, and it's not as if we or our children ever had plans to go back there and live. No, I doubt that any direct descendant of the Mollettes or the Clines will ever again make that piece of ground come to life under his hand. I know that in some ways it's a shame to let it lie fallow, to grow over in cheat grass and honeysuckle. But then again, just building an A-frame there on the creek bank wouldn't exactly be the legacy that land deserves either. It was made to be worked, trod upon by kids and dogs and a cow or two—looked at every day for what it could be, not merely what it is. After all, that piece of earth more or less supported four generations of my family. From my earliest memory, we worked a garden there. Later on, selling off a house seat or two gave my daddy a start on what ultimately became a right good living for him and Momma.

I should say right here that I doubt that a one of my people ever worked that ground because they wanted to. Best I can determine, theirs was a have-to existence from the first. None of them that I know of ever had much choice of whether to stay or go. In my family, the notion of preference pretty much originated with my generation, and most of us didn't have the good sense to know we had that power till we'd about squandered it.

Our kids, though—early on Sister and I gave them so many choices that it just about immobilized them. We've been lucky that they finally got their legs under them and are doing okay. Or maybe it's they who are lucky, but you can bet on one thing: I assure you that not one of the latest generation of Cline-Mollettes has ever considered going back to live there at Three Forks of Greasy Creek. There are three of them, my progeny and Sister's—direct descendants of old Elias Mollette—who will someday hold title to what is left of the Lige Mollette property. Yet not a one of them would know the meaning of the word "grubbing," much less how to go about doing it. Amanda McKinley Greer, Ryen Preston Greer, and Brett Preston Scott—the end of our Mollette line, at least for now. What do they see as they look at that piece of ground? Yes sir, I wonder. They have a history on that land, a history as manifest as the land itself, for the demands of that piece of ground shaped four generations of Cline-Mollettes. For good or bad, our history lives on in every one of us, its legacy continuing to give meaning to all we touch. Terrain shapes history, too; don't think it doesn't.

I am the fifth generation of Momma's people to have worked the ground at Three Forks of Greasy—the second, maybe third, generation to have been born in the log-and-batten-board house on that property. If Momma or Daddy were here, they'd be sure to remind all of us that I worked that piece of earth as little as I could get away with. I guess I'll have to admit that's close to the truth, but I was the first generation whose sustenance never depended on working that ground.

By the time I came along, my mother's people had lived off that land from the time old Elias Mollette (1783–circa 1865) left Scott County, Virginia, for the trip through Pound Gap in the head of the river to join his half-brother, Nathan, in Kentucky. Elias settled on Greasy Creek, in what was then Floyd County, probably by laying a land warrant on all the property that hadn't already been claimed by somebody who got there earlier. Might be that better-off folks from the central part of the state had already claimed some of it, but in those days their claims could often be bought for very little cash money. No, the flatlanders hadn't bought that land with an eye toward working it, since they considered those hills and hollows pretty close to worthless. Such land was too hard to work—unless you were a poor man, that is.

When I was in school they taught us that the Pilgrims and the Puritans made that treacherous trip across the water to avoid religious persecution. What the history books of that day did not make clear, however, was that once those colonists got here they were just about as narrow and inflexible about religion as the people they had been trying to get away from. For all our talk of freedom, that hasn't changed a lot today. From Hardshell Baptist to bred-in-the-bone nonbeliever, people are seldom willing to keep their mouths shut about what they see as the truth, and they'll follow their pronouncements with laws, too, if you let them. Since my family has had its share of heretics on all sides of the religious issue, I want to believe it was a desire for independence that drove old Elias to make his way through that wild, green country from the head of the river (Levisa Fork of the Big Sandy) to the head of Greasy Creek. It's more than likely, however, that Elias followed in the footsteps of his half-brother, Nathan—who'd come nearly a decade earlier—because back home in Virginia neither had much choice about whether to stay or go.

A man had to eat, and in order to do that he had to make his own poke. That meant he had to get himself a piece of ground to work, a cow for milk and butter, and a pig or two to provide fried meat and grease for his gravy. He also needed a wife to put up that food, make soap out of the wood ashes and meat grease, clean and mend his clothes, and have some younguns to help with the pure old drudgery required to keep a place going. Love and companionship were one thing, staying alive was another, and everybody knows it takes a family to work a place.

Sometime before 1815, Elias married Sarah Gibson (1795–circa 1870), who provided him with the comforts of a wife and family. By the time Elias and Sarah got their call to Glory, they had brought forth nine children to whom they passed along their good name as well as almost all the land on the Middle and Left Forks of Greasy Creek. Their next-to-last child was my great-grandfather, one John B. "Big-eye" Mollette (1822–1907). The story goes that there were so many John Mollettes that they had to go by their nicknames: Big-eye, Little-eye, Good-eye, and Cutfly. Since the story says Cutfly was so named because of his ability with a whip, I know that leads to some curiosity in regard to eye size in my family. Well, I've looked, and let me say right here that far as I can tell, my eyes and those of all the Lige line are quite normal—not one big-eye among us.

In 1864, Big-eye married Amanda Wells (circa 1843–circa 1876), a union that produced six children, the fourth of whom was my grandpa Elijah Mollette (1872–1939). Though he died almost two years before I was born, the person Grandpa Lige was and the life he lived with my grandma Emmy, lives on in stories and in images that are as clear to me as people and events that happened directly to me in my own experience. Though the Mollette home place was located in Johnson County, during Grandpa Lige's growing-up years Three Forks of Greasy had its face turned more toward Inez (Martin County seat) than Paintsville (Johnson County seat). The road system that ultimately positioned Greasy Creek almost midway between these two county seats had not been built, which meant no real obstacle lay between Greasy and Inez, while the Levisa Fork of the Big Sandy River separated the 250 or so folks who lived in Paintsville from residents of the eastern part of Johnson County. It is no surprise, then, that when young Lige met and courted a girl, he took himself a wife from Martin County.

By the time Elijah Mollette married seventeen-year-old Emma Cline (Grandma Emmy always told that she married at sixteen, but records belie this) and brought her to Three Forks, his family owned a couple hundred acres that encompassed parts of Left, Middle, and Right Forks of Greasy Creek. He would have carried her from her home in Martin County in a wagon drawn by two horses—his own horses, by the way, which indicates he was a little more prosperous than the everyday fellow of the time. When Emma Cline married Elijah Mollette, he was a young man with good prospects. He even had a house to bring her to, a circumstance not common in that day and time.

From stories she told me, I can picture Grandma Emmy as a young girl. She was tall, straight-backed, and rail-thin, her waist-length black hair swept back and anchored with combs at her crown. Her distinctively dark Cline face—not yet wizened by age and sunshine—filled with optimism for a promising future as the wife of young Lige and mother of his children. Both of the youthful Mollettes cut a fine figure then, when Lige stood tall and straight, before some combination of illness and hard living made him into what barely passed for a man.

Don't misunderstand here; I do not believe my grandmother had any illusions that her future would be anything other than filled with hard work. Pure drudgery was the standard for country women in those days—a life filled with birthing, nursing, and bringing up as many babies as the Lord sent, while continually laboring in both house and field. Billie Edyth Ward recalls her own mother saying, "I just accepted that I would have several children. I never gave it a thought." I can recall Grandma Emmy commenting to Momma that one or another local woman had "done good" when she managed to put considerable space between her babies. By the mid-twentieth century, as the economy shifted and the land ran out, children became more of a burden than a blessing. I am not sure where or when Grandma Emmy picked up that negative view of female fecundity, but she certainly passed it along to Momma, and both of them said as much to me many times. Though there were few reliable methods of birth control, I was given to understand very early that it reflected badly on a woman to bear a number of children.

The strenuous labor necessary to work a place was not new to Emma, for even as a bride her hands were not uncalloused. As her nephew Bob Allen says, "All of them worked the ground their whole lives, but no doubt about it, Aunt Emmy had it the hardest." By "all of them" Bob meant the four Cline girls, Louan, Laura, Emma, and Eliza, and their only brother, Grover. Their growing-up years had been far from easy, since their father, Jacob Cline (1849–circa 1937), could not be depended on to do much of anything around the home place. Though U.S. Census records for 1900 still list Jacob as head of the household (indicating that he did not leave his family for a woman who lived over near the train station in West Virginia until Grover, the youngest, had passed his sixteenth birthday), Grandma Emmy told a different story.

She always said her daddy had done all but move out before she left home to marry Grandpa Lige on the third of December in 1891. According to her, old Jake could not even be bothered to come home for Christmas the last few years she lived at home, leaving her to help her mother make Christmas for the little'ns, Eliza (1881–1956) and Grover (1884–1959). Even before Jake Cline left the family for good, he spent most of his time with that sorry old rip from West Virginia. He used his job taking tickets at the train station in Kermit as an excuse to spend weeks at a time away from home, leaving his two younger girls, his only son, and his wife, Martha, to work the land they lived on. But then Jake never was one to stay at home much, which you can tell by looking at the birth dates of the kids.

When country women discuss private matters with each other, they are likely to cup their hands around their mouths so nobody else can hear. They might remember that "little pitchers" have *good* ears, as well as big ones, and proceed with caution. Birth control—or the lack of same—was one of the primary topics requiring the cupped-hand mode.

"You know poor old Janie Lee Bowens is pregnant again. Bless her heart."

"How many does this make anyway . . . a dozen?"

"I'm gonna say this'll be her tenth, but seems like she lost a couple, so . . . Lord, this'n may be her thirteenth, and she's still a young woman."

"Why, I'd bet you money she's not thirty years old. Humph! She must be weaning them early."

The cupped-hand version of the Jake and Martha story holds that when the young couple set up housekeeping just two years after the end of the Civil War, "folks well knew what made babies." Reliable methods of preventing them from coming every year or so while being a dutiful wife to a man? Well, that was another question. Much of the folk wisdom held that a nursing mother couldn't get pregnant, so a lot of women nursed babies for two years as a means of spacing their children. Grandma Emmy proudly pointed out that she bore a child every three years, from Lizzie in 1894 to Grace in 1915.

Back then, almost any widow woman would tell you that when you see more than four years between a couple's kids—another cupped-hand topic—you don't have to look hard to see trouble of some kind. Could be a sickly woman, might be a miscarriage or two, or could be a man gone for some reason or another, but you can bet there's trouble of some kind behind it. Jacob and Martha's first baby, Louan (1867–1913) came just a year into their marriage, followed by Laura (1868–1937) nineteen months later. For reasons we can only guess at, seven barren years passed before Martha delivered her third child, my grandma, Emma (1874–1953). Unless there was a miscarriage, maybe even a couple, that could mean "trouble," or it could be that Jacob simply left home to find work.

What we do know—if Grandma Emmy is to be believed—is that by the turn of the twentieth century, Jake had left the home place to go live with one Joshia Brewer over near where he worked in West Virginia. He might even have married the woman—and she may well have been an upstanding woman, but not in the lore of my family—for Grandma Emmy always referred to her as a "mean woman." According to Billie Edyth Ward, who taught with Aunt Stella at the Middle Fork of Greasy grade school, Aunt Stella said Grandma Emmy despised "mean women" because of what her daddy had done. As was the custom of the day, when Great-Grandpa Jake left home, any source of cash income left with him, hence Great-Grandma Martha was left to eke out a hard farm living for herself and her two youngest children. The Cline's family home place consisted of more than one hundred acres, a good bit of it in bottom land, set off to the left of a broad curve on what became Kentucky Route 40 heading east into Inez, which was then called Eden. Naturally, the only son, Uncle Grover—the baby of the family—would inherit the home place, thereby making it incumbent on the Cline girls to marry their living.

When Emma Cline married Elijah Mollette, she had every reason to expect that he would be a good provider, so she sat proudly on that wagon, looking forward to her first Christmas as mistress of her own house. She'd done well for herself by all the standards of that day. Married up, she had—the only way for a woman to advance herself in those days. And just what had she advanced herself to? Well, first there was the house; we know quite a lot about that house, because it stood until the late fifties. About a mile or so off the main road, just past the first blind curve heading up Greasy Creek, and to the left of the dirt road in a little clearing sat the house. It was right at the Three Forks of Greasy Creek—nearly two hundred yards above where Left Fork wound past Mandy Walters's store and Little Friendship United Baptist Church, and about one hundred yards shy of where Middle Fork and Right Fork separated in front of the schoolhouse bottom.

According to Billie Edyth Ward, the more than one-hundred acre farm, Lige's place, "began at Left Fork stream . . . included the mouths of Middle Fork and Right Fork . . . and [across Greasy Creek] . . . up Right Fork to . . . the Ora Dutton place." Though by today's standards the house would be considered small, back then Ms. Ward recalls it as "a big double-log house." She further writes:

> I believe the house may have been built long before the turn of the century. The weather boarding covered the logs which I'm guessing the main house was made of. The farm where Calvin Daniel now lives was known as the "John R. Mollett[e]" place as far back as I can remember. (John R. was a half-brother of Elijah.) Of course, they had moved away—died most likely—when I first recall, but they still had ownership. Almost all the land in the Middle Fork and Left Fork (Buttermilk) was owned by the Mollett[e]s and their descendants. I can't recall just where John B. (Lige's father) was said to have lived, but one of my grandpa's brothers told about "going in Big-eye's cornfield and getting corn for [his] oxen." That means it was somewhere in the Middle Fork, maybe near the mouth of the creek as he was going home to Spring Knob.

I was born in 1941, and the house on my grandmother's property never changed over my lifetime. By the time I came to know it, the house probably had not been whitewashed in many years, but I never thought it looked as if it needed paint. The structure sat up on a small bank on the left-hand side of the dirt road as the hills backed off enough to allow the three forks of Greasy Creek to flow into each other. The Lige Mollette house sat in a clearing between Left and Middle Forks of Greasy Creek across the dirt road from Right Fork and came into view as you rounded the first blind curve going up Greasy Creek. It was less than a mile off the main road.

There was enough space for Daddy to pull his car to the top of the bank and come to a stop hard up against the black iron kettle that sat on a raised circle of rocks over a charred space at the far southwestern corner of the yard. I saw my grandma use that old pot for rendering lard, making soap, and boiling hogshead for souse (a spicy sausage). She said she had also used the kettle to boil her apples, tomatoes, and beans for large-quantity canning in the days when she had so many kids at home, but I never saw that happen. By the time I was around, she did her canning on the coal cook stove in the kitchen.

About ten steps from the left car door was a huge green apple tree that during summer filled out to completely cover the yard. That old tree was so big that I was about grown before I could get me a handhold to climb it by myself, but with a little start-up boost from Gwen, I found it to be one great climbing tree. One summer Daddy hung me a rope-with-board-seat swing from the lowest limb. Well, I swung and twisted so much I wore all the grass from the yard underneath it, and Grandma Emmy made Daddy take my swing down. We were not the kind of folks who "swept the yard" even if it meant briggidy (exuberant, show-off, smarty pants) little girls had to give up swinging. That tree wasn't just for fun either. It produced hard golf-ball-sized apples—a multitude of them—that were just right for cooking but too sour to eat. Of course, we ate them anyway, though Momma always warned they'd give us the bellyache.

The house itself had faded to palest gray, and there was no hint that it had ever been painted—no chipping or peeling—more like it might have been whitewashed sometime far in the past, and whatever white had been there had been long devoured by the wood itself.

The porch extended completely across the front of the house, and there were three chimneys—one on either side of the structure and another, which you couldn't see from the road, off the lean-to kitchen out back. Two rocking chairs and a swing occupied the front porch, and ladder-back, cane-bottomed chairs were brought from the front room as necessary. Most of the time, however, when there were more visitors than could be comfortably seated in the swing and rockers, folks just sat on the edge of the porch. Once I got too big to sit on Grandma Emmy's lap, my favorite seat was on the porch at the top of its two steps. Although the steps were stone, they consisted simply of a double layer of big flat rocks stacked flat on the ground—stone, but no mortar.

Several times I heard Daddy offer to build Grandma Emmy some good wooden steps, but she would have none of that. "Those steps have been there since I came on the place and they'll outlast me," she said. And they did.

My grandmother was survived by more than her old stone steps, too. The stand of sweet peas that grew ever larger just outside the apple tree's shade, near the southeastern edge of her yard, remained long after she died, but the morning glories that grew up the four skinny porch posts never came back, though Momma planted new seeds for several years. The dirt around that old porch was so hard-packed it's a wonder my grandmother ever got anything to grow, but she always had a way with her flowers.

Two doors provided access from the front porch into Grandma Emmy's house. The left entrance led directly into what we called the "front room," and the door on the right entered the "upper room." Heading toward the kitchen required walking directly through the front room, negotiating your way between a grouping of wooden ladder-back and rocking chairs gathered 'round the fireplace off to the left and the two quilt-topped iron beds, one in each corner on the right. Just before the door to the dining room was a narrow enclosed stairway leading up to the loft, which consisted of one plain room. The walls were exposed timber, with no ceiling or insulation between the room and the roof. Nails had been driven into the walls of the loft to substitute for wardrobes. The better clothes were placed on hangers—two or three to a nail—and sometimes four or five garments per hanger, while work clothes drooped directly from the nails. The loft was outfitted with four quilt-topped iron beds, identical to those in the front room, placed end to end in each of the four corners of the room. There in the loft each family member had a nail and a hanger, as well as a cardboard box for his or her personal garments, for there were no closets or chests in my grandmother's house.

The dining room was the center of Grandma Emmy's house, though the absence of any heat source rendered it unusable on winter's coldest days. It led from the front room into the kitchen and was furnished with two trunks, a pie safe, and a long, narrow table that could seat a dozen. Other than the loft, it was the only room in the house that did not have either a stove or a fireplace, so it depended on the leftover heat from the coal cook stove in the kitchen and the front room fireplace.

The only other room in the Mollette home place was what was always called the "upper room," for reasons I cannot fathom. This room, accessed by the right door on Grandma Emmy's front porch, was filled with four more iron beds, placed exactly as were those in the loft. Like the front room, the upper room also had a fireplace, but there were no chairs around it. A quilt horse hung from the ceiling of the room and was raised and lowered by heavy twine that stretched to each of the four corners of the room and was caught on small hooks placed in the ceiling corners and halfway down each corner.

All the family spent enough time there to attest that little had changed about the home place between 1891, when Grandma Emmy married into it, and 1953, when she was carried from it to be buried beside her husband in the tiny graveyard within sight of the front porch swing. Oh, the house got electric lights in 1949, when the Rural Electric Association (REA) brought electricity off the main road and lit up Greasy Creek all the way to Pigeon Roost. Despite having lived past the middle point of the twentieth century, however, Grandma Emmy never had running water in her kitchen, or an indoor toilet, or a bathtub. The house never had central heat or even a coal furnace. The two front rooms were heated by open fireplaces and the kitchen by a coal cook stove, leaving the dining room and attic with no heat source. Though the stark description of Grandma Emmy's home place sounds severe, I do not recall ever thinking of it in that way. She always had enough coal to fire up the cook stove and always had something to cook on it.

One of the problems with attempting to chronicle the life of Grandma Emmy—her paralyzed husband, her nine children, and the grandchildren she took to raise for periods ranging from a week to a lifetime—is that all the hardships make it appear so serious and sad that you just wonder how they managed to get up in the morning and keep going. Well, whatever images I recall from my time spent with Grandma Emmy at Three Forks of Greasy Creek, the accompanying soundtrack is laughter.

My Grandma Emmy was a strongly religious woman—never one to cuss or use any other kind of bad language—but she did have a strong sense of fun. Probably the harshest word she'd ever say was "shucks." She did, however, have expressions indicating her displeasure with situations, one of which I had forgotten until I rediscovered it in the cache of letters I found after I was well into work on this book. Inviting someone to "kiss my butt"—or a more graphic version of same—was an oft-used expression where I grew up, but I never heard Grandma Emmy say it that way. Instead she used a somewhat cleaned-up version, which I had flat forgotten until I found a 1943 letter written by Momma shortly after a visit to Kentucky. She writes that "Linda said she told Cake-a-bony [my doll] to 'smell old mossy.'" In this packet of letters, written between 1941 and 1946, Momma indicates on several occasions that she has tried to keep me from playing with children who use bad language. Moreover, she often writes to my grandmother about inappropriate things I have picked up from Daddy. In this instance, however, it is clear that my mother knows the genesis of "smell old mossy," and I'd be willing to bet that Grandma Emmy laughed as she read about it.

The biggest fear of my grandmother's life was that Uncle Burns would die in the war, and I know she prayed about it often. One evening, however, as she sat around the fire in her front room with Momma, Daddy, Leon, and me, Momma began to voice her concerns for "Buddy" (Momma's name for Uncle Burns) being "in the fighting over there." Grandma Emmy listened for a few minutes, then set her mouth and said, "Huh! Burns is about as likely to drown from falling drunk in a ditch line as he is from getting shot!" "Why, Mommy!" Momma exclaimed, her mouth wide in horror. The rest of us laughed. My grandmother loved Uncle Burns better than she loved all the rest of her children put together. Everybody'd have to agree that was the case. She was worried to death about him. We all knew that. But there was considerable truth in her assessment of his situation that night, and I guess Grandma Emmy figured if the truth is going to hurt, you might as well laugh about it.

By the time my mother was born on June 28, 1915—the baby of the Elijah Mollette family—she had been preceded by four brothers (though little Jake had died at age three) and four sisters. She was born into what neighbor Billie Edyth Ward called an "upstanding family."

The men in the Mollette family, Momma's brothers, were strong starters—good minds, good hearts, even—but they never learned how to finish anything they started. If it didn't come easy, they fell by the wayside. The ethic seemed to be "let somebody else do the dull." What's more, all three boys were bad to drink. Momma—and Aunt Amanda—always said their brothers took after their daddy in this, but some have taken exception with this version of the Lige Mollette story. Said he was just a sick man, as opposed to one who drank himself down. Since I don't know the facts of it, I'll try to give as much of the public story as I've been able to uncover.

Perhaps the article announcing Elijah Mollette's death, entitled "Boons Camp Citizen Dies," that appeared in the *Paintsville Herald* on June 8, 1939, will be of some help.

Elijah Mollette, Former Deputy Sheriff Ill 11 Years

Elijah Mollette of Boons Camp, former deputy sheriff of Johnson County under George Spears, and one of the county's best citizens, passed away Wednesday morning May 31, after an illness of more than 11 years.

Mr. Mollette was the father of Mrs. Kash Holbrook, who has taught in the Paintsville City Schools for many years, and of Representative John B. Mollette of Van Lear.

He had been a merchant and farmer of Boons Camp prior to his illness. He also was one of the superintendents of the Rockcastle Lumber Company, which operated a large camp in Martin County and a narrow gauge railroad in both Johnson and Martin Counties.

A great many of Johnson Counties [*sic*] citizens became acquainted with Mr. Mollette through working under him on the railroad and in the lumber camp. He was one of the ablest supervisors and one of the most beloved by his fellow men.

Mr. Mollette's physical suffering was not half so great as his mental anguish through all the years he was powerless to do any work. He had to sit idly by and see his family carry on while he could not assist them.

The nature of his illness was a form of paralysis which grew continually worse until at the last he was unable to speak above a whisper.

When he was so weak that he could not talk to his many friends who visited him during his last days he still made them know they were recognized.

When his dear friends would call and he could not talk to them, the tears would stream down his face, and his mental agony was almost unbearable.

Besides Mrs. Holbrook and Rep. Mollette, Mr. Mollette is survived by his wife, Mrs. Emma Cline Mollette, and the following children: Mrs. T. F. Fletcher of Inez; Mrs. Ray Colvin of Thealka; Mrs. Jay Preston of

Williamsport; Fred Mollette of Van Lear, and Burns Offutt Mollette of Staffordsville.

Funeral services for Mr. Mollette were held at the family home at 10 o'clock Thursday morning with Rev. John W. Butcher, Dr. J. R. Fairchild, of Inez, and Rev. Millard VanHoose as the officiating ministers.

Burial was in the family cemetery.

This account bears out Billie Edyth Ward's report that the Elijah Mollette's were an "upstanding family" as well as that for a time they ran a small store there at the home place. While Ms. Ward does not remember the store itself, she recalls her mother saying she "went to Lige Mollette's store." That visit would have been after Ms. Ward's mother married into the Greasy Creek community in 1902. Her mother spoke of John and Fred as "little boys" at the time, so the store must have existed sometime between 1902, when Mrs. Ward's mother moved to Greasy, and 1915, when Uncle Fred would have been twelve years old. I never heard my mother, who was born in 1915, mention that her parents had run a store.

Neither Momma nor Aunt Amanda ever spoke of Grandpa Lige's having been superintendent of a lumber company, though both discussed at length their father's stint as a lawman. I always understood that he was high sheriff of Martin County, and since it was in Martin County, I figured it must have occurred before he married Grandma Emmy. I also thought all the work history occurred before 1915 or so, which was when Momma said he got down sick.

Perhaps the greatest split between my received memories of Grandpa Lige's story and the version in the newspaper lies in the number of years my grandfather was sick, as well as the nature of his illness. Momma was quite clear—with confirmation by Aunt Amanda—in saying that for most of her life her father was unable to do much around the place, which would estimate his illness at nearer to twenty years than eleven. Momma was born in 1915, and she said many times that she never saw her daddy do a day of work in her life. Moreover, Momma credited Grandma Emmy with having to wait on Grandpa Lige, in addition to carrying out virtually all the farm tasks that usually fell to the men.

When Uncle Burns left for some sort of highway work in 1930, Grandpa Lige was the only male on the place, and he was unable to do anything for himself, much less do the heavy farm labor. Sometime earlier Grandma Emmy's mother, Martha Cline, had come to stay with the family. Great-Grandma Martha was able to help out around the house and with Grandpa Lige's needs, but she was eighty-some years old when Uncle Burns left home, so the farm work was all done by Grandma Emmy, Aunt Gladys, and Momma. When Great-Grandma Martha took sick sometime in 1933, she returned to Martin County to stay with one of her other daughters, where she died in January 1934.

While the picture Momma—and Grandma Emmy—painted of Aunt Gladys was always one of weakness and disability, Ms. Ward believes Aunt Gladys did her part around the farm, including plowing. In a letter describing her memories, Ms. Ward writes: "I can recall that they had a team of mules and Gladys was the oldest girl at home at that time. I recall passing—going to the post office most likely, and Gladys would be turning ground—a hard job for a strong man—in preparation to planting a corn crop. This would be in the bottom land—(tow slopes) and not exactly on the hillsides."

Momma considered herself a good worker but swore she never labored as hard after she left the home place as she was required to in her growing-up years on Greasy. After Aunt Gladys died in May 1934 and Momma moved to Paintsville to get work, Grandma Emmy was left alone to manage. Both Momma and Aunt Amanda often confessed wonderment at their mother's having kept that hardscrabble farm going until her death. In response to my questioning how my grandmother was able to get by alone, Billie Edyth writes:

> Emma had livestock which could be sold, crops, vegetables, all could be turned into the small amount of money that a family simply had to have. Emma would have "workin's" and the men of the community would show up to grub and clean up the ground she wanted to plant—early in the spring.
>
> I recall that after we bought a mowing machine, Lee (my oldest brother) would mow hay for her free of charge. Also we kept a bull and charged a small fee to people who wanted to "drive their cow" but Emma was never charged although she offered payment. I recall she would come *within sight* of our house with some boy, stop, and wait until he returned from the barn.

Ms. Ward and I spoke of the expression "drive" the cow, which meant to have the cow bred, and admitted that neither of us have even heard or used that phrase for many years. As for the reason for my grandmother's practice of not even walking all the way to her neighbor's house? Ms. Ward—who taught me to multiply fractions and conjugate verbs in eighth grade—and I agreed that for Grandma Emmy to pass the time of day with the Wards would have meant acknowledging what was going on in the barn. Ms. Ward and I also agreed that times have changed.

As for what specifically was wrong with my grandfather, Ms. Ward says that in her memory Lige was always sick, and somewhere she heard that he had scrofula (tuberculosis of the neck). She says Grandpa Lige's problem was so severe that Grandma Emmy could not leave him alone for any period of time, not even to attend church right across the branch. From Ms. Ward's earliest memory, my grandfather was always paralyzed, with Grandma Emmy or one of the children leading him from place to place. He was unable to communicate so that anyone outside the family could understand, so a family member would be called into service to interpret for him. In warm weather, one or another family member would lead him to the yard and seat him under the green apple tree, where he could watch folks pass along the road. According to Ms. Ward, the family said he enjoyed passersby speaking to him though he could not speak back.

Ms. Ward's earliest memories of Grandma Emmy take place in the schoolhouse bottom about two hundred yards up the creek above the home place. Before Little Friendship Church was built on Left Fork of Greasy, the United Baptists would hold regular meeting time at Three Forks of Greasy School across from the home place. Though Grandma Emmy couldn't leave Grandpa Lige to go to the service—she was a Methodist then, anyway—she would go stand in the schoolhouse yard around the time church was to break and invite those in attendance to come across to the house for dinner. Some would go over home with her, and those who did not—especially the preachers—would stop by to speak to Grandpa Lige as they passed by the house. Most of the folks would be walking, since few owned cars in those days.

Grandma Emmy was a religious woman, from a family of Martin County Methodists, but she became a Freewill because they believed in foot washing, while the Methodists did not. Two of her children, Amanda and Stella, became Methodists, while Lizzie, Fred, John, Burns, and Momma sooner or later joined the Freewills. Nobody seems to know what religion, if any, Grandpa Lige pursued. Given that he had been somewhat wild as a young man, he was down sick long enough to have had plenty of time to come to the Cross. A man with any sense doesn't sit for twenty-some years in the stare of G. Reaper without doing some big-time repentance, so I figure he had to have become something religious, though I don't exactly know what. The newspaper's suggestion that three ministers preached my granddad's funeral sounds more United Baptist than anything else. What's more, his sister Aunt Liz Sturgill also lived close by on another patch of the old Mollette property, and her boy N.R. "Little Nim" Sturgill was a big United Baptist, so it could be that they converted Grandpa Lige. Ms. Ward also suggests that Grandpa Lige had regular access to the United Baptist faithful: "I recall that Emma could not leave to go to the United Baptist meetings held in the school house just across the creek but she would usually be there at dismissal to invite folks home with her for dinner."

Upon reflection, I'll have to say that I kind of hope my grandfather became a United Baptist, because that would mean, whatever his background, he had experienced remorse and redemption. United Baptist is not an easy faith to follow, and if my scalawag grandfather was redeemed by that bunch, I'd be betting it took. Not that other faiths won't have their place in Heaven, but the Uniteds—well, they're devoted, and it would ease my heart if I knew my grandpa threw in with them.

Well into my mother's generation, the basic need for survival ruled and the methods of surviving had changed little from the day Elias Mollette settled on Greasy. With no farm machinery, no electricity, no indoor plumbing, and no central heating, simply living from day to day required a full measure of labor on the part of every household member. While more modern conveniences—hence an easier life—might have been available in towns or cities, the very lay of that land isolated its inhabitants.

Perhaps my people chose that country for its sequestering qualities; maybe they just found themselves there. In any event, the greatly cherished Appalachian landscape did not lend itself to easy access. What with the lack of dependable transportation and close-at-hand jobs, as well as the general mistrust of outsiders, there was little opportunity for an unskilled country boy to find work. Over time, however, the coal companies brought work right to his door.

There can be no doubt that some pretty negative things happened to folks—and to their land—as a result of the introduction of coal mining into Appalachia, but some fairly positive opportunities opened up, too. Trying to work land that verges on the vertical can be less than ideal, and the existence of those who must live that way includes more than its share of desperate moments.

For people whose children routinely died of a variety of mysterious "fevers," the accessibility of a coal camp doctor was clearly a mark on the plus side of the ledger. By contrast, generations of children raised in coal camps, who never learned the skills necessary to work the land their fathers abandoned for the coal fields, were left close to helpless when the mines worked out some years later. It is not difficult to find arguments on both sides of this issue. It should be noted, however, that controlling people—however much caretaking is involved—is hardly ever good for their development. This is true whether it be black folks brought to this country as chattel or country folks who gave up their legendary independence for the safety of a regular paycheck and the assurance of food, lodging, and medical care provided by the mining company.

Shortly before the turn of the nineteenth century, the first coal mines came into the area, and records show that on November 15, 1846, the first coal contract in Johnson County was signed. Family legend holds—and public records support the fact—that during the latter part of the nineteenth century, many of the residents of eastern Kentucky's hills and hollows sold off rights to any minerals that lay beneath their land. The full effects of such contracts, which (back then) must have appeared to be an unexpected blessing to those landowners, have not yet been fully realized. One of the largest buyers of coal rights was Paintsville resident John C.C. Mayo, who on September 16, 1901, incorporated Mayo Coal Company.

Few eastern Kentuckians can be impartial about the coming of coal mines to our part of the world, hence John C.C. Mayo is both revered and cursed for having played a major part in that negotiation. As for my family, we've got folks on all sides of that issue, and my own position shifts daily. Both my momma's and my daddy's people were established in eastern Kentucky years before the coal people came, so I guess we own the idea of the place as much as anybody. And I suppose if you looked hard enough, you could find that some sharpie from "away"—

or from town—took advantage of some poor, unschooled ancestor or another and had him sign away the rights to whatever minerals we sat on. Whether the mines and the folks who owned or operated them were God or Satan depends on where you stand to view it, too.

As far as I can determine, prior to 1920, no member of the Cline, Mollette, Ward, or Preston families had ever worked in the coal mines. From the time I was born in 1941 until I graduated from high school in 1958, coal mining appeared to me to be the preferred career choice for most young men in that area who wanted to stay close to their roots. In truth, coal underwrote every aspect of my own family's life up to and including my daddy's death from complications of smoking and black lung disease.

I come from people who worked the land for a living, and, up until my parents' generation, each son was able to provide for his family by moving one patch away from the home place. Whole hollows were settled a patch at a time as each boy grew up, found a wife, and built a house on a distant piece of his daddy's property. Traditionally, boys "married on" and girls "married off," so the process was a little different for a female. Taking a man's name was just the beginning of a woman's commitment to her husband; indeed, she became part of his family, his community, and his work. Though, on occasion, folks in her new environs might remind each other that some wife or another had been perhaps "a Barnett from over on Hammond," the woman's identity was expected to be completely submerged. Even in speaking of the woman, folks would use past tense: "Elmer Jackson's wife *was* [not *is*] a Barnett from over on Hammond."

While a girl was expected to become part of her husband's family, when a boy married he was usually given his own piece of ground on the periphery of the home place. Each son was expected to move to the outer edges of the farm, build him and his wife a house, and work the ground just as his daddy had done. Even today, such property is referred to as "the Joe D. piece" or the "John B. piece," though both Joe D. and John B. went to their reward in the thirties. My son currently receives a few dollars each month from a gas well on the Sam A. piece, though he has never stepped foot on this property. What's more, he most certainly could not find it without a deed and a surveyor, and would have a tough time even tracing his roots to Sam A. or naming the decade in which Sam A. died.

The patch-off tradition was responsible for settling many an eastern Kentucky hollow and accounts for the fact that kinship patterns are somewhat easier to trace. Even today, I would be hard put to find a house on Greasy Creek where folks were not some distant kin to me or whose forebears haven't been on one fork or another as long as mine have.

Billie Edyth Ward was born and has lived her whole life in the family home about a mile above the Lige Mollette home place. In 1945, when she taught at the head of Greasy—about a mile above her home place— she enrolled around fifty students, only ten of whom were *not* descendants of one Joshua Daniel. Ms. Ward says, "Today there are about a dozen households above us, and all but ours and three others are J.W. (initials for Joshie Way) Daniel's descendants."

Though it is impossible to attribute motives, especially after so many years have passed, I suspect that old Elias Mollette and his half-brother, Nathan, never would have come into eastern Kentucky if they'd had a choice. Instead, it's likely they would have patched off their home place in Virginia. In all probability, they were deprived of that choice because their daddy ran out of land.

A piece of ground, however fertile, will just support a finite number of people, which means there can be only a limited number of patch-offs before somebody has to get a job. When the land ran out on us, the situation was ripe for the coal companies to move in. At least such appears to be the case for the Mollettes on Greasy Creek. In Momma's family, all the boys ended up working the coal mines at some point or another, though only Uncle Fred moved to a mining camp and made a life of it. I do not believe that one of my Mollette uncles would have gone to the mines if they had thought they could support themselves and their families by staying on the land. Their choices were limited by their love of home, their lack of education or training for any other job, and their vision of the probabilities for making a living in the world outside those confining but protecting mountains.

I know this will be read by some as a justification for coal mining and the pure misery it has brought many of the descendants of my daddy's generation of coal miners, as well as the rape of the entire region. I don't want sludge in my front yard or the mudslide in my back door any more than anybody else, and today's mine owners have to take credit for such atrocities. I honestly do not believe, however, that those folks who bought up mineral rights from Great-Grandpa John B. could have envisioned the sludge-and-mudslide problem any better than old John B. could. Billie Edyth agrees that, "Big Eye and the others could not imagine today's trappings." And speaking of one of her distant ancestors, Will "Coojer" Ward, she says, "The $150 Coojer got for the mineral rights meant a fortune, and not even the buyer could foresee when 'all subterranean products' might mean something not visualized by Will Coojer Ward."

Did they obtain mineral rights as cheaply as possible? Of course they did. The fellow who bought those rights was making a living, as was my great-grandfather, who sold them off. I also doubt that the selling of such rights or the presence of coal camps in the region were seen as anything but positive by my parents' generation. To the contrary, the mining of coal in or near home had to seem a blessing to my three uncles, since it provided a way to make a living and stay in the area. In 1920, as a boy of seventeen, my uncle Fred Mollette was ready to begin his life and had no way to support himself. The land he might have counted on to patch off just a generation earlier was already overcommitted, supporting his paralyzed father, his mother, two younger brothers, and three younger sisters—the youngest being my five-year-old mother. I believe my uncle Fred is representative of a number of native-born Appalachian boys who chose to go up to Van Lear, or Wayland, or over in West Virginia, and work the mines.

My forebears have been portrayed as having chosen to become coal miners because they were just not as bright as those who made other choices—poor country boys who unknowingly took part in the destruction of their homeland. Certainly some were slipshucked by the mining industry, which used them up and threw them out just as it took their beautiful countryside and ruined it. I believe, however, we need to look at the choice to work the mines in light of the prospects of my uncle Fred when he first went to the mines in the early twenties. At that time, my uncle was not choosing between coal mining and accountancy, or law, or much of anything else that would support him, and he did not go immediately into the mines. First, he was a school teacher, but he couldn't make enough money to leave home, marry, and support a wife and children. And he had to leave home, because by then the land his family worked had been so overworked the soil was played out. Once Uncle Fred wanted to be on his own, he needed a place to live, and the Mollette land was worn out and had run out—no more patch-offs.

How could Uncle Fred have conceived that moving into a coal camp house—a house with more creature comforts than the home place he moved out of—would someday rob his children of the habits and skills necessary for working the land? Since he was brought up on his people's land, Uncle Fred took those skills for granted. To him, progress meant *not* having to do those things, so why would his kids ever want to learn them? Today we can see where this attitude resulted in the powerlessness of whole generations of folks left at the mercy of mining companies, unions, and of city-bred academics, who often appear to value the welfare of the environment over attempts at understanding the choices of the inhabitants of that environment. Uncle Fred's letter from the Wheelwright coal camp, postmarked May 6, 1945, says, "[W]hen we moved up here we moved in a apartment but we have a house now. We have a house with gas and hot and cold water in it and has a bath in the house so I have it made don't I? Ha Ha."

My people have made some choices—choices that in light of the past sixty years seem ill-considered. We need to remember, however, that those choices were made without benefit of recent history. Moreover, when they were doing the choosing, a scant supply of choices presented themselves. That infamous Appalachian commitment to home and family was at work here. If a boy wanted to stay near home, the coal mine offered the best living available at the time. Initially, coal mining offered an unskilled laborer a way of sheltering, feeding, and clothing himself and his family. This enabled many a man whose family had outgrown their land to remain near to home and not starve out.

Today, it is easy to deplore the consequences of coal mining on the area, but speaking as one whose every need was bought with coal money and the sweat of my coal-miner daddy, the presence of the mines made all the difference in my own family's existence. Instead of taking the land away from us, coal mining enabled us to remain on our land and continue to practice and pass on those survival skills lost to those who moved their families into coal camps. But before Daddy moved us back to our own piece of patch-off land in Kentucky, we lived for a time in a McDowell County, West Virginia, coal camp. One of Momma's letters from that camp expressed her satisfaction—indeed her delight—with the lifestyle and conveniences offered there as she says:

I have been so busy that I can hardly breathe. We washed our bedroom walls down Saturday. They are painted green. I still have my kitchen walls to wash down.

Well, I started this yesterday afternoon and Jay came in from work and I had to get supper so I'll try to finish it now.

Cooking isn't much of a job for I have the best stove I ever saw. It cooks things in just a few minutes and it doesn't heat the kitchen up so badly. I have been scrubbing all over the place today. We have the biggest long porch & it is shady from before noon until night. It has dressed flooring & I have to scrub it nearly every day.

We are crazy about the place here & we have the nicest neighbors I ever saw. Last week the woman that lives out from us brought me a mess of lettuce & the woman that lives on the other side of us gives us ice from her Frigidaire any time we want it. The girl and boy that lives in the other two rooms are the nicest people. I think the world of her for she is so good to me. Her husband's people are from over on Rock House.

I am sorry we didn't get to go to Daddy's grave, but as you know, it was impossible. I studied about him all week nearly. [My family used the term "studied about" to mean "thought about."]

How is your garden coming? I miss the mustard and poke but we have some awfully good meals. You can get two pork chops for a dime & Jay gets 2 every day—one for his breakfast and one to go in his lunch.

I am getting my things pretty now. Jay went down to the shop & made me the prettiest water bench. [The water bench held the water bucket and dipper for drinking and a shallow wash pan for washing up. The pump was outside the door.]

We live up so high I can see Jay as he starts up the railroad from the shop. I am going to close now for I want to go down to the office [All my people called the post office the "office."] & come back as he comes from work. I see him coming. . . .

In a letter written near the same time, Momma again comments on how good they found life in Hemphill:

Got your card today [Monday] . . . I went to the store after groceries & to the office & got it.

Did you have a crowd Sunday? I got a tiny bit homesick & Jay laughed at me for it. We stayed home all day & I got a good dinner. We had steak, gravy, green beans, lettuce, fried potatoes & hot biscuits. I made fruit salad tonight for supper. We have plenty to eat, and it isn't costing nearly so much. We sent the money to pay one of our notes off today & paid some on another. Jay got every day's work last week. . .

Both my parents would have been content to live in a mining camp, and I doubt they would have tried to move out of it if Daddy's work had not been so far from their parents. Though jobs in the coalfields were labor-intensive, they offered a young man a dependable wage and a degree of creature comfort that was hard to match on the hardscrabble farms of eastern Kentucky. Still, it would be hard to pin down any single cause for the rush to leave the land for the mines. The land ran out, the ground worked out, and the money from mining coal provided a ready alternative for folks unaccustomed to having any choice other than to starve out on their daddy's land.

To Lifie Jay and Grace, the decade of the forties dawned looking much like sunset on the thirties. It found them living across the road from Pop Pop and Grandma Alk, spending any free time they had with one set of in-laws or another. Sometime in early August, Momma passed out in Grandma Emmy's garden and had to admit to her mother that she was pregnant. From all the stories handed down to me, everybody termed it a blessing. After all, Momma and Daddy had been married nearly four years, which was a long time to wait for a pregnancy in those pre-Pill days when birth control was by no means certain.

There is no way to determine just when Momma first began to be sickly, but she took on considerably with this pregnancy, so much so that she made frequent visits to the doctor in Paintsville. It was still unusual for women who lived that far out of town to have a doctor attend a birth, but from the time Momma found out she was pregnant, she secured Dr. Picklesimer's agreement to deliver the baby. Moreover, he agreed to come ten miles out of town and half a mile off the main road to carry out this task. Though some folks pointed out that the doctor would have to come three miles past Grace and Lifie Jay's own house to go to Greasy Creek, Grace insisted she wanted "to be with Mommy" and that's the way it was. Thus, on February 20, 1941, Dr. F.M. Picklesimer delivered Linda Sue Preston on a featherbed in the upper room of the Lige Mollette home place at Three Forks of Greasy. The baby was quite small, which made some folks say right from the first that she took after her mother—sickly. Momma always said she had not ever been hearty, but giving birth to me really got her down.

In a letter postmarked February 28, 1941, Aunt Lizzie, whose health was more robust—and outlook more optimistic—wrote Grandma Emmy: "Heard about Grace's baby and am so glad it's over. I worried about her but tell her when she has as many as I have she will not notice it. Ha!" At the time of this writing, Aunt Lizzie had a sick husband (Ray) and five children, ranging in age from Frances, who was nearly as old as Momma (1915-1994), to Lois Ann (1939-2001), who was just a toddler. Aunt Lizzie certainly had her share of burdens, but she goes on to say, "As soon as I can I'll get the goods to finish those quilts, as soon as Ray gets able to work. He weighs 118 pounds. He looks awful bad. It is a lot of worry and us such a big family." She ends with a message to Momma, who was still in bed (from the birth eight days earlier).

Aunt Lizzie's letter offers encouragement—and a slight nudge—to her baby sister, as she writes that a former student from Momma's school teaching days "had a little baby the other day, her 2nd one and they never did get any doctor . . . and she was up doing her work in 5 days." Aunt Lizzie was not alone in chiding Momma a little for staying in bed longer than maybe others did with childbirth. By planting time, however, Momma was up, moved back to Two-Mile, and ready to turn her hand to the usual sowing, hoeing, harvesting, and preserving yield from the Mollette and Preston gardens.

As the thirties ended and the forties began, the coal mines were laying off rather than hiring on, and Daddy was still doing pick-up carpentry and whatever else he could find. Though Momma and Daddy were somewhat disappointed that Daddy had not yet been able to get on at a Johnson County mine, his steady pick-up work, plus what she canned and preserved from the gardens, brought in enough for our family of three to live on. Thus, autumn of 1941 still looked as if the forties would be much like the thirties for Lifie Jay and Grace, simply with three instead of two in that little house on Two-Mile.

On December 7, 1941, the Japanese attack on Pearl Harbor changed everything for members of my parents' generation. However isolated eastern Kentucky had seemed, it was no more. We were at war, and that "we" included everybody in my family. For all the traditional Appalachian aversion to war and leaving family, folks in our section of the country were superpatriotic. I don't know about everybody else, but if the Wards, Prestons, Clines, and Mollettes are any indication, most of the boys who didn't get their call in early '42, went down and joined up. Everybody of an age to go wanted to get about doing their part in the war effort.

Even those not of an age to go wanted to do their part, as evidenced by Momma's oldest brother, John B., who was past forty—thus not eligible for the draft—but joined up anyway. Grandma Emmy's youngest boy, Burns, was called into the army immediately, and all three of Aunt Lizzie's boys joined the navy as soon as they came of age. Then, despite the fact that he had a new baby and had always resisted leaving his parents, Daddy volunteered for the army.

When my mother wanted something, she employed an impressive array of skills ranging from reason through argument to all manner of persuasion. As Daddy said, "It's hard to stand agin' her." Still, over five years of marriage she had been unable to convince Daddy to move any farther than across the road from his mother and daddy. What Momma had been unable to accomplish in five years, however, the war brought about within months.

Frankly, the fact that my daddy volunteered for the army is antithetical to every other thing I know of him. Moreover, I am quite certain that offering himself up for military service is the only time in his life my daddy ever volunteered for anything, for he was the single most self-deprecating person I have ever known. Even when he applied for jobs, Daddy was reluctant to brag on his skills and abilities, hiring on at entry level long after he became a skilled carpenter. If an opportunity required that he put himself forward and tell why he would be the best person for a job, Daddy simply took himself out of the race. Had World War II not come along, I don't believe Momma ever would have persuaded him to move out from under the shadow of Pop Pop. After Pearl Harbor, however, Daddy saw no choice, so he joined up and he and Momma began making plans around his inevitable commitment.

Unlike Momma, who experienced every moment of her existence as a near-death experience, Daddy thought himself strong, robust, and capable of mastering almost any physical task. Thus, he was crushed when he failed the army physical. Along with his friend Junior Ward, he had taken the train to Ashland one afternoon and was examined all the next day. Apparently the doctor who listened to his heart asked him if he had undergone any treatment for his heart condition, and when Daddy said, "What heart condition?" the physician told him he had a double heartbeat. Then the doctor said his heart condition was severe enough that Daddy wouldn't have to go to the service.

Daddy then asked to be reexamined the next day, for he believed the extra heartbeat problem was caused by his having had to stay overnight in a strange place and with strange people. He always claimed that if those army doctors had retested him once he became comfortable with the surroundings, he would have passed and gone on into the service. As Billie Edyth Ward writes, "No man wanted to be 4-F; 4-F was a putdown in our part of the world."

During the sixties war protests, I once asked my daddy why on earth he had volunteered to go fight. At first he gave me no answer. I pressed him and he said, "Seems to me like this [country] is the only place on earth that ever gave a poor man a chance." I pointed out what I considered to be some basic inequalities in this country, and he said, "Poor man might not have much of a chance, but he's got a chance. If a man's worth a damn, he can get out on the road and make it."

"But what made you trust the government enough to think we were right and those fighting against us were wrong?" I asked. He sat silently for a long time, as was Daddy's way. He'd never give an opinion on anything unless you kept after him. Finally, he said, "We didn't have no say in it. *They* come after *us*. And how d'you reckon it'd be, girl, if they'd busted our ass [in World War II] instead of the other way around?"

My daddy was not in the habit of stating his opinion, much less defending it, and that is probably the most I ever heard him say in justification for his behavior. We both knew he didn't owe me any explanation, but I appreciate him making his case for me.

After trying unsuccessfully to get the army to reexamine him, Daddy was so ashamed of failing his physical that after riding the train back home, he took the next bus directly over to Welch, West Virginia, where he got a good job working in the West Virginia coal fields. Because Daddy was considered "family," Polly Blevins managed to find him a place in the boardinghouse she ran for the coal company. As soon as Daddy got his first paycheck, he came back to Kentucky for his car and to make arrangements for Momma and me to join him. The way Daddy moved the three of us to West Virginia was gradual and followed much the same pattern of other families in eastern Kentucky as they went to find work in West Virginia's coal camps.

He wanted us to go back with him then and there, but the Blevins's boardinghouse was fully occupied and Daddy was last on a long list of miners in line for coal camp houses. At first Mrs. Blevins made up a pallet for Daddy on the floor of the room of some other miner, then gave him a single room as soon as the next miner moved out. Best I can judge from a letter Daddy wrote postmarked October 1, 1941, he was in line for a double room and expecting Momma and me any day, but my parents' activities leading up to that letter were brought about by a series of connections that were typical of our people. First of all, Daddy went there because he could not get into the army but wanted to be part of the war effort. He chose to go to Welch because Polly Blevins ran a boardinghouse there.

Polly Blevins had been Polly Ward—Frank Ward's sister—and that set of Wards had been on Two-Mile for as long as any of us could remember. Frank Ward raised his whole family just a couple hundred yards from Pop Pop, and two of the older Ward daughters, Becky and Agnes, were as close to Momma and Daddy as sisters. My point here is that people from Two-Mile and environs take home with us in that we are not inclined to move cold into a bunch of rank strangers. We have connections—the best kind of connections—and those connections provide instant community.

I would suggest that though the Blevins's boardinghouse was physically located on Pitch Holler in Hemphill, West Virginia, it was simply an extension of Two-Mile, Greasy, River, and Bob's Branch. Those who lived in that boardinghouse had a kind of dual citizenship. West Virginia was where they worked, Kentucky was their home, and they were just as transient as their brothers who were in the service.

Momma, Daddy, and I made the trip from West Virginia to Kentucky and back at least once a month, though often Momma and I would stay back in Kentucky to help Grandma Emmy. By the time I was five years old, I could recite the names of all the train stops between Kermit and Welch, West Virginia, and the terrain was embossed on my memory forever. I knew we were entering West Virginia when our bus crossed the Tug River and I had to gather my things so we could transfer to the train. Otherwise, there was little change in landscape. The creeks and hollows of eastern Kentucky are no different from those in West Virginia—same with the coal camps. Folks who have never been to Appalachia have never seen how the most remote woods abruptly give way to a trail of coal dust, a cluster of shotgun houses, a school, a church, and a company store, punctuated by a coal tipple or two.

To my growing-up eyes, the coal camp's attendant slag heap appeared as much a part of a natural act as the trash left in our sycamore grove by a flash flood on Two-Mile Creek. As a kid, I could not determine the distinction between a man-made mess and one caused by nature. Both creeks and coal camps were simply part of the reality of my life, one no better or worse than another. I knew that the Tug Fork of the Big Sandy River, about twenty miles to the east of Two-Mile, ran black, while the Levisa Fork, some six miles west, flowed brown, or sometimes green. I never thought to ask why, and it never even occurred to me that the color or condition of one river was somehow preferable to the other.

Though Daddy worked the mines for a quarter of a century, the only period when we did not raise hogs, chickens, and a garden was during the war years, when he worked in West Virginia. Even then, Momma and I often spent most of the summer with Grandma Emmy so we could keep a hog there and raise our own little patch of vegetables, which we canned and took back to West Virginia to tide us over the winter. Had it not been for the war, I don't believe Daddy ever would have left Two-Mile, and certainly Momma and I would never have spent time away. Indeed it is the only period of my parents' nearly sixty years together for which I have any written record of their lives, separately or together. Momma regularly wrote Grandma Emmy letters chronicling the minutest detail of our coal camp days.

Though I also have letters from all of Grandma Emmy's adult children, I have only one from Daddy. In his letter to Momma, Daddy outlines his attempts to get us into the Blevins's boardinghouse, not exactly the easiest process. Scrawled in the top margin before the beginning of the letter proper are the words, "Did you get yer money." Then Daddy begins:

> Hi sweethearts will try to answer your letter recvd. Yesterday. Was glad to hear my girls was alrite. I'me o.k. I reckon I just got up an I feel a little better I was talking to Aunt Polly [Polly Blevins] last nite she said she was going to let me have those rooms just as quick as she could she said if Cara an Edd [Mrs. Blevins' daughter and her husband] got out she could move the old man down in the other end. Or still let us have two rooms they [Cara and Ed] think their going to get a house purty quick. The super told him yesterday he thought the store had decided not to take that house or if they didn't he could have the house.
>
> Buddy [Daddy's affectionate name for my mother] you do what you want to about coming out here. I just don't know what to say about the moving. If Edd gets out it won't be but a day or 2. Ever downstairs room is full now an if you was to come you would have to come upstairs to stay an you know about what that would be. Cara an Edd is in that room they sent Ben out of.

The top floor had small rooms where individual miners slept on double beds, with not so much as a dresser in the rooms. Momma said there was no such thing as twin beds in those days (though there must have been in the army), and if they were really hard up for space or somebody really needed cheap accommodations, the miners doubled up two to a room. Sometimes a miner and his wife would stay in such a room, but no children were allowed. Since Polly—whom Daddy and Momma called "Aunt Polly" and Momma sometimes called "Mom Blevins"— was so close to our family, she had made an exception for Daddy to bring a child and stay in a small upstairs room.

Daddy goes on to say: "You go ahead an get yer clothes any kind you want." I assume the clothes are the reason he sent the money he asked about in the top margin of this letter. Momma had probably written asking about buying something new for her and me so we could make a good impression when we got there. That sounds like Momma, who was always "dressed till a fly wouldn't light on her," and she made certain Sister and I looked even better than she did. It was also like Daddy to send the cash in the next mail, for I don't think I ever heard him deny Momma anything she wanted. Then he gets back to the subject of his letter: "Just do what you like about coming out here. It don't make no difference there is a possibility that I may get those rooms any day now. Can't say for sure But I hope so."

Daddy would have written that it made no difference to him, for he would not have wanted Momma to do anything she didn't want to do because of him. Momma and Daddy were both reluctant to say outright what they wanted for fear they'd push each other into doing something they'd both regret. Given what Momma and Daddy have told me about that time, I would guess both of them wanted desperately for Momma to get on the next bus, but were unwilling to say so.

The letter continues: "I want to save for that note as much as I could. I want to cut it down so I can cosign it if I can an I only have 2 more pays to do it in. I want to pay 50 dollars on it if it can be done atall." Daddy's car—the one Pop Pop bought him (used) in 1934—had quit on him the month before I was born, so he had taken out a note to pay Dr. Picklesimer for delivering me and to buy himself another used car. I don't know the make or model of this particular car, but I am pretty sure it wasn't a Ford, because Daddy never trusted Fords. That generation had strong loyalty to this brand or that—at least my daddy did. Daddy didn't trust that car to make the round trip back to Kentucky, which, along with gasoline rationing, was why the three of us took trains and buses home to Kentucky every month or so.

Daddy thought it was important to have his car in West Virginia, though, if just for us to drive around on the weekends. Cars were very rare in the coal camp, but my daddy always had to have a car. In all likelihood, the car was a Plymouth, for Daddy was partial to Chrysler cars and at that time he was unable to afford a Dodge or Chrysler. Near the end of the war, Daddy traded this nameless vehicle in on the first car

I recall us having—a '41 Plymouth, which Daddy kept till he traded it for a '49 Plymouth in the early fifties. A year or so later, Daddy switched to General Motors cars when he bought a blue Chevy station wagon to enable him to haul more riders to the David mines and gave his '49 Plymouth to Momma. He bought the family's first-ever new car—a '57 Chevy, black with a lime green tail fin—in 1957.

"If you take a notion to come out here Be sure an write me before youre coming so I won't pass you somewhere on the road." It was necessary to include this caution, for there were no telephones within ten miles of Momma, who was still with Grandma Emmy, so they could have been on trains or buses heading in opposite directions.

"Well I guess I will close an try to go to the office with this." Daddy then signs off with: "So long I'll see you sometime——Jay." My daddy was not one for endearments. I never heard him speak of love to or about my mother—or anybody else, for that matter.

Some few years ago I was part of a psychology workshop up East and was involved in a group discussion about intimate relationships. One of the participants—a thirty-something mental health professional from New York—suggested that she counted herself among the many young women who are chronically unable to sustain a relationship with a man. She then laid her inability-to-commit problem squarely at the feet of her father, saying, "In my entire life, my father has never told me he loved me. I think he is incapable of saying those words." At the time, I was nearly twice the age of that young woman and my own daddy was clinging to the last days of his life. My first thought was that my father had never said those words to me either, but it never occurred to me that he didn't love me. We just were not the kind of people where men go throwing around the word "love"; *I love you* was just not a part of the vocabulary of Appalachian men of my father's generation.

Daddy lived for seventy-seven years—fifty-eight of them with Momma —and I was around for fifty-three of those years, but I never heard him speak words of love to my mother. Yet I cannot imagine a man loving a woman any more than Daddy loved Momma. I believe he went to his death believing he was the luckiest man walking to be married to my mother. As for his love for Sister and me? That was never in doubt either. Daddy was not an openly affectionate man, but Sister and I never questioned that he adored us.

I spoke of my East Coast group discussion experience to Sister shortly after it happened, then forgot all about it. Five years later, however, when I read this letter, I thought about that New York psychologist's distress as I read Daddy's final declaration. There, tacked on as an afterthought to the only letter I have ever seen in my daddy's slapdash handwriting is: "I love my girls." Think my daddy didn't love me? There it is, finally, in black and white—well, gray and tan. *I love my girls,* he says.

Shortly after this letter, Momma and I did indeed get the bus to Kermit, then the train to Welch, where Daddy met us at the station and proudly carried us to Polly and Lindsay Blevins's boardinghouse. It was located in Pitch Holler, about a quarter mile across the Tug Fork of the Big Sandy from #2 Tipple, where Daddy worked. Despite the lack of space and privacy, all three of us thrived there.

In January 1942, Momma wrote Grandma Emmy: "I washed Monday and have been drying my clothes along all week. I finished my ironing yesterday all but a bedspread & two sheets, & a gown. I just brought them in today. I guess I'll wash some tomorrow but that's my 'little washing.'" This "little washing" was done on a washboard in a tub of water on the back porch of the boardinghouse, and then ironed in the parlor. For both washing and ironing, Momma had to wait her turn behind Mrs. Blevins and her daughters, Ruby and Carrie. The wet wash was hung on a clothesline strung out back. I'd be willing to bet, however, that Daddy was one of the few miners—perhaps the only— who wore freshly starched and ironed clothes to the mine every day.

My mother fondly spoke of her time in West Virginia, however uncertain and sporadic it may have been, as the happiest of her life. She constantly wrestled with homesickness—was torn all to pieces at having to leave Grandma Emmy—but enjoyed something close to a mother-daughter relationship with Polly Blevins. As much as Daddy needed to be alone, Momma loved a crowd and enjoyed living in the boardinghouse and having all those people at supper every evening. Momma was proud of the job Daddy held—contributing to the war effort in that way—for both Momma and Daddy were superpatriotic.

During our years in West Virginia, one slogan captured the imagination of coal miners and their families. As common as Burma Shave signs on the highway, the assertion was splashed on barns we could see from the train. It read: *West Virginia—Heart of the Million Dollar Coal-fields.* Momma, Daddy, and I always felt a sense of pride when we read that slogan on the side of buses or on billboards. Momma would repeat it for emphasis: "West Virginia, Heart of the Million Dollar Coalfields." My daddy worked in those coalfields and he was proud of holding a regular job, working that job, and supporting his family. All those emotionally freighted, sense-of-self sorts of attitudes rode on the back of that adage each time it was repeated.

Though I was quite young when I lived there, some memories of Aunt Polly Blevins's boardinghouse are vivid. I clearly recall being the center of attention and Daddy Blevins calling me his "big-eared Melungeon." I don't recall ever asking what or who a Melungeon was or even why I was called that. (Later I learned that it's a regional term used by some to refer to those who are descendants of a mixed-blood group.) Momma said Daddy Blevins was just teasing by calling attention to my having inherited Daddy's big stick-out ears and my skin being darker than that of most babies. My mother was a fierce fighter of what home folks called a "hillbilly necklace"—a black sweat ring around the throat. According to Momma, "I used to scrub your neck raw because you were so dark-skinned that your neck and knees always looked dirty."

My days in West Virginia were spent with Momma and Aunt Polly as they worked around the boardinghouse, cleaning and cooking and listening to music and war news on the radio. Now and again some song would come on and Momma would say, "There's my Bing." I thought that was the name of the song but later learned she was referring to Bing Crosby. I don't recall listening to Bing much after we moved back home, though. In Kentucky, our music—like us—was country. From the time we got electricity in the Two-Mile house, country music—which we called "hillbilly music"—provided the score for my family's life as the radio played from sign-on to sign-off in my house. Sometimes we'd turn it down while we ate supper, but that was not standard practice. Though our supper table conversation never lagged, we loved to hear music with our meals. At the Blevins's boardinghouse, the radio was not only left on at suppertime—it was turned up. Then folks just talked over it, unless somebody heard something he wanted to listen to and hushed the rest of us so he could hear.

We'd go in to supper at a long table set for eight or ten people. The plates were face down on the table with a fork lying crossways across the back. Huge bowls of food were already on the table, and everybody would take their places, turn their plates over, and begin ladling food from the bowls as they were passed around. I don't recall ever seeing either a knife or a napkin on the table, and if somebody wanted some butter, he just stuck his fork in the big round cake of what we always called "cow butter." I don't know why we called it that. This was in the days before we'd even heard of margarine, so cow butter was all we had. Later, we differentiated between cow butter—our own, in a round cake, direct from Grandma Emmy's cow by way of her churn—and that which came in sticks bought from the store. One of Momma's letters to Grandma Emmy says, "The Prestons' cow has gone dry so I don't guess we'll be getting any more butter." I'm not sure when my family took up the butter knife—somewhere between my adolescence and Sister's, probably. I imagine TV had a lot to do with our abandoning the practice of individually forking out our butter, or maybe some fancy home economics teacher brought the enlightenment.

Conversation at the boardinghouse table was spirited and usually jolly, even though the war was going on and much of the talk dealt with war news. The gist of discussion about the war seemed always to be that we were justifiably kicking ass either in Europe or the Pacific, and there was much conversation about where each named place happened to be. Since everybody had brothers, nephews, cousins, and friends over there somewhere, there were always discussions just trying to place precisely where we were fighting.

My memories of the Blevins's boardinghouse have been helped along by two of Aunt Polly Blevins's nieces—Betty Ward Keys and Peggy Ward Crutchfield. As young girls, both visited their aunt's boardinghouse. As Peggy says: "Bet and I remember when we went to visit there was always a lot of laughter and fun. Bet remembers the swing on Aunt Polly's porch falling and a two by four hitting her on the head (I tell her that's why she has migraines) and I remember that they always told me I would be 'fat like Aunt Polly when you grow up.' There was (and is) something about our branch of the Ward family that uses the word 'fat' as a dirty word. Don't know where that came from."

Let me point out here that both Bet and Peg are as bone thin as my mother was, and Peg's comment that her branch of the Wards using "fat" as a dirty word is an interesting contrast to the ways my own people used that word. Of the many wartime letters I have between various members of Momma's family written to Grandma Emmy, few of them are without mention of somebody, usually children—okay, usually me—being "fat as a pig." When a member of my family spoke of someone getting fat or being fat, that was a sign of well-being. When someone reported that a child was "a big 'un," "fat as a pig," or "mean as a snake," that meant the child was in good health. So letter after letter reports how much the family had for supper, how much the writer ate, and how one or another ate.

In a letter dated March 12, 1942, Momma reports, "Linda is fine. She gets fatter all the time." And on December 5, 1942, Momma says she has been "breaking Linda from the bottle" and goes on to say, "She eats like a pig and we buy pasteurized cows milk for her & she just soaks it down. She is such a big girl now." In at least a dozen letters between 1942, ending with her last letter to Grandma Emmy in February 1945, Momma repeats the mantra, "Linda is fine & as fat as a pig." Pictures from those years, however, reveal that I was not a particularly robust child.

In the only letter from Uncle Fred in Grandma Emmy's packet, her second son reports that his new baby, Donnie, has "growed so much and is as mean as he can be boy he is a bear dog." In a July 13, 1943, postcard from the TB sanitarium, Uncle Tom Fletcher says, "Tell Grace if she will stay in the bed like I do she will get fat, too." No doubt he was responding to one of Momma's messages about how sick she was and how much weight she had lost. In a February 16, 1945, letter, in discussing her attempt to cut back on smoking, Momma writes, "I feel better, too & eat like a pig. Guess I'll get fat now."

One way Momma gauged the state of her health was by discussing how little she had eaten and how much weight she had lost. Over the years, Sister and I cannot recall a time Momma ever spoke of gaining one pound. Instead we calculate that our mother lost thousands of pounds over her lifetime, and Sister and I found *every one* of them.

One expression we had for explaining that a person was getting better—not so bad off anymore—after a sick spell was to say "he's taking nourishment." Another step toward good health was when he was "up and taking nourishment." Over the course of her lifetime, Momma took very little nourishment, forever claiming to be too sick to eat. She would carefully chronicle all the food made available to her, pointing out how little she ate of it. This was the case whether she had cooked the meal or someone else had. The first written reference of Momma's refusal of food as a sign of illness is a May 1942 letter from Momma to Grandma Emmy wherein Momma describes a typical Sunday boardinghouse dinner that fits in with Bet's and Peg's memories and my own. Momma reports, however, that she did not even taste the chicken and ate only greens, which was Momma's way of saying she "couldn't keep anything on [her] stomach."

The Ward girls, Betty and Peggy, also lived in a West Virginia coal camp in Kingston, West Virginia, which their brother, Charlie, wrote about in the book *Silk Stockin' Row*, so they are more familiar with Kingston than Hemphill. After I began asking them questions about their memories of Aunt Polly's boardinghouse, Peggy talked with one of her former schoolteachers, Betty Smith Holley, who had lived at the Kingston camp's boardinghouse. Though the details of the Kingston boardinghouse are not identical to those of Aunt Polly's place on Pitch Holler—I do not recall any single women at Blevins's, for example—there are similarities. Peggy writes: "The women kept their own rooms clean, and clean sheets were furnished once a week. The house had a coal furnace . . . and a coal stove in the kitchen. The meals were full meals (chicken, steak, roasts); no sandwiches were served. . . . Breakfast was not especially a 'sit down together' thing but lunch was served at 12:00 and dinner at 5:00. . . . There were three long tables and the food was served 'family style.' There was good conversation and camaraderie at meal times."

Bet remembers that one of Aunt Polly's children lived in Kingston at one time, and says, "We remember the two grandsons who had cerebral palsy and were severely handicapped. Our dad was always close to his brother Frank (on Two-Mile) but kind of lost touch with Aunt Polly." Aunt Polly and Momma were generally the best carriers of war news, since the Blevinses had a big radio down in the boardinghouse living room, and she and Momma spent many afternoons sitting before that radio, sewing or mending or writing letters. What's more, Momma was a regular correspondent with Aunt Lizzie's three boys—Gene Ray, "Pick" (Fred Thomas), and Roy Mitchell. We had sepia-toned pictures of all three boys in their sailor uniforms displayed on the dresser up in our room. Big, burly, and blond Gene Ray and Gig Young look-alike Pick were both reduced to three-by-five gray cardboard frames, while Roy Mitchell, those white curls spilling out of the front of his sailor cap, could have passed for God's own angel. Momma had lived with Aunt Lizzie off and on before she married Daddy, and she loved those boys as her own. Keeping company with the Colvin boys on Momma's dresser top was a two-by-three black-and-white picture of a nearly bald one-year-old Linda Sue Preston, an American flag waving in the background, with Momma's hand holding my right arm—to keep me from falling out of the picture booth, perhaps. Rounding out the picture grouping was a smiling Uncle Burns in his army uniform.

Momma corresponded with all three of her nephews, but she received the most letters from Uncle Burns, maybe because the Colvin boys were often on sea duty and could not send or receive mail regularly. Uncle Burns, however, wrote often, both before and after he was shipped out to Europe. I got to hear each of Uncle Burns's letters several times, since Momma would read parts of them to Aunt Polly, again to Daddy as he washed up before supper, and then she would take them to the table and share pieces of them with everybody. My uncle Burns wrote great letters. He not only chronicled every rumor about where the latest "big push" was on (sometimes the censors had marked that part out), but he also had news of how many of our own had been killed or injured, as well as how many of theirs we'd taken out. Though we didn't exactly cheer at the news that whole villages were leveled, the winning feeling was unpolluted by regret for the innocent. It may be that the grown-ups felt some remorse and I was just too young to make the inference. Uncle Burns also included descriptions of his own romantic exploits, some of which Momma censored for the supper table. Despite Momma's taking on when Uncle Burns divorced, I don't recall her expressing much dismay at his fooling around all over Europe. Everybody knew my uncle to be a rounder, so not much got left out of his descriptions of the "girl in the red-checked shorts," and we were left to imagine the rest. Whenever Momma would read such passages, Daddy would grin and shake his head, while Daddy Blevins laughed and slapped his leg and Aunt Polly always said, "Law, that Burns!"

Our living conditions—and place of residence—varied during the five or six years Momma and I moved back and forth between Kentucky and West Virginia. First we lived in one room on the top floor of Blevins's camp boardinghouse. Then two rooms came available and we moved downstairs into them. Then half a house (one bedroom and a shared kitchen) came available on the hill around past #2 Tipple. We shared that house with Mary and Ray Engle until they moved out down on the road and we took over that bedroom and had the kitchen to ourselves. Then another half a house came available down on the road and we moved down there. The houses on the main road were preferable because they had water and a sink in the kitchen, where the houses up the steps only had a pump outside the kitchen door. First we shared the house on the main road above #2 Tipple with Lahoma somebody and her husband, then with a fellow called Johnny Bull. At one point we had that house all to ourselves.

While those were the only places we lived in West Virginia, there was no orderly progression from the boardinghouse through having the #2 camp house to ourselves. Whenever Momma and I would go back to Grandma Emmy's for as much as two months, Daddy would give up the family quarters and return to the boardinghouse. Then when we returned, we had to get on the housing list all over again. If it happened that there was no housing shortage when we came back, he would simply move back into the house or half a house we'd left before we returned. Because we were never sure where we would be or how soon we would be settled, all our clothes, pots, dishes, spices, drugs, and cosmetics were packed into two trunks, which spent time between and among our various houses and the storage room of the Blevins's boardinghouse. The same could be said of our utility cabinet, refrigerator, and bedroom suite, though the last few times we moved out of the #2 house on the main road, Daddy just moved the headboard and dresser, leaving the mattress, refrigerator, and utility cabinet to the family who took over the house. Almost everybody in Hemphill lived the same sort of itinerant lifestyle during those war years, and neither Momma nor Daddy complained about it—then, or later, when we discussed it.

Aunt Stella's son-in-law, Morris Young, was in the army, and Aunt Stella's letters to Grandma Emmy spoke of her daughter, Veva, and her sons traveling back and forth between Texas (where Morris was stationed), Lawrence County, Kentucky (where his parents lived), and Inez, Kentucky (where Aunt Stella and Uncle Tom lived). Sometimes Veva took her baby—and later, babies—with her; sometimes she didn't. It was wartime, and many young folks were on the move. Thus, members of families whose older generations had never traveled outside Kentucky were suddenly taking up temporary residence in California, Texas, Washington, or New York. Then on November 23, 1944, Aunt Stella writes: "Veva is still in Texas. Her boy has been sick but is better now." At that point Veva's sick boy was staying in Kentucky with Aunt Stella and Uncle Tom. Momma and Daddy were disapproving of folks who left their kids on the grandparents. In a letter postmarked November 2, 1944, Momma writes: "[W]hat does Veva mean by leaving her babies—and Tom & Stella both sick, too. not that I blame Veva if she wants to, but I wouldn't have gone & left Stella & Tom by themselves & them both sick."

While nearly all of Momma's letters were filled with "Linda cries to come stay with you" statements, I was only allowed to live with Grandma Emmy when Momma was back in Kentucky. So long as my mother was on Two-Mile, she could leave me with my grandmother for days—sometimes weeks—but she and Daddy never allowed me to stay back in Kentucky while they went to West Virginia. If Momma went to Hemphill, so did I.

Just as Veva was on the move—with or without babies—from Kentucky to Texas and back to Kentucky, so were we on the move between Kentucky and West Virginia, then a round-robin rotation between and among boardinghouse rooms and different coal camp houses. Though folks' lives were disjointed, at best, I could find no complaints about living conditions in any of the hundred or so cards and letters from eight of Grandma Emmy's children written between 1935 and 1945. While they often described situations that were severe, not one ever suggested that his or her housing, food, or working conditions were as bad or worse than he had left on Greasy Creek. In fact, most of the time they expressed concern that Grandma Emmy's situation was worse than theirs.

Every one of the girls invited Grandma Emmy to visit, and Momma and Aunt Stella pleaded over and over for their mother to come live with them, indicating how much easier it would be for her if she would just leave the home place. In a letter written in 1944, Momma says:

Mom, I can't tell you in a letter all I want to tell you but here's this much anyway & don't think I'm being unreasonable or asking the impossible. Jay feels about it the same way I do. Why don't you come stay with us? You could rent your place or do anything you wanted to with it. Jay said if you would come & stay with us he would do everything he could do to please you & I'll swear you wouldn't ever have to turn your hand to do a thing—or ever have a short word spoken to you in any way.

After all, that farm doesn't mean a thing to me & you mean everything. What good is it going to do for you to kill yourself there? You've spent 50 years on that place & it isn't going to do any of us any good after you're gone. I'll wait on you as long as I live if you'll just come & stay with us. If Daddy was alive you know he wouldn't want you to stay there & you sick. I don't want you to live with us because I think it's my duty. I want to take care of you because I love you & want & need you to stay with me. Jay says tell you he feels the same way I do about it & he's worried to death because you & Leon are there by yourselves.

If you won't come & stay here I'll move home if you & Leon will come & stay. You can have all the say-so you want & it will be your home same as mine. I know if I was sick you'd come & take me home & take care of me. You know you always did.

She then speaks of Daddy's having been offered a "bossing" opportunity in a camp ten miles away, where the camp "is clean & quiet & on the railroad. Big gardens & fenced in yards & company store. We can get a big house & have all the room you want if you'll just come."

I know Daddy wanted Grandma Emmy to stay with us so she wouldn't work herself down on the home place. Even after we moved back to Two-Mile, he and Momma tried their best to get Grandma Emmy to come live with us right up until she died. Also, given that Daddy was never willing to take a bossing job, I suspect Momma was hoping that if she could get Grandma Emmy to come to West Virginia, Daddy would take the job so as to get us the bigger house.

Jay says if you won't come then I'll have to come & take care of you there & you know as long as you're there you will work some. Please, Mommy, say you'll come. You could get some good renter to take care of the place & any time you got tired of us you could go back.

You always said when you got too old to work you'd not be like Aunt Mary & try to stay by yourself. You know you would be satisfied with us.

Your getting well is all that matters and you won't even have to worry about a thing. Jay is young & strong & plenty able to make a living for us & he wants to, he said to tell you.

You know Granny [Martha Cline] stayed with you and you liked for her to stay.

Well, Linda just got up & I put her clothes on & she's eating her break-fast. She's fat as a pig.

Mom, do you reckon if Jay brought the car & came after you, that you could get Lizzie to come & stay there & let you come up for a week or two & rest & see how you like it? He could come & get you.

Aunt Polly says she's coming down to Beaver Creek to the hospital the first of the month. Write & tell me what to do about all this & please try to see things my way & I'll never ask you for anything else.

She asks if Grandma Emmy has seen Aunt Stella recently and given her the books we brought on our recent visit and reports that she has written to Uncle Tom in the TB sanitarium and sent him a carton of cigarettes. Momma goes on to say how much she knows Grandma Emmy enjoyed having "Lizzie's kids and Linda" there when we were last home and finishes: "We'll talk it all over when I see you. Try to manage to come for awhile anyway & *Don't Work!* If I come down there I'll make sure you don't. (Ha) Be sure & let me know, Mom, & don't tell me not to worry for I am nearly crazy with worrying about you."

In just about every letter her daughters wrote to Grandma Emmy they cautioned her about working too hard, for each of them knew from experience how hard life could be on that piece of ground. All of them had worked it when they were young and strong, and they knew it was too much for their aging mother and her grandson. Both Momma and Aunt Amanda spoke of how they worried for Grandma Emmy's welfare, and they agree that she was "stubborn as a mule" when it came to leaving the home place.

Though I have no record and do not know the occasion, I do recall Grandma Emmy coming to visit us in West Virginia once. She and Grandma Alk came together—rode the train and everything. Daddy drove us to the Welch railroad station, where we waited for the train, waving madly as soon as it came into view. Grandma Alk was by the window, and she smiled that sweet Ward smile the moment she glimpsed us on the platform. Momma had hold of one of my hands, and I was jumping for joy as they alighted. Wearing a navy serge dress with a gold-colored cameo brooch at her throat, Grandma Emmy stepped off the train first. Then Grandma Alk, in her black crepe with a white collar, disembarked. I don't know who was the happiest, but the time they were with us was sheer joy for all five of us, and Momma and I cried all the way back from the train station when they left for home.

Though they seemed to enjoy each other's company, my two grand-mothers were not one bit alike. Grandma Alk was one of those pleas-ant, peaceful women who couldn't be riled by Satan himself, while Grandma Emmy was droll, opinionated, and tougher'n a pine knot. Grandma Alk was delighted with having made the trip and all the new experiences of riding the train, while Grandma Emmy took it in stride, and both grandmothers were tickled to death to see how good we had it in the coal camp. Daddy drove us all over the place, he and Momma in the front seat and me in back, passed from lap to lap and sometimes just sitting wedged between my grandmothers. We rode past the club-house and "silk stocking row"—where the bosses lived—down to the company store, over to the trestle to watch the trains go by, and even to a couple of other coal camps so they could see that Hemphill was the best.

When I was about five years old, Momma and I were on one of our going-to-stay-with-Daddy trips to West Virginia. We were sitting at the supper table in Blevins's boardinghouse when a man came running in and said the Havaco mine had blown out. This announcement cleared the table as every man jumped up, crowded into cars, and headed for the mine. Included in this band were the only three females present for the announcement—Polly Blevins, Momma, and me. About half an hour later, Daddy parked at the foot of the hill, and we joined the throng of people milling around just above the tipple at the mouth of the mine. The man who had come running into the boardinghouse had said that they needed all the manpower they could get to help, but at first there seemed to be little anyone could do. Once assured that the mine was safe for reentry, however, Daddy put on another miner's hard hat and disappeared with the rescue team into the yawning chasm in the side of Havaco Mountain. Meanwhile, I enjoyed the excitement as Momma and Aunt Polly Blevins were left to roam the crowd, comforting, gathering information, and repeating the explosion story that had been developing since our arrival. I had no idea why some of the women seemed so upset, and I was agitated when Momma would not allow me to play with one or more of the many children chasing each other up and down the hill.

Eventually, Daddy and Daddy Blevins came back, said there was too much slate to get to those who were trapped, that the mine was putting the next shift to work with picks and shovels and sending everybody else home. As we drove away, most of the crowd was dispersing, but a determined little group of women huddled together near the drift mouth (the cavity leading into the mine from the outside) of the mine. I suppose they were the soon-to-be-widowed.

By Daddy's twenty-fifth birthday, on March 12, 1942, Momma, Daddy, and I were still living in one room at the Blevins's boardinghouse, as Momma reports in a letter to Grandma Emmy: "Today is Jay's birthday & Ruby [Blevins—Polly's daughter] is baking him a cake. He's happy as a coon this morning—singing and whistling all over & rocking himself. First time I've ever seen him happy for awhile. Bet you have a bushel of work. If we don't get rooms soon I think I'll come home & stay & raise a garden. Maybe Two-Mile is O.K. after all. (Ha)"

Though Momma loved the boardinghouse, she liked it much better when we had a two-room arrangement downstairs. Shortly after that letter, Momma, Daddy, and I did get rooms downstairs, and the next year we moved off Pitch Holler for the first time into our own half a house located on the hill just above #2 Tipple. We had our own bedroom and living room but shared a kitchen with a single miner who bunked in the second bedroom. There was no indoor plumbing, but there was a pump with cold water just outside our kitchen door, and the shared toilet was out the living room door and about thirty steps up the hill. The other fellow sharing the house went back to his home in Tennessee when the mines went out on strike in the spring, and we moved into the rest of the house. In April 1943 Momma writes: "We've moved into the kitchen and little back room we were telling you about. We have both porches now & our kitchen looks like it did at home [on Two-Mile]."

By September of '43, Daddy's name had been shuffled along the list long enough so we made our final move directly down about sixty steps to one of the camp houses on the road above #2 Tipple. I recall that house as really fine, with a bedroom, living room, and a kitchen with water in the sink. The toilet was a long way up the steps, but Momma and I took no notice of that, since neither of us ever used it. Daddy carried the slop jar to the toilet before work every morning, and Momma potty-trained me on a two-quart paint can that I became so attached to we carried it back to Kentucky with us in 1947. Okay, so some have their blankies; I had my paint can. Besides, Momma washed both paint can and slop jar with lye soap every morning, and Daddy had painted my paint can cream-colored, the same shade he painted the living room.

Not everybody could afford slop jars, and even those who could usually refrained from using them until they had to do a number two. For number one, folks customarily had their own paint can—at least the women did. I don't know about other folks' families, but my daddy never used the slop jar. If he needed to do serious business he went to the toilet, so I figured that was a man thing.

The years in West Virginia were harsh ones for Momma and Daddy, no doubt about it. Food, cigarettes, and housing were hard to come by, so it was a real blessing to us that Momma and I were able to be with Daddy at all. The war was on, the mines were running double time, and Daddy worked six and often seven days a week. The mines ran nearly nonstop, with a daylong shutdown now and then, probably for maintenance. I don't know why or how often it shut down, but when they'd gear it up again, Momma would always say, "That old tipple's singing again, Jay." After spending the first year or so in a boardinghouse, Momma, Daddy, and I moved to the cluster of camp houses back of #2 Tipple. The noise made by the #2 coal tipple in full cry was a keening sort of hum—pitched higher, I think, than most mine operations. The sound verged on a croon, and Momma always termed it the "singing" tipple.

Illness—some real, some imagined—often swept through the camp, felling somebody new every day. In addition to the usual colds and flu, kids got chicken pox, measles, whooping cough, and scarlet fever, while adults got down sick with anemia, blood poisoning, and tuberculosis. During our time in West Virginia, my family was visited with every one of those diseases, and we were not at all unusual. One affliction or another raged through the camps, carried by folks crowded on buses and trains who caught something in Ohio and took it to Tennessee, where somebody picked it up and brought it to Kentucky. Then, some one of us passed it from Kentucky to West Virginia and beyond. As for illnesses that were not catching, unsanitary living conditions took care of us there.

None of the houses in our row of camp houses—or on the hill above us—had indoor toilets; the ones on the hill didn't even have water in the kitchen, only a pump outside. This meant that at least seven families—perhaps twice that many—used the same toilet up the steps at the top of the hill. Momma and I did not visit that shared facility. After Daddy had emptied our white slop jar with the fine red ring around its lip into that toilet every morning, Momma scrubbed the life out of that old chamber pot. Then, with the same determination, she attacked the two paint cans she'd emptied into the slop jar prior to Daddy's morning chore.

As for sanitary conditions at the company store, nobody ever wore rubber gloves when they sliced the meat or ground the hamburger either. The fact that we cooked our food to death probably saved us many a time, but the bologna, pickle loaf, and cheese was sliced and sometimes fed to the grinder by hands not exactly sterile. We lived close up to each other, a situation that did not lend itself to optimum health.

All of the above problems were complicated by the fact that both my parents were so connected to their extended families in Kentucky that neither of them could bear to stay away from home—Two-Mile and Greasy—for any prolonged period of time. Thus, as often as every couple of weeks, they packed up the baby—me—and headed home for a couple of days. An aerial map reflecting the proximity of Johnson County, Kentucky, to McDowell County, West Virginia, in no way illustrates the problem of Lifie Jay and Grace's trek homeward in the forties. Here's how it really went down.

Daddy worked the early shift at the mine, leaving the house just before 6:00 A.M., and if he got no overtime, his quit time was at 3:00 P.M. In those days the mines ran full out seven days a week, and the miners' schedules varied week to week or month to month, so we were never sure which five or six days a week Daddy would be working. Sometimes he would work fifteen, twenty, or thirty days in a row, then take off for four or five days. This sort of staggered schedule worked well for Daddy, since that allowed us to go to Kentucky on Saturday and stay through the next Tuesday or Wednesday.

The trip itself was arduous. On Friday before we'd "head to th' house," as Daddy always called it, Momma would pull the small cardboard suitcase out from under their bed, open it on top of the bed, and wipe it thoroughly with a rag barely dampened with Clorox water. The unlined suitcase was made of extra-strength cardboard, pale cream inside and out. On the outside, the cream background was crisscrossed with deep tan and brown lines, creating the illusion of checks around the bag's middle and rows of lines around both ends. It was the only suitcase my family owned until after it burned up in our house in 1955, and for all its wartime travels, it was in great shape right up to its incineration.

I was kind of proud of our suitcase, a pride I inherited from Momma and Daddy. First of all, not everybody owned a valise of any sort, and we certainly saw all kinds of carrying items on the trains and buses. The traveling servicemen had huge navy blue or army green duffel bags, closed with thick ropes caught tight at the neck, while others carried everything from carpetbags or leather satchels right down to big paper pokes rolled down at the top. I never saw a knapsack, attaché case, hobo bundle, or makeup case, and I never saw a suitcase that trumped ours. The Jay Preston family traveled in style, at least in my young head, which brings me to the second source of pride in our suitcase—we owned one.

The fact that we owned a suitcase meant we were folks who traveled, and for all the hardships of my parents' lives in a West Virginia mining camp, both were proud of the fact that we were the kind of folks who went places. There was an air of excitement about every single trip we ever made, whether a Sunday drive to Broke Leg Falls or a trip back to Hemphill, West Virginia, to visit the Blevins and Kish families in the fifties after we'd moved back home. That frisson of excitement was not missing on those exhausting trips to Kentucky in the wartime forties—not ever.

Momma would place two folded pairs of khaki pants, two short-sleeved button-up shirts, plus a daily change of undershirt, socks, and undershorts for Daddy in the bottom of the suitcase, then she would turn to the real job—sorting through her clothes and mine to select just the right daily outfits. Even then, Momma and I had a truckload of clothes, all starched, ironed, and done up within an inch of their lives.

No matter that the suitcase would be stuffed so full that Momma would have to dampen and press every item with Grandma Emmy's stove-warmed flatirons; we weren't going anywhere without being dressed till a fly wouldn't light on us.

By the time Daddy got home at 3:15 P.M., Momma and I had been in a flurry of trying on everything we would wear when we got to Kentucky, choosing the right shoes and hair ribbons to go with same, changing our minds and beginning all over again, and finally carefully folding it all and packing it. The final items to go in the suitcase were Momma's and Daddy's cigarettes, a pack a day each. Most of the time cigarettes were easier to come by in Kentucky, but they took no chances on running out. After supper, where we talked about who we'd see and what we'd do when we got to Kentucky, Momma would clean up the kitchen and Daddy would put me to bed and read me a story, then we'd try to get to sleep early so we wouldn't be too tired to travel in the morning. Daddy never read me a story unless we were leaving for Kentucky the next day, and once we moved back to Two-Mile, he never read me to sleep again. I don't recall that ever being mentioned in our house, but I probably assumed it was because I was a great big girl—nearly six years old—by the time we moved back and had simply outgrown the practice.

Early Saturday morning, somebody would drive us to the Welch railroad station, which was a big enough station for the train to make a regular stop—unlike our destination in Kermit, where you had to signal in order to disembark. The fact that Welch (*our* station) was big enough to have its own scheduled stop was also a source of pride to us. The train left early, though I don't recall how early, and it's not in any of Momma's letters. Because the letters were all written from West Virginia, she gives detailed descriptions of the inbound trip, nothing about the outbound, so I must reconstruct from memory.

Once on the train there were certain unspoken rules of behavior following along the lines of "women and children first," with one exception. Though Daddy would stand for any woman, child, older person of either gender, or someone obviously impaired in some way, this was wartime and both he and Momma would stand to give a seat to a serviceman. Most of the time the soldier or sailor would not take the seat, especially from Momma, but neither of my parents ever failed to offer. Lots of times Daddy stood all the way from Welch to Kermit. If the train happened to be not quite full and he got a seat in Welch, however, he still had to get up and offer in Williamson, Iaeger, and any other small place where somebody flagged down the train. In a letter written August 9, 1943, Momma reports: "I believe we had a very good trip. Jay stood up from Inez to Kermit [a woman, older person, or serviceman must have boarded the bus in Inez] for the bus was crowded but we got a seat on the train & made it fine."

Another unspoken rule was that we never carried snacks on the train, ever. Other folks could be seen taking peanuts or a pickle jar of water or Kool-Aid from a paper sack and passing it among their traveling companions, and it was not uncommon for some to snack on a sausage biscuit. My parents were adamant that if I wanted something to eat, Daddy could afford to buy it. We were not the kind of people who carried biscuits from breakfast to snack on later. Maybe this had something to do with their having lived through some very hard times. Neither Momma nor Daddy ever went barefoot—even around the house—and if we had leftovers, we ate them at the next meal or we gave them to the pigs. We did not carry them in a poke sack and eat them right out in front of anybody as if we couldn't afford to buy ourselves a snack. That wouldn't look right; we were not that kind of people. My daddy often referred to himself as a "poor man," as in "trying to make a poor man's dollar" or "life's hard on a poor man," but he never allowed us to engage in any of the behaviors that he and Momma saw as clear markers of poverty.

Once the train had reached our destination—Kermit, West Virginia— we got off at the station and waited for the bus that ran once a day, maybe twice, between Paintsville and Kermit. We rode the bus from Kermit, through Warfield, Inez, and Tomahawk in Martin County, then across the hill through Spicy Gap, down to Ern Ward's store and the Boons Camp post office, where we pulled the little cord over the window and got off. From there, we walked the remaining mile or so up Greasy Creek to Grandma Emmy's house. Most of the time, if Grandma Emmy knew we were coming, Leon would meet the bus. Then, after helping Momma and me disembark, Daddy would continue to ride the three or four miles on around to Pop Pop's house on Two-Mile. If Leon didn't meet us, Daddy would carry our suitcase to Grandma Emmy's, then stay the night before walking the next day to Pop Pop's.

Many among my cache of letters detail our travels, for once we were back in Hamphill, Momma always wrote my grandmother to let her know we got back and to tell her about the trip. One of my favorites is Momma's October 18, 1943, description of our first trip home without Daddy:

> . . . got back O.K. Had a good trip. The baby never went to sleep on the bus & we got our ticket & left the suitcase with the station agent & went out & got her some ice cream. About 10 minutes before train time the engineer on a coal drag missed his orders & pulled in on the track between the station & the track # 16 [the train running from Kermit to Welch] runs on & boy was there excitement for awhile. The station agent grabbed my suitcase & put the other station agent in charge of me & Linda & he went through the freighter & flagged 16 & held it till the coal drag pulled out.
>
> Three of the conductors put Linda & me on & one found us a seat. Linda went to sleep in three minutes & slept into Yeager [Ieager]. She wasn't one bit of trouble the whole way home. Jay brought Mom Blevins's car & met us at the Station. A sailor took my suitcase off & Jay took us to a restaurant for supper before he brought us home.

One of the reasons Momma enjoyed living in Hemphill was dining out. If Daddy's car was running and he didn't have to work on Sunday, we would go to the Blue Swan restaurant in Welch at noon for Sunday dinner. Daddy always wore a suit and tie, and Momma and I dressed like we "stepped out of a bandbox." After our dinner we would often drive out in the country somewhere in McDowell County, where we could pull off the road, sit in the car, and watch the trains go by about a hundred yards away. In nice weather, we'd get out of the car, and I could wave at the people as they passed by on their way to somewhere.

Momma always knew the names or numbers of the trains, and we'd imagine where those folks were going and what they might be doing when they got there. All three of us would make up stories about who was going where and what lay ahead of them. Momma would say, "You remember Johnny—that red-headed soldier we met on the train last month? Well, he married his girlfriend, Betty, while he was home in Virginia and he's taking her back to camp with him. If you'll look closely, they're in the dining car eating chicken and dumplings." She would go on to describe Betty's hair and clothes and tell how many suitors she was disappointing by eloping with Johnny. My doll, Cake-a-bony, would recall soldier Johnny, too, and would look hard to see the newly married couple as the train whistled past us.

The trains ran in the direction of what Momma always said was Wyoming. "Over there's Wyoming," she'd say. Once I went to school and learned of the state by that name, I felt some familiarity with it because of the times I'd watched trains headed in that direction. In the late seventies, when Momma and Daddy drove west the first time, she was telling me about the states they'd gone through, and I reminded her about those trains we thought were going to Wyoming. "Oh," she laughed, "that was Wyoming County, West Virginia."

Some of the trains were new and special—one of those was the Powhatan (which was pronounced Pow-Tan and I thought was spelled that way until I studied history) Arrow. We didn't see it on Sundays when we drove out in the country. It was a through passenger train that ran in the early evening and could be seen from the trestle just up the hill from the swinging bridge over to Pitch Holler. When we lived at the boardinghouse, we'd walk up to the trestle after supper and watch for the trains—especially the Powhatan Arrow. I'd wave at the fancy folks eating their supper in the dining car.

Momma finished her October '43 trip report saying: "Linda told everybody she had a big time. I've found out I can come home by myself so I'll come often now. (Ha)" Just a year later, Momma speaks of another trip "by [her]self": "10/24/44, . . . Had a good trip except for the rain. Got a seat on the bus and train and the baby was the best I ever knew her to be. She went to sleep just after we got on the train and slept until I woke her to put her coat on to get off after we passed Iager [Ieager]. Jay had the car and met us. He said he didn't much look for us but was glad we came."

When we first began riding the trains, only a few of them were airconditioned, but by 1944, we'd come to expect it. In a June 1944 letter she says, "We got home O.K. The air conditioning busted on the train & it nearly steamed us to death & we had to stand up to Williamson but outside of that we made it O.K. Got home around nine o'clock."

Now and then there would be some old friend or acquaintance—a soldier returning to camp, maybe, or someone on the way to visit a relative—on the train or bus who would provide company. Momma was always glad to exchange war news and hometown gossip with such folks. In a letter dated April 26, 1945, she reported one such incident to Grandma Emmy: "We got home O.K. Linda fussed all the way home about not getting to stay. Cora Lewis was down at the post office coming to Norfolk, VA to see Walter & we came all the way home with her. I sat with her on the train. Some people got on the bus with children with whooping cough & later got on the train but the conductor let us go in another coach. I was so glad to come this far with Cora & she was glad, too."

There were rules about not riding the train if you had a contagious disease—especially TB—but conductors were pretty good about shuffling folks about so that they had minimum exposure. Though Momma often refers to them maybe not letting us on the train if we were coughing, I don't recall anyone ever being refused a ride, and she never reports such an event.

Nobody's house or business was air-conditioned then—not even the company store. As for the buses we rode to the train and back . . . Well, I'll let Momma tell you about one of those buses:

August 2, 1945

Well, we got home O.K. although we had the awfullest time I ever saw. That storm struck just after we got in Martin County & the bus windows wouldn't roll up on one side, the rain blew in until it was 6 inches deep under our feet & the bus drowned out over on Stafford & there we sat with the lightening running all over the bus.

Linda had to get out & pee & we got wringing wet. It stormed all the way into Kermit & she was so wet & cold I went out & bought her a new dress & changed her panties & sox in the station. When we got home it hadn't rained at all here that day.

Our car-to-train-to-bus-to-foot trip to Kentucky took eight hours or so to cover around one hundred miles, but the roads were so steep and winding that it took four or five hours by car. In that time, in that part of the country nobody got anywhere very easily. Though most of our trips to Kentucky were of the train-bus-foot variety, sometimes we traveled by car. Either we'd catch a ride with someone who was going, or we would drive somebody. In a March 1945 letter, Momma says: "Mom, we will be down in a week or so. Aunt Polly is pretty bad off. Her heart, you know & she wants to come."

Though it was common knowledge that Aunt Polly had a bad heart, she routinely did all the drudge work (washing, scrubbing, mopping, and cooking for the multitudes) at the boardinghouse. Illness did not provide downtime for working people. Momma continues: "Frank [Ward's] oldest boy, 'Little Frank,' has been overseas over three years & he wired them he was in California & would be in on furlough soon, so she wants to come down & I guess we'll bring her. She hasn't been at all well for awhile & wants to come down there for a few days."

Not many folks had a car, so we usually went in our car or Daddy would drive the Blevins's car. Aunt Polly did not drive, and Daddy Blevins would not drive their car on long trips, so when they needed to go to Kentucky Daddy drove them. Though Momma had a driver's license, I do not recall her ever taking the wheel during our West Virginia years. If we needed to go somewhere when Daddy was at work, we walked.

One of my favorite memories of the Hemphill coal camp is of Momma and me walking down the road past our row of houses. We were walking to the corner, turning left just past #2 Tipple and continuing to #1 Tipple, where we knew it would be quitting time for Daddy. We were dressed alike, me and Momma, in black-and-white-plaid pinafores that she had run up for us on her pedal-foot sewing machine, and we both had on white sandals. The road consisted entirely of coal dust, at least as far as I could tell. It may have been a dirt road at one time, but there were no signs of earth anymore, just coal dust. I begged hard to be allowed to go barefoot, but Momma wouldn't have any of that. *Civilized people wear shoes,* she told me, time and again. It seemed to me, even then, that the scant leather strapping that constituted our footwear was hardly different from bare feet. Momma, however, was sure of her position here, so she was adamant—no bare feet for her Linda Sue.

Nevertheless, I know the freedom of going barefoot, because when Momma left me with Grandma Emmy, I was allowed to go for days without shoes. Grandma Emmy's yard and garden were just full of unexpected objects that hurt my tender feet. The coal road, on the other hand, was most inviting, consisting entirely of what Daddy called "bug dust"—very fine coal dust—no stones, no bees, no lumps of coal. I know how pleasant it is to go barefoot on this very road, because whenever we would go out without Momma, Daddy let me take off my shoes. The squishy feel of the fine dust between my toes beat shoes all to pieces. Just before rounding the bend to our row of houses, Daddy would dip the corner of his white handkerchief in the narrow, black creek that ran through the camp. Then he would take that wet corner, wipe my feet, dry them with the dry parts of the handkerchief, and buckle my sandals back on me.

I'm pretty sure Momma knew about Daddy's and my secret. After all, she's the one who rubbed the black out of Daddy's handkerchiefs on a washboard the following Monday. Momma was also the one who insisted that Daddy carry a handkerchief in the first place, instead of just blowing his nose through his fingers like most men. What's more, sometimes Daddy let me walk barefoot all the way to Mrs. Blevins's boardinghouse, where everybody got a kick out of Linda Sue's black feet. Of course I didn't walk every step of the way to Blevins's on Pitch Holler; Daddy always picked me up and carried me across the swinging bridge over the black Tug River. We often stopped in the middle and talked to the ducks. Yes, the river was coal black, but a paddling of ducks often swam fifty feet beneath the bridge.

But on this day I was with Momma, just a few straps of leather saving us from barbarity. Our pinafores were clean, starched, and ironed to a crisp so that the rows of white rickrack trimming shoulder ruffles and skirt tails stood out from the black background. Momma was shining there, giving off that glow she had so much of in those days. She thought we looked good and I knew it, so maybe we were strutting a little. As Daddy joined us, he got a lot of teasing from his buddies getting off his shift and commented to Momma that we might not want to walk all the way to the tipple next time, because "the boys shit me about it." He ducked his head and grinned a little, so we knew he didn't mean it.

Though he worked at some coal mine or another for thirty years and always called himself a coal miner, my daddy never mined coal. Coal mines, especially big ones, needed carpenters, and Daddy was a carpenter. Most of his work was outside the mine shaft, working on coal camp stores, offices, and houses; building and repairing tipples; and occasionally shoring up timbers inside the mine itself.

Daddy had considerable pride in his ability and willingness to work. He and Momma shared in the belief that success is not about outcomes; it's all about giving more than a full day's work for a full day's pay. Both believed that working hard at whatever they were assigned to do was more important than holding a title, and Daddy said that sometimes the title itself caused people to think they were too good to do the work.

"Stuck a straw up his ass and called him boss and sumbitch ain't done a lick of work since" was the way he put it. I doubt that anybody ever chooses to work the mines because he believes he will *like* the work. Then again, I don't come from the kind of people who entertain a variety of choices when it comes to how they'll make a living.

As a young man, my daddy made three life-altering decisions: He dropped out of high school; he got a job at the mines; and he started smoking. Those choices were made with a youthful mind that asked "Why not?" Given what we know today, it would be easy to fill a book with reasons why *not*. It might behoove us to remember that today's judgment has been informed by sixty-some years of going to school on case histories of people like my daddy and by looking at the results of more than one hundred years of coal mining on these hills he loved. There can be no doubt, however, that coal mining—the good and bad of it—shaped the lives of every member of my family.

Daddy started working in the mines because of the good money and because, after failing his army physical, it was the only way he could serve in the war. He got another chance at soldiering, though, when they called him for another physical in 1944.

In an April 7, 1944, letter to Grandma Emmy—written over the signature of "Linda Sue," Momma wrote: "Mother has been sick in bed again. She almost has pneumonia & is coughing her insides up. Daddy has been sick, too. Daddy says we have something the matter all the time for two months now. He's going for Mother to go back to the Hospital as soon as she gets able & have that lung checked on. Her nose bleeds so much and she coughs so.

"Daddy got his reclassification card to May 3rd. Guess his call will come then. He says he'll be glad to go."

In the same envelope is a one-paragraph letter:

Dearest mom,

Jay got his call yesterday. He will have to leave Paintsville at 7 o'clock Monday Morning so he will be down Sat. Don't know if I'll be able to come or not. I can't move around at all hardly, and the Dr. said I'd have to stay in bed. So if I'm not able he'll have to come Saturday. Linda said she was coming with Daddy. I hope I'll be able to stand up. Hope you are better. I don't feel so good this morning.

Well, Jay will see you even if I don't.

Daddy didn't pass this exam either and had to content himself with contributing to the war effort by continuing as a carpenter at the mines rather than as a soldier. According to Momma he was pretty downcast about it, and in a letter postmarked October 1944, she says, "Jay says he can't believe something like his pulse can keep him out of the service. He says if they wanted to they could ask any boss he ever worked for how hard he can work. I don't know what they would do without him here though, since he works six and sometimes seven days a week. The mines are running all day, all night, with no stop and he gets an hour or two of overtime almost every day."

Daddy was proud of being a coal miner and a union member. He joined the United Mine Workers union as soon as he got on at the unionized mines in West Virginia, and he remained a union man as long as he lived. He thought meetings of any kind were a waste of time, however, and routinely paid fines rather than attend union meetings. Though he felt some miners took advantage of their union contracts to slack off work, Daddy refused to cross a picket line even when he thought a strike was uncalled for. He wouldn't scab, because he saw the union as the only way to balance power between the company and the workers. Daddy was a fiercely independent thinker, however, and believed a man had to do what he thought was right. In keeping with that belief, for two months in 1943 Daddy crossed the union picket lines six days a week to work in the Hemphill mines. He never talked about it, and I would not have known it had Momma not divulged it in a conversation shortly before she died. Then it turned up in my grandmother's letters.

In a letter to Grandma Emmy, postmarked June 26, 1943, Momma says: "Jay has worked every day through these strikes & believe me it has been like sitting on a keg of dynamite. He refused to come out [on strike] and the country at war & I've lived in suspense for two months. He got two hours overtime yesterday and didn't get in until 5 o'clock & I was actually sick I was so worried." She goes on to say, "It hasn't been very pleasant." As I read this letter almost sixty years later, my first thought was, *I'll bet it wasn't very pleasant. I'll just bet.* But the words that come back to me are those Daddy spoke to me thirty years after he served his country in the only way they'd let him: "Seems to me like this [country] is the only place on earth that ever gave a poor man a chance."

THE FAMILY CHORUS

During the war years Grandma Emmy did not have one child who lived close enough to walk to her house, and for our people that was unusual. Though Momma wrote home often, she was five to eight hours away under good travel circumstance. Uncle Burns and Uncle John were off in the army. Both Uncle Fred (at Van Lear until he had to move to Wayland) and Aunt Lizzie (at Muddy Branch) still lived in Johnson County, but not near enough to come home often. Aunt Stella lived on a farm over in Martin County, and Aunt Amanda was all the way over in Jackson, Kentucky.

Though I am sorry my grandmother did not have her children to lean on, I am most appreciative of the letters they wrote to her, for these messages provide a description of where and how they lived. The Lige Mollette family was very close and seemed to keep few secrets from each other, so the letters they wrote to their mother describe their triumphs and concerns about themselves. Momma worried about her brothers and sisters, and her letters are filled with her perceptions of their experiences. The letters from her siblings also provide a context for what each was thinking and the lives they led during the war years. Burns was Momma's favorite brother, and she often worried to Grandma Emmy about some real or imagined problem Uncle Burns might be having.

At the time he went into the army, Uncle Burns was married to a woman named Elizabeth "Libby" Baldridge, who probably had her hands full with my favorite uncle. That marriage was not to last much beyond Uncle Burns's completion of basic training, and Momma tried to sort it out on paper. She wrote to Grandma Emmy, "Mom, I don't know what about Burns. . . . I don't know why he doesn't write you or why Libby doesn't send you some word. I just don't know what to make of it. He is giving Libby her divorce." Uncle Burns was a pretty faithful correspondent, but he was far more open in his letters to Momma than he was to Grandma Emmy. In Uncle Burns's letters to Momma, he always included the warning not to tell "Mom"—Grandma Emmy—whether it was about impending orders to be shipped out or involvement with the women. Divorce was not so common in those days, but everybody in the family blamed it on his soon-to-be-ex-wife, Libby.

Though the whole family admitted to Uncle Burns's problematic behavior—he was a drunk and a womanizer—Momma forever took his part, defending his every behavior. In a letter to Grandma Emmy, postmark unclear, Momma is beside herself with worry about her "Buddy" and makes no bones about who is at fault in the divorce:

> Well I got a letter from Buddy yesterday—and an official card that he was at the port of Embarkation. Mom, I will write you what all he wrote me when I get so I can. I can't see or think now—I didn't know it was going to hurt this way. He is giving Libby her divorce. Says he doesn't want her hanging after him for he has plans of his own when he comes home. He wrote me what all to do & I am so crazy I don't know what to do. May God have mercy on that rotten soul of that _____ if I ever see her again.

In such situations, Momma would repeat that "Blood's thicker than water and after all family is family." She continues:

> Mom, if she sends his silverware—he wrote her she had to send it to you, be sure and put it in the trunk so the mice can't get in it. He was afraid they'd eat the chest. I'll bring his letter for you to read when I come home

& I'll write you what he wants to do when I get so I can. Jay is about to die over it. I never thought it could be so awful. I ought not to be writing this way but if I can't let it out some way I'll die. You and I are all he has now—God knows I'll never fail him. He knows it, too. Mom, he says he'll be in New York two or three weeks in port.

Momma could take on when she got a notion to, and her tendency toward overstatement was legendary. I seriously doubt that Daddy was "about to die over" Uncle Burns's divorce, but Momma was forever propping up her own opinions by attributing them to Daddy. She then cautions:

Try not to worry. Maybe this blind sickness will wear off after awhile. Linda is fine. We will try to come in pretty soon. I would have given a thousand dollars to have been there yesterday & last night. Write me Mom. This is awful. I've just about cried till I can't. I'll try to write in a day or two.

Mom, don't worry about me. I guess I'll be alright after awhile. Burns would be ashamed of me if he knew I was acting this way.

Uncle Burns was always more likely to take responsibility for his actions than his family was to hold him responsible, though occasionally Grandma Emmy would make a pointed and perceptive remark. Though he wrote Grandma Emmy religiously, she got the expurgated version of Uncle Burns's correspondence. Those of us at Aunt Polly Blevins's table were left to read between the lines a bit, too, for everyone knew about Uncle Burns's drinking. While he often wrote of going "on a toot" and even ending up in jail, we knew it probably happened more often than he admitted.

The last time Uncle Burns came to West Virginia, just before he was shipped out, he got so drunk that when we put him on the train, Daddy gave the train conductor an envelope with my uncle's destination written on the back. There was a dollar inside along with a note repeating Uncle Burns's destination and asking the conductor to see that my uncle made it back to camp. I was just a kid, but I can distinctly recall Momma backing (addressing) the envelope and writing that note. Then Daddy gave her the dollar to put in the envelope, and Daddy Blevins rode along with us to help put my drunken uncle—so out of it, he had no idea where he was—on that train full of soldiers.

I imagine the conductor was tolerant because he saw a lot of that sort of behavior from soldiers on their way to the uncertainties of war. In the case of Uncle Burns, however, the last leave home was just one more excuse for a good drunk. I don't think my uncle was ever particularly remorseful about his behavior. Oh, he was sorry about hurting Grandma Emmy, but not about the drinking. Right up until the Lord saved him late in his life, Uncle Burns just thought of his drinking as a part of him. That was the way he was, and it always appeared to me that he liked the way he was. No excuses—the drinking was just part of the package.

Along with Grandma Emmy's wartime letters was a cache of pictures, many of Uncle Burns, a number of which show him with his arm around a variety of women—often one on each arm. One picture in particular is special to me, for he carried it in his billfold and used to show it to me and speak of how much this girl reminded him of Momma. This photo shows a young woman standing in front of a tall fir, holding the skirt of her long, white dress out on either side of her. From the tilt of her head to the shape of her face, she does indeed favor my young mother. In truth, the girl in that photograph looks more like the Grace in West Virginia than any picture ever taken of Momma in the flesh. On the back, an inscription—in German—is signed and dated 1945, which is when Uncle Burns had last been in Germany. In the mid to late fifties, when Uncle Burns stayed with us off and on, he was still receiving occasional letters from this German woman. He would smile a sly little grin as he carefully skinned off the stamp for my collection.

Law, that Burns.

In an attempt to understand more about the life on Greasy and Two-Mile before I was old enough to remember it clearly, I called upon Billie Edyth Ward's memories, especially concerning Momma's older brothers and sisters. During one of my visits with her, she ventured that some folks do not believe my characterization of the three Mollette boys in *Creeker* was fair to Uncle Fred, and maybe not to Uncle John either. This is not the first time some neighbor has suggested to me that I should not classify Uncle John and Uncle Fred in the same category as Uncle Burns, and they're right, of course.

The degree to which my infamous uncle Burns was allowed to muck up his life and the lives of those who loved him so far outdistanced anything attributed to his older brothers that there is no comparison. I suppose Momma—and I, too—lumped them together because the whole family blamed the wrongdoing of all three on the well-known fact that each was terminally charming but could not resist strong drink. I never heard my mother do anything but defend her three brothers to any outsider who might mutter a disparaging word about any one of them. Privately, however, her opinion of their actions never changed. She and Aunt Amanda agreed that all three of the boys, like their father, were bad to drink. While Momma loved her brothers John and Fred and always treated them with sisterly affection, Uncle Burns had Momma's whole heart. It could be that she spoke of all three boys' drinking problems in the same way as a means of minimizing the extent of Uncle Burns's affliction. Taken separately, however, their stories reveal very different men.

A dead ringer for his once-handsome daddy, Uncle Fred was the best-looking of the Mollette boys, and the truth is I never saw him drunk—not *down* drunk, anyway. He grew up at the home place on Greasy and married a thirteen-year-old neighbor girl named Alma Wells. Maybe if Alma's health had not failed, Uncle Fred might have turned out to be a good husband, father, and provider, but that is not how the story played out. As it was, Alma got tuberculosis shortly after giving birth to a daughter, Barbara, in 1932, when their older child, Leon, was five years old. From that time until her death in 1938, Alma was in and out of the hospital and the TB sanitarium, while her family and Uncle Fred's took on child care for the sick woman and her young husband.

Until fairly recently, I had no idea that Uncle Fred had abandoned his only daughter—or even that he had a daughter. We all knew, however, that after Leon's mother died, Uncle Fred hauled him home to Grandma Emmy, and she brought him up as her own. Apparently, when Uncle Fred gave Leon to Grandma Emmy and Barbara to his wife's side of the family, he simply forgot about them both. That sort of behavior is hard to explain, especially in light of the whole "family first" ethic we were brought up with. What could he have been thinking? We all wonder. Even without having knowledge of Uncle Fred's daughter, there is no justification for his treatment of his mother and his oldest son.

When he brought Leon to live with Grandma Emmy, Uncle Fred effectively tied her to the home place for the rest of her life. Letters indicate that in the first six months of 1945, my grandmother had a sick spell bad enough to be reported in the *Paintsville Herald*. In a letter to Leon dated January 28, 1945, his aunt Virgie Wells writes: "received your card and sure glad to hear from you and to know you are o.k. I saw in the Herald where your Grandmother is sick tell her I hope she gets well soon."

Over the next three months, each of Grandma Emmy's daughters invited her to come live with them. None of the offers, however, included Leon. While every letter asked about Leon, often inviting Grandma Emmy to bring Leon and come stay for a few days, nobody ever mentions the two of them living with any one of the families. It is not hard to justify the daughters' reluctance in light of their own personal situations in 1945.

Aunt Lizzie had a sick husband—Uncle Ray died in April 1947—and her oldest child, Frances, had divorced and moved back home with her son, six-year-old Tommy. Aunt Lizzie's oldest son, Gene Ray, had served nearly three years in the navy—at war and at sea. On March 10, 1943, Aunt Lizzie wrote a postcard to her mother saying: "Just a line to let you know that Gene is safe so far. He has been in Pearl Harbor in the Hawaiian Islands & was gone 20 days & he came back to the States & loaded up again with ammunition and left last Monday for parts unknown said he was fine but awful seasick. The destroyer's airplane and submarine guarded them over."

Nineteen-year-old Fred Thomas, nicknamed "Pick," had also joined the navy, and as her May 10, 1944, postcard suggests, Aunt Lizzie was proud of her boys. Still, even my unflappable aunt clearly had her hands full, what with Uncle Ray down sick, a house guest, two little kids—Lois, age eight, and Tommy, age six—and sixteen-year-old Roy Mitchell pushing to join his brothers in the service. She writes: "Ray's sister from Wayland came Sat. & stayed till today & I could not come over. Tommy cut his foot awful bad & can't walk. Tell Grace we got a letter from Gene yesterday, he wrote it May 16th. He had got her letters. His feet have been bothering him someway & he has been to sea again. I got both their pictures yesterday enlarged. They are awful pretty. Tell Grace to come up again before she goes home & bring me some onions & lettuce."

Momma's sisters were famous for helping each other in whatever way they could, from sharing and carrying everything from books to old clothes, to fresh vegetables, to cow butter. At some point, Aunt Amanda, who was both childless and financially better off than the rest of her sisters, offered to adopt Aunt Lizzie's Lois. Depending on who tells the story, she did it because Lois Ann looked so much like Aunt Amanda or because Aunt Lizzie was having such a hard time keeping body and soul— or at least her family—together. I suspect it was some combination of motives, but whatever it was, Aunt Lizzie was hurt by what she saw as the suggestion that she was not able to take care of her own kids and refused outright to hear of such a thing. Meanwhile, Aunt Amanda was hurt that people would suspect her motives when she was just trying to help out her sister. Momma sided with Aunt Lizzie, because in her opinion Aunt Amanda was "too funny-turned" to raise a child anyway. None of this was even whispered in public, but privately those waters churned for forty years. In any case, Aunt Lizzie was in no position to take care of one more person, much less two. It was simply out of the question that Grandma Emmy and Leon would move to the Muddy Branch coal camp with the only child she had who had a big family of her own.

Her second daughter, Stella, lived down on Rockcastle Creek in Martin County with her husband, Tom Fletcher, and sometimes their daughter, Veva, and her children. Under normal circumstances, Aunt Stella could certainly have taken in her mother and her nephew, but circumstances were far from normal. Momma and Aunt Stella were a little more high-strung than their other siblings, or maybe they were just differently strung. In a November 1944 letter, Momma says she has heard from Aunt Stella, reporting that "She said she hadn't heard from her X-ray but she went to Dr. Hall last Saturday & that her lungs were perfect that she had a nervous condition."

Even in ordinary times Aunt Stella was easily rattled, so when Veva's young husband had to go to war, leaving her with one, then two babies, and Uncle Tom contracted TB and had to go to the sanitarium, my aunt was beside herself—and one Aunt Stella could be quite enough. It could be said that every member of Momma's family had an intensity about them that when not leavened with humor could be a bit much, and Grandma Emmy could lose patience with what she termed Momma's and Aunt Stella's "nerves." Apparently in December 1944, my grandmother had written Momma that her complaints were "just nerves" when Momma responded: "As you say I guess a lot of it is nerves but I can't seem to pull out of it at all."

When Aunt Stella commenced to worrying about money, she was like Momma describing her various illnesses—intense. The irony here is that with the exception of Aunt Amanda, Aunt Stella was probably better off financially than any of her siblings. Still, like Momma and her sick, Aunt Stella's letters are replete with references to what things cost. In a March 16, 1943, card she reassures her mother: "Our car wasn't torn up so bad. That man [who was at fault in the accident] wouldn't have it fixed. Curtis said it would cost 20 or 25 dollars to fix it. But it could have been torn all to pieces & us killed." And in May of '45, after Uncle Tom was home, she worries about the cost of help on the farm, saying, "We had to pay a man $2.75 to work one day and he just worked a little over 7 hours then."

One letter, written in September 1944—with Veva and the babies at her in-laws' house in Lawrence County—after Uncle Tom had to go back to the sanitarium, reveals Aunt Stella living alone, trying to cope with her worries, yet cautioning Grandma Emmy not to worry: "I am getting along alright—am teaching every day. I got Veva to call about Tom today and the line was down and she sent a telegram and they sent her back one, collect, and she then called me and it cost her about $5.50. She could almost have gone as cheap. They wired '*Taking more nourishment, seems stronger, otherwise no change.*'" When my aunt speaks of calling about Uncle Tom, that was not as simple as picking up the telephone in her own home. According to Jane Allen, the first telephone in Inez was at the gas company office, and a bit later there was a phone in the drugstore. If Aunt Stella needed to get word of her husband's condition, she had to go to the gas company and call the sanitarium, which I believe was near Ashland. If she could not talk to the doctor then, he had to call back to the gas company office (reversing the charges) and they would go get her and have her call him again. Since Aunt Stella had no home phone, it was easier to have Veva call from her in-laws' house in Louisa, unless the line was down.

She continues: "Veva didn't go yesterday to see him. She was feeling too bad, but she said she was going Friday or Saturday one. I've talked to her twice today. She is coming up next week to stay a week. We'll try to come over when she's here. I am so afraid his mind is bad again by them saying 'no change.'" When she speaks of fearing that "his mind is

Asbury (brother of Elizabeth Ward Preston) and Laura Bell Ward, Daddy's maternal grandparents.

Paris and Alice Ward Preston, Daddy's parents.

Grandfather Elijah Mollette.   Grandparents Preston.

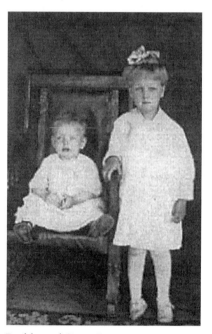

Grandparents Mollette.   Daddy and Sister Irene, ca. 1917–18.

Grandma Alice Alk Ward Preston, Great-Grandma Laura Bell Ward,
Aunt Irene Preston Potts, Linda Sue Preston, Robert Jay Potts,
and Jo Imogene Preston, ca. 1944.

Leon Mollette, son of
Fred Mollette.

Auntie Lizzie and Auntie Amanda.

Betty Ann Mollette
(Uncle John's girl).

One of the many pictures of my infamous uncle Burns in the company of women.

Uncle John in center.

Uncle John, Uncle Burns, & ???

Mollettes, unidentified. I am told that Momma is the blond child on car hood.

Momma and Daddy, 1936, after they were first married.

Daddy and Momma before they met. He's 18; she's 19. Their favorite early pictures of themselves

Daddy on porch of Coal Camp house in West Virginia, 1940-something.

Daddy and Linda Sue, 1944.

Linda Sue with Momma, at two, in 1943. Look how fat she was!

Daddy with Sister and Linda Sue, 1950.

Momma and Daddy, 1966.

Auntie Stella Mollette
Fletcher.

Daddy and Brett Preston, 1967.

Gwen's husband, Wallace Williamson, at the Cabin he built up the hollow
from the Holbrook homeplace—a favorite spot of all at the reunion.

Brothers Preston: Mitchell, Jay, and Glen at Aunt Irene's funeral.

Rosa Daniel Rice (Kat Holbrook Daniel's daughter), Gwen Holbrook Williamson, Linda Sue, and Augustine Franklin Holbrook (Bud's wife) on Holbrook Reunion Decoration Day 2000.

Sister on Decoration Day.

Momma's and Daddy's bench, Decoration Day 1995.

Sisters, Linda Sue and Pat, 1997.

Christmas 1995. Aunt Amanda, Brett Preston, and Arthur.

Generation Next, 1998: Brett, Amanda, and Ryen.

bad again," she is talking about Uncle Tom's losing confidence in his ability to get well and his resulting depression. Between 1942 and 1945, Uncle Tom was in and out of the sanitarium three different times, once for nine months. His postcards are all upbeat, perhaps because he did not write when he was "down in the dumps."

Aunt Stella continues outlining her recent expenses:

Don't you go to bringing me any money, Mama. You don't know when you'll get sick and need it, and it is just like pouring water in a sieve to give it to me. I was counting up tonight and I've spent $145.00 in the 9 weeks since Tom has been gone, and not paid any debts either. It just goes for these trips and telephone calls and other things. One trip, the one Frank Conley sent his car was $20.00.

Another time we had to stay all night and I had to pay the driver's expenses. In that [$145.00] was feed, gas bills, about $12.00 on soy beans, $3.50 for bringing my calf home, a hat, pair of shoes, 4 pairs of stockings, and dozens of other things. You know how it is—it just melts and money doesn't go anywhere these days.

You keep yours. I am not going to pay my debts until I see how Tom gets, for I may have to go stay some at the sanitarium later. I studied about going this week, and then the girls are going tomorrow and I'll hear [about Uncle Tom's condition]. I am not going this weekend unless he gets worse.

Grandma Emmy taught her girls to believe in the power of prayer, not to make their predicament better, but to make them better able to handle whatever circumstance arose. Aunt Stella continues:

I know Mama God is with me. I couldn't go on and carry the load I do if he wasn't. I trust he will let Tom get well. I *sure* was glad that he knew us and talked to us.

Mama, don't worry about me—I am alright. I weigh 120 now and feel pretty good most of the time. I do know that if Tom doesn't gain some that he'll never be here very much longer. The head Dr. is having them give him nourishment every hour.

Despite all her worries, she looks forward to a singing convention and perhaps a visit with her mother: "There's a singing convention at Inez Oct 6th. Plan to come if you can. Come over any time you can. I studied about coming [to Greasy] some night but the bus runs after dark now. Don't worry Mama and maybe things will work out somehow."

It is interesting that none of Grandma Emmy's girls ever made obvious complaints about their living conditions. In fact if anything they all seemed thrilled to have the conveniences available to them—Momma with her coal cook stove, Aunt Stella's car that kept needing one repair or another—and all of the girls frequently sent detailed accounts of plentiful food both in their gardens and on their tables. A sampling from Amanda: "We've been having potatoes dug and the renter started gathering corn this week." Stella: "Veva got beef at town and we fixed the best dinner." And "I canned 7 quarts of tomatoes last Sunday and we made 6 gallons of kraut yesterday evening." Lizzie: "Tell Grace to come up again before she goes home & bring me some onions & lettuce. Ha! Ha!" And Momma, describing their dinner after Daddy had worked Thanksgiving Day 1944: "[Jay] ate too much Thanksgiving. He worked yesterday so we had our meal last night. We had cooked & baked chicken, dumplings, dressing, shuck beans, mashed potatoes, candied sweet potatoes, pumpkin pie, chocolate pie, fruit cake, hot biscuits, cornbread & coffee & milk."

While all four of Grandma Emmy's girls, whatever their circumstances, would have been happy to make room in their houses—and their lives— for their mother, none of them felt able to take in teen-aged Leon. I believe they genuinely cared for the boy. He is mentioned, asked about, written to in every single letter. Many times he is invited to "come over" for anywhere from overnight to a week, but not forever.

Leon was not without problems, the exact nature of which I cannot determine, for he was out of my life before I gained any understanding of such things, and I haven't been able to find anyone who knew him any better than I did. I know he was slow in school and had to take the eighth-grade exam three years in a row before he passed it and could move on to high school. Questions about Leon and that exam abound in the letters, the last one written by Uncle Tom on January 7, 1943: "Is Leon going to pass that 8th grade test this year?" I assume Leon must have passed in 1943, for there were no further inquiries of this sort.

Leon also had some vision problems that were not discovered until he had some sort of eye test at school and got glasses. In a November 16, 1944, letter Momma inquires: "Are Leon's eyes any better since he got his glasses?" Then in 1945, Leon was called for the army. In a June 25th letter Momma writes: "Leon should have his papers by this time. I'm surely anxious to hear if he passed or not."

Leon failed his physical and did not have to go into the service, so Grandma Emmy kept him in school until he completed high school, though it took him five, maybe six years. Scattered in among Grandma Emmy's letters are random, yellowed pages of Leon's homework. Two of those pages, written in his shaky scrawl, contained one of Leon's algebra assignments. I think of that homework each time one of my college students tells me he or she is math phobic. In all likelihood, Leon fretted over those lessons sitting at the kitchen table, working by the light of a coal oil lamp before retiring upstairs to the unheated attic. Despite my grandmother's attempts to make life better for him, it is hard to imagine a childhood more unrelenting than Leon's. Though they certainly loved each other, Leon was trapped with Grandma Emmy, and she was trapped with him. The person responsible for that was Leon's father, Uncle Fred.

In my grandmother's letters, the first mention of Uncle Fred occurs in a letter from Aunt Stella written March 15, 1945: "Had a letter from Lizzie Tuesday. Said Fred was fired from Van Lear, and he had gone to Wheelwright. She said he stayed drunk a week and they fired him." Then, in a postcard dated May 1, 1945, Aunt Stella writes: "Got a long letter from Fred. The first one in life." As for letters from Uncle Fred, Grandma Emmy's collection includes only one letter written by him, and it was to let Leon know his new address:

5/8/45
> Hello Leon,
> How are you by now? I guess you thought I wasn't going to answer but I have been so busy. We have been moving again. Leon how are you getting along now and how is Mom getting along?

Since Aunt Lizzie informed Aunt Stella of their brother's move in mid-March, the date of this letter indicates that Uncle Fred waited at least two months to let Leon know his change of address and to check up on the health of his son and his mother. He goes on, "Leon you ought to see Donnie now he has growed so much and is as mean as he can be boy he is a bear dog."

At the time Uncle Fred is bragging on his younger son, he is married to, living with, and supporting the two older sons of his new wife, Laurie, while his oldest child, Leon, hardly even hears from him. "Boy, I didn't know what to think to hear from Stella I was glad to hear from her." Knowing my aunt Stella and her tendency to take family members to task for their transgressions, I would like to see that letter. I'd venture a guess that the tone of my aunt's letter was what prompted Uncle Fred to write his son the only letter that survives the two of them. He asks:

> When have you heard from Burns. I got a letter about a month ago and I haven't heard since. So the war is about over in Germany so he might git to come back to this side. I hope so.
>
> Leon I am coming down in a week or two and I will come over and see you and Mom. If your school is out I want you to come up and stay about a week with us when your school is out.
>
> Well buddy I guess I will close as I don't know much to write so ans soon and come up when you can.
>
> ans soon
>
> Fred
>
> Laura said to come up some time
>
> My box number is 395

The lackadaisical attitude toward his son, in addition to Aunt Lizzie's report of his losing his job in the Van Lear mines after a weeklong drunk, paints a better picture of Momma's brother Fred than anything in my memories of him. But then, self-control and personal responsibility never were strengths of any of my maternal uncles, Burns, Fred, or John.

Uncle John, the oldest, was perhaps the most successful of the three Mollette boys, having served in the Kentucky State Legislature for a term or two. Like his younger brothers, until he got religion Uncle John drank his way through a number of opportunities for success. According to Momma and Aunt Amanda, Uncle John's worst mistake was losing his first wife, Maggie, who was a smart, attractive, and down-to-earth lady, who put up with far more than she ever should have with my charming uncle. The fact that everybody in Momma's family cast all the blame for their divorce on Uncle John is proof conclusive that Maggie was not in any way at fault. Grandma Emmy and her daughters maintained a life-long attachment to Maggie, and Momma always said she believed Maggie loved Uncle John until the day she died.

While Uncle John was not an admirable husband, he was a good father to his only child, Betty Ann. Once he was saved and went into the church, Uncle John became an even better grandfather to Betty's children. Before he got religion, however, I recall his carrying Betty's first child, Johnny Doug, to our house on Two-Mile and showing off the baby's vocabulary. He walked down Two-Mile from Maggie's house carrying his grandbaby and sat in one of the steel chairs in our front yard, where we were all resting one summer's evening. I don't recall the exact age of the baby, but he was just beginning to talk.

Uncle John would say: "What is that, son?"

The baby would say, "Doggie."

"And what is that, son?"

"Kitty-cat."

"Whose boy are you?"

"John B.'s boy!"

"And what does John B. say?"

"John B. say, 'Hell's bells!'

"Hell's bells" was just the beginning of a long list of slightly indelicate phrases that "John B say," according to his grandson. I never saw him drunk in front of his grandchildren, but drunk or sober, Uncle John was a cut-up and we were an appreciative audience.

Uncle John had a great love of the sort of fox hunting done eastern Kentucky style. The men took their dogs out to the woods and sat around a fire telling stories all night while the dogs presumably chased foxes. This is as much as I know about fox hunting, because it was one of those male bonding rituals closed to women. According to Billie Edyth Ward, who taught his grandson in eighth grade, John B went fox hunting over on Rock House, and before dark he collected samples of leaves, rocks, and fossils. He brought the bounty he'd collected back to Johnny Doug, then helped his eighth-grade grandson sort and label leaves for his natural science project.

This story is so very typical of Uncles John and Burns. Both were avid readers, interested in a little bit of everything, and everlastingly kind to children. I must have asked Uncle Burns a thousand dumb questions, and I don't recall his ever getting short-tempered with me. My uncles were exceedingly patient with me, and both were excellent resources. They were just bad to drink.

Enthusiasm and hope leavened my family like soda in sorghum for a winter's breakfast, expanding and lightening the heavy molasses while cutting the sweetness by half. Our laughter saved us from a syrupy sentimentality—laughter with an edge to it. The improbable we tried with heart. The impossible we just laughed about. Our thinking was that if you can poke fun at the devil, it gives you some control over him and over the inevitable outcome of his acts. Had old Lucifer in our sights, we did.

Momma and Daddy moved back to Two-Mile essentially unchanged. They laughed a lot, loved their family, worked hard, and liked to have a good time. The West Virginia years in the Hemphill coal camp had changed one thing about my parents, though—their names. In the early forties, Daddy and Momma had gone off to West Virginia as "Lifie Jay" and "Grace." In the late forties they returned to Kentucky as "E.J." and "Grayce."

When Sister was born in 1947, that ended West Virginia and the traveling life for me and Momma, since two kids were one too many for us to just up and go follow Daddy from job to job. While Momma would have preferred to stay in Hemphill, Daddy never got broke from home enough to see himself living that far away from Grandma Alk and Pop Pop. Fortunately, we had the option of moving back because—thank the Lord!—Daddy was part of the patch-off tradition. We had land. When Daddy married Momma, Pop Pop had deeded him a little piece of ground right across the road and the creek from where Pop Pop lived with Grandma Alk and Daddy's youngest sister, Jo. To an outsider it may have appeared that there wasn't much to the Lifie Jay piece. To Momma, Daddy, and me, however, it was "home" in every sense of the word, and it tied our little family to Two-Mile and to a rural Appalachian lifestyle that was all but destroyed by the industrialization of the American landscape.

The point could be made that the patch of hillside land across Two-Mile Creek was not a substantial gift, since the property wasn't good for much of anything, not even a very good house seat. It was, however, the only piece of ground Pop Pop ever gave any of his children, since he knew early on that he would need to leave anything he accumulated to provide lifetime care for Jo, his severely retarded youngest child.

The Lifie Jay piece was a rolling patch of land about two hundred feet deep and three hundred feet wide that lay between the hill and the graveled main road that ran between Paintsville and Inez. Daddy and Pop Pop built our house on a fifteen- to twenty-foot shelf of flat land that lay between the ten-foot flood plain south of Two-Mile Creek and the precipitous rise of the hill behind it. There was hardly a foot of level ground to be found on that side of the road, but Daddy set the house on stilts in front and level with the yard in back, which settled our home high enough so we were out of any but the worst flash flood danger from Two-Mile Creek. The land on the right side of the house undulated just slightly over about fifteen feet to the branch, which only flowed full in the springtime. The hill back of the house, where rock was barely covered by soil, was less than three feet from the southwest corner of our house. The backyard widened to maybe forty feet behind the house before giving way to the branch that ran from a natural spring up the hollow. Our outhouse sat on the hillside across the branch about twenty feet downhill from the pigpen on the slope.

I recently spent a year in eastern Kentucky, which provided me opportunity to plumb the memories of a number of folks who grew up where I did, when I did. While we do not agree on everything, there is consensus when it comes to what we see as modern conveniences and unanimity as to the very last of those conveniences we would give up. While we enjoy central heat and air conditioning and can hardly imagine life without electricity, indoor plumbing tops our list of luxuries necessary for a civilized world.

When my family moved from West Virginia back to Kentucky, we didn't have a bathroom either place, but there had been a sink with running water in the coal camp house and Momma had become accustomed to that bit of home improvement. Daddy promised Momma if she'd move back to Two-Mile, he'd not only put water in our house, but he'd also put us in a bathroom. It took him five years to deliver on that promise, and though Momma was pretty stoic about it, she loathed that damned toilet with a pure searing hatred. My mother seemed to have no problem using Grandma Emmy's toilet (or anybody else's when we went visiting); she just felt when she was home she shouldn't have to walk across the branch to the outhouse. While she kept our toilet scrubbed as clean as possible, her repugnance at doing any personal business there was duly noted by Daddy, who knew in his heart that if any woman ever deserved a bathroom, Momma did. As had been her custom in West Virginia, Momma did not use our toilet. Day or night, she did all her business in the slop jar (also known as a "combinette" at the local hardware store).

Once we moved to Two-Mile, though, I began using the toilet for number two. I suppose Momma thought I might as well get used to it, since I'd have to use a public toilet when I went to school. I always assumed slop jars were to keep women from having to go to the toilet, but when I entered school at Meade Memorial in 1947, I had to get accustomed to using the outdoor toilet for both numbers one and two. As a first-grader, I was pretty wide-eyed at the entire execution of this act. As I recall, the structure was about a six-holer, and some of the girls squatted with their feet on the seat, some sat right down on the boards, and some kept their feet on the floor and hovered just above the bench. There really is no comfortable—or aesthetically pleasing—method of using outdoor facilities. Thank goodness we moved into the new school building when I was in fifth grade, and they tore down those stinking outhouses. To my way of thinking, indoor plumbing is just a hair above central heating on the list of the Lord's blessings.

Though our house on Two-Mile Creek had a coal bank in the left-hand edge of the yard, we never owned the mineral rights to anything mined out of there, and Daddy never worked there either. But even if we owned not a piece of it, I thought of it as "our" coal bank simply because of its proximity to our house. It fronted on the main road (Kentucky Route 40) and sat about thirty feet above Two-Mile Creek in the western edge of our front yard. A small tipple stood in front of it, through which coal could be dumped into a pickup truck backed up on the bridge crossing the creek less than one hundred yards from our front door. The mine cavity itself entered the earth approximately eighty yards left of our front porch, cut through the hill, and exited just above Pop Pop's strawberry patch, about one hundred yards up the hollow behind our house. Rail lines ran from front to back of the mine, I think, but I couldn't swear to it, since I was forbidden to go inside either end of the shaft. On occasion, Gwen, Sister, and I would sneak maybe thirty feet into one end or another of that hole through our hill, so I know there were tracks laid back that far and assume they went all the way through. I don't believe they ever had more than one small coal cart on those tracks, and a sway-backed old mule pulled the cart.

Our yard to the left of the house—the side with the coal bank—declined so precipitously that Gwen and I loved to ride my tricycle down it, until we were way too big to be riding a tricycle. It was on that very hill that nine-year-old Gwen Holbrook broke what was by that time Sister's tricycle while the four Prestons were all inside the house at supper. That steep little hill was also where everybody on three front porches watched Daddy set my skinny hind end on the seat of my new— well, just purchased from Junior Pack, but new to me—twenty-eight-inch, maroon-with-a-white-swoosh boys' bike. All and sundry then saw me ride that big sucker down the bank, plow straight through Momma's stand of blooming sweet peas edging the yard, cut a path through five or so feet of wild honeysuckle thicket, and come to rest with the minnows and crawdads right smack-dab in the middle of Two-Mile Creek.

Gwen says she loved to be at our house at suppertime, because when Momma made Sister and me come to supper she was left with all the playthings to herself. One of her favorite stories is about swinging high out over Two-Mile Creek in the rope swing Daddy had hung from one of our big sycamore trees. When it broke, sending her flying into the creek, her cries brought everybody from our supper table and her house across the road. Gwen and I have long assured folks that while we might not be famous anywhere else, both of us made a big splash on—or in— Two-Mile Creek.

I cannot ever recall thinking that the up-and-down sloping nature of the property or the proximity of the coal tipple took away from the desirability of our place. Even now, I think of my home place as beautiful. I don't know precisely who owned the coal bank, but somehow I think I.D. Preston (no kin to us) or Chip Whitten maybe had something to do with it. It was said that some folks with coal banks on their property would go out and pick up coal to burn in their fireplaces and coal cook stoves, but I don't recall our ever doing that. Seems to me that Daddy had our coal delivered, periodically adding to the coal pile that sat to the right front of our house just before the branch off the path to the toilet.

That coal bank worked out and the tipple fell down a number of years ago, but my family took no notice of it. I don't even know who hauled away the debris or when exactly the tipple fell down. The matter did not concern us. The land was ours; the coal bank belonged to some-body else. That it existed was just a fact of our lives, mattering to no one—at least to nobody who counted.

By today's standards, the house itself was small, originally four rooms, but it was pretty much standard issue for Two-Mile, and I don't recall ever feeling jealous of Gwen or Easter, whose houses were bigger. No-body gave much thought to the standard-of-living questions that seem to consume so many of today's young people. I mean, I knew we weren't rich, and I even had some idea of what rich was because John C.C. Mayo's house—later turned into a school—stood in Paintsville. In my head, *that* was rich—the Mayo Mansion.

A cut or two below the Mayo family—who were long gone from

Johnson County by then—were Momma's sister Amanda and my uncle Kash, and Daddy's brother Mitchell and my aunt Ogie. For me, and I suspect for most of my friends, rich and poor had to do with the size and value of a family's house and car. Uncle Mitchell was a builder, lived in a brick house in Pikeville, and drove a Cadillac; Uncle Kash was a traveling salesman, lived in a big house in Paintsville, and bought a new Chrysler every year. My rich relatives, then, informed my definition of the word "rich," but "poor" was harder to define.

In my young head, my family belonged in neither category, nor would I have slotted anybody else on Two-Mile as rich or poor. The Packs— Aunt Wid's boys and Daddy's first cousins, who lived in large brick houses down near the mouth of Two-Mile Creek—were well-off, but I didn't think of them as rich, probably because they drove neither Chrysler nor Cadillac. Though my house was smaller than Gwen's and Easter's, they came from bigger families and needed more space, so I always thought us equally well-off. The same could be said for poor. Early on, I got it in my head that poor folks lived in shacks, and even today I cannot think of a house on Two-Mile that I would have termed a shack. Grandma Emmy, who never had any cash income, was certainly not poor; she supported herself with the land she lived on, and she always had grass in her yard. Poor, as I saw it, meant having to sweep the yard instead of mow the grass, and everybody I knew on Two-Mile and Greasy Creek had plenty of grass to mow.

Our house had about 850 square feet, though it didn't live that small, and Daddy and Momma kept it in much better condition than I've ever been able to keep my own place. Daddy was forever improving something or another, and he could hardly get something fixed up before Momma set to cleaning it. Billie Edyth Ward recalls Aunt Stella's report of a conversation where Daddy joked that he thought he'd take the living room wallboard down, turn it over, and put it back up again.

Aunt Stella: "Why would you even think of that?"

Daddy: "I've painted this side so many times I just know the stuff has soaked through and there's a good coat on the back side."

Bless her heart. Aunt Stella was about as serious as Daddy was funny, and he so enjoyed kidding her.

Since I can recall a time when nobody on Two-Mile had indoor plumbing or central heating, it is clear that everybody my age enjoys a better standard of living than Sister's and my parents. In the context of today, our house and land may not sound like much of a home place. In light of what we have come to expect, it is hard to describe the Two-Mile house and land as favorably as it exists in my memory, but then—and now—I'd call it a close to perfect place for a kid to grow up. Pop Pop's generosity in providing us with our own piece of ground meant we never moved into a coal camp. And that made all the difference.

Though we probably had enough tillable soil on Two-Mile to grow a small truck garden, our house sat on the only piece of our land that wasn't straight up and down. Wherever we lived—West Virginia or Two-Mile—we always kept a garden on Grandma Emmy's land at Three Forks of Greasy. After Daddy got on at Princess Elkhorn Mine at David, Kentucky, we never had to leave Two-Mile again, and our family was able to continue to work two pieces of the Mollette land. Despite a work-day—and commute—that ran from 4:00 A.M. to 5:00 P.M., in the summer Daddy always put in another couple of hours working the ground up at Three Forks. On summer mornings, Momma hoed corn, weeded tomatoes, or picked beans around on Greasy, then spent most afternoons back on Two-Mile canning or preserving whatever fruit or vegetables that were in at that time. During my growing-up years, we all helped Grandma Emmy in her garden, and she in turn helped us with ours. From February 14, when we put in our lettuce and onions, through November's hog-killing season, I never saw either of my parents do much of anything other than work. Even in the evenings when we would sit out in the yard or on the porch, just visiting, Momma always had a lap full of beans to string or peas to shell and Daddy'd be fixing some small piece of equipment that needed work.

Country people did not take up hobbies to relax, and I don't believe that changed much over the 150 years between Elias Mollette's time and my own. Physical labor was seen as work, and the only relaxation was freedom from same, which means folks of my generation have bought into modern conveniences in a big way. While I persist in believing that camping, hiking, and jogging are a waste of valuable energy, Sister is six years younger than I am and therefore somewhat more highly evolved in terms of openness to new ways of being. Early on, Sister embraced the practice of camping, and for the past twenty years she has walked three to five miles a day, pursuing fitness and enjoying nature.

In the early nineties, when Momma and Daddy were down sick, Sister and I spent a good deal of time running back and forth to eastern Kentucky trying to see to their welfare. During the five years immediately preceding their deaths, Daddy wasn't "at himself"—a circumstance my mother constantly denied. Every day as Sister headed out for her walk, Momma never failed to comment on how much her hike through the River Narrows, or down Bob's Branch, or to the "upper end of town" would hurt Daddy. "Daddy'd be ashamed" was the recurring message. Momma's reaction to Sister's hikes was that "People will talk, Linda. You know they will. They'll think she's quare." While I always took up for Sister, explaining to Momma the whys and wherefores of such unnecessary activity, I must admit that I too think it's more than a little "quare" to engage in all that unnecessary movement. As Sister has pointed out, the only way I could ever be caught running is if something big and bad happened to be chasing me.

I don't think I learned to wipe my own nose until I started school. If I had a cold, Momma had a hankie under my nose before I noticed it was running. Just like her insistence that I wear shoes, Momma was desperate to differentiate between our family and what she viewed as those folks who didn't know any better or didn't care that their dirty children ran wild and talked worse. One of the reasons she agreed to move back to Two-Mile was that she thought home folks took better care of their children, and she wanted me to go to school with kids who knew how to act.

In 1947, when I entered first grade at Meade Memorial School, it was standard practice for our teachers to educate us in personal grooming, hygiene, and manners. My third-grade teacher, Mrs. Ellen Wells Pack Dutton, was one of those most committed to this little contribution to civilization, and—being a Wells—she was quite sure of the ground she stood on. Let me say that if I don't always behave as a proper lady, it is not because Mrs. Dutton did not teach me how to act. God knows she tried. Her rules were as strict as Momma's, and each of those women was sure of the righteousness of her own interpretation of every rule.

Billie Edyth Ward was teaching with Aunt Stella at the two-room elementary school at Three Forks when, as a seven-year-old, I was double-promoted into Mrs. Dutton's third-grade classroom. Aunt Stella shared a story with her colleague concerning an apparent misunderstanding in regard to the practice of carrying a handkerchief. According to Billie Edyth, Momma kept Kleenex tissues, a practice unusual for that time and place, so I was sent to school with a small packet of these tissues. Mrs. Dutton, however, held to a more conservative version of the hankie rule and declared that "it must be a washed, ironed square" of cotton or linen. Billie Edyth writes "which Linda promptly lost before the day was over." She further suggests that "at five hankies per week, G.C. Murphy's dime store [in Paintsville] had a good customer."

Sister recalls Mrs. Dutton most fondly and had no trouble complying with the rules when she reached third grade six years behind me. I have always attributed this to Sister's superior malleability, but now I wonder. By the time Sister came along, many of the customs were changing, and in terms of social awareness she and her cohorts were light-years ahead of me and mine. It may be that Momma never sent Sister to school with Kleenex, or perhaps Mrs. Dutton had relaxed her position on the hankie/tissue question. Or, it just may be that over the six years elapsing between my experience and Sister's there had been some cultural slippage on the part of the whole country in matters of hygiene and deportment. While I do not recall that particular hankie incident, Billie Edyth's story suggests that Linda Sue Preston did not break new ground on the handkerchief question.

In matters of dress, taste, and deportment, Momma routinely went along with whatever the school required. Daddy followed Momma in such matters, and, over time, I learned not to resist any of their rulings. I know my daddy was proud that Momma never let herself go, did not use bad language, and even ironed our sheets, but she was never quite able to civilize him. As he got old and sick, Daddy lost energy, but his character, taste, personality, and language never changed one whit.

Although Momma and Daddy made new friends and were cordial to their neighbors when they lived in West Virginia, their closest relationships there were with folks whose extended families were residents of Two-Mile. Thus, when they moved back to Two-Mile, my parents rejoined their original community and took up the lives they had left five years before.   .

Even though Daddy is an offshoot of the Wards and the Prestons, and Momma descended from Clines and Mollettes, their story is not bound by blood but by community. It includes stories of Packs and Wallens—who have a lot of Preston in them—and Holbrooks and Daniels—who have a lot of Ward. Moreover, there are several sets of Prestons and several sets of Wards, all of whom have some common ancestor. The reason we are family, however, goes even deeper than blood and speaks to the sense of community we shared on Two-Mile. And if you back up one generation, Bob's Branch and Greasy Creek must be included in that family/community spectrum. We are of a kind, we rural, hill-country Appalachians. We are common folk, misunderstood by scholars, thus not often seen in books. We are family.

Our Two-Mile kin's most unforgettable character, by far, was my great-uncle Keenis Holbrook, who moved his family into Pop Pop's place across the road from us in the spring of '48. We called him "Uncle K." and he could be counted upon to provide information along with entertainment almost any time. He was tall and lean with a shock of salt-and-pepper hair, which he took to his grave, and he could beat all hell with his version of just about any everyday happening. Like other adults on the creek, Uncle K. taught us life's lessons through story and example, but his stories were a cut above everybody else's in that they were harder to forget. We repeated the stories to each other partly because of the exaggeration and partly because of Uncle K.'s colorful language.

Uncle K. was a man of strong opinions, which he would share at the drop of a hat. His expression was hampered somewhat, however, by his religion. He was a deacon in Old Friendship United Baptist Church, which precluded his taking the Lord's name in vain or falling to swearing in any form. It probably did not help that his closest male neighbors, Daddy and Frank Ward, were two of the most creatively profane men I've ever known. Uncle K. got around all of this by adopting as his own the word "Hellll-o," accent on the *h-e-l-l*. To this day, the mere use of that word accented in that manner can bring vivid Uncle K. memories to every one of us who knew him. Each time I see the list of overdue taxes in the newspaper, I am reminded of Uncle K.'s view of such deadbeats. He would turn to that page of the local weekly newspaper, slowly shake his head and say, "Hellll-o, pure outlaws!"

Uncle K. is best remembered sitting with his legs stretched across the seat, leaning back against the sidebar of one of the swings on his front porch. This was the best perch on Two-Mile, since it provided a ringside seat to all that was going on. The Holbrook porch was about thirty feet above the road and allowed its occupants to see what—and who—was coming from about a quarter mile in both directions. From March to October—indeed on any mild evening year-round—Uncle K. could be found reared back in his swing dispensing news and narrative alike to those who chose to visit on the porch as well as to any passersby on the road. He was by no means the only raconteur on Two-Mile, but his way with a story attracted folks to the Holbrook porch to get Uncle K.'s take on the latest tidbit we'd heard. When he worked as a vacuum cleaner salesman, he brought back tales from Meat House to Marrowbone, Beauty to Bee Branch. Door-to-door sales was a perfect fit for Uncle K., and every one of us benefited from what he gleaned during his workday.

During the fifties, in our region, we looked forward to seeing the traveling salesmen who came by now and then. Such men were treated with admiration and respect, for they provided some respite from the day-to-day. If we were doing sit-down work, we'd get the fellow a glass of iced tea or a cup of coffee and continue our work while he tried to sell us insurance or demonstrated his wares. If we were doing something that needed close attention—canning tomatoes, let's say—the salesman was invited into the kitchen to sell us as we worked. Much of the time, however, we took time-out from whatever we'd been doing to sit and pass the time with the fellow. I don't recall any of these salesmen as rank strangers, for the first visit by any seller required that he begin by tracing for us his connection with someone who had some familial association with Two-Mile. Once we had established his *bona fides,* we treated him with the same degree of cordiality we would any resident of the community. Sometimes we bought, sometimes not, but the visitor was always asked back.

The salespeople I recall best were the Jewel Tea man and Bill somebody from the Bankers Life and Casualty insurance company. In the fifties, it was not uncommon for the salesman not only to sell his product but also to return monthly to collect the premium or payment. This meant Uncle K. was our monthly messenger to and from all points in Johnson County, sometimes beyond. Though I cannot say for sure that he was a good salesman, I cannot imagine that he was not, for he certainly had the gift of gab. The rest of us didn't get out that much, so Uncle K. gathered tales and brought them home to Two-Mile for our information and entertainment.

Though Uncle K. was a United Baptist deacon and took his responsibility seriously, I never once heard him preach or attempt to proselytize Daddy, Pop Pop, or Frank Ward—good men, all three, but unsaved, as best I recall. Oh, he'd invite them to church at regular meeting time if the opportunity arose, but he didn't go out of his way to come by and give them the Word. If, however, Daddy happened to be in our front yard as Uncle K. was on his way to church, he'd holler cross the road, "Better go with me, Lifie Jay." "Aye, not today, I reckon," Daddy would reply. Uncle K. would get into his car, and that would be that. Now, generally folks who were as religious as Uncle K. often felt called upon to teach by bearing witness more than by example, and they could get a little hard to take. Though Uncle K. was one fine storyteller, in this case he knew when to seek another venue.

Back before improvements to Route 40, once folks drove more than a few miles east of Paintsville's Stafford addition, there were very few places that had room to pull all four wheels of a car off the road. The mountains are bunched up close there, so if a driver needed to stop, he generally had to turn into somebody's yard.

On his way to the barn one morning, around 5:00 A.M., Uncle K. noticed that a semi truck had pulled off the road at the foot of the hill in front his house. After doing his milking, Uncle K. went down to the truck and banged on the window until he woke up the driver. Apparently the long-distance trucker had gotten sleepy in the middle of the night. At the first wide place in the road, he pulled himself and his load over for a nap before continuing his journey. His sleep was ended by one Keenis Holbrook, who—over the trucker's protests—hauled him up to the house for breakfast. Aunt Exer was not at all discommoded by this stranger in her kitchen at five in the morning. She just poured the man a cup of coffee, fried up another couple of eggs, put on a few more sausage patties, and made a tad more sawmill gravy. After he'd told his story and had his fill of breakfast, the trucker went on his way.

For a number of years after that incident, whenever that trucker drove through Two-Mile, he stopped by to see the Holbrooks, always bringing a little jar of jelly or some Stuckey's candy. Depending on the time of day, he'd have a bite to eat with Aunt Exer and Uncle K. According to Uncle K.'s daughter Gwen, the trucker stopped by in 1971 and was told that Uncle K. had died. He never visited again.

Uncle K. may not have been the worst driver on Two-Mile, but most of those who survive him cannot recall anyone who could even compete with him for that honor. Stories abound of Uncle K.'s misadventures with the two or three old cars he drove over his lifetime on Two-Mile, and I will try not to attribute these to any specific rememberer for fear somebody may recall it differently. When Clifford Preston—no mean storyteller himself—married Uncle K.'s daughter Bonnie, he became one of the best repositories of Keenis Holbrook stories. One of Clifford's best concerned the evening he and several family members were roosting up on the Holbrook porch as Uncle K. swung his car off the road and headed up the bank to park near his back door. Clifford's car was parked at the foot of the hill, and as Uncle K. passed it his rear bumper caught on Clifford's front bumper, ripping it off the car and dragging it several feet up the bank. Uncle K. continued to the top of the hill, stalked into the kitchen, got himself a glass of tea, walked through the house and joined the group on his front porch. Once he was settled in his swing, where he had a clear view of Clifford's car, Uncle K. drew back in astonishment, saying, "Hellll-o Clip, somebody's tore your car all to pieces."

For much of my childhood, the Holbrooks did not have a car, but in the early fifties, when Uncle K. went out on the road to sell Electrolux sweepers, he bought some kind of little humped-up Chrysler—late-thirties vintage. The car ran just fine, but getting it started was a bit problematic. Since Uncle K. liked to get on the road early, during my sixth-grade year I needed no alarm clock, arising as I did before daylight to the Chrysler's keening. *Whiiiiine-whiine-whiine-whine-whine . . . whiiiiine-whiine-whine-*

whine-whine . . . whiiiiine-whiine-whine-whine-whine . . . then, Uncle K.: "Hellll-o, I wish th' black bitch was in Chinie!"

Most of my memories of Uncle K. dispensing his wit and wisdom from the Holbrooks' front porch swing take place of an evening as we gathered about him for his recounting of the day's adventures. Meanwhile, our own days had not passed without incident. We'd lived and developed our own stories, many of which resulted from encounters close to home. After all, we were lucky to have the Williamsport post office—the gathering place for anybody who could take a morning break to go pick up the mail. Along with our mail, we kids would pick up the latest intelligence, passed along with good sense and sagacity by Leonie and Mitchell Wallen and the patrons of their store. Those who sat around on empty carbide cans and turned-up pop cases or leaned against the door frame were, for the most part, old men who had done their morning chores and headed for the post office so as to be out of the way while their wives got dinner.

The stories they told—of folks who may or may not have engaged in the behaviors described—served as powerful examples of unwritten rules that were to be ignored at the peril of anyone who violated them. Along with Gwen, Sister, and various other kids from the creek, I was provided with examples aplenty of sin and sainthood. We came to admire those old men, and I believe they cared about us, too. In today's climate of suspicion and folks looking for sexual motivation in just about any relationship, it is difficult to explain the bonding of different generations that routinely took place in that day and that time.

For many years, Jeff "Squire" Davis had been postmaster at Two-Mile, but he retired and turned that job over to Leonie Wallen shortly before—or maybe just after—we moved back from West Virginia. I knew him pretty well just from seeing him when we all gathered at Leonie's store to pick up mail on summer mornings. Most of the time, however, I was busy hanging out with Gwen and didn't get that close to the old men, including Jeff Davis or the Preston brothers, I.D. and N.M. Sister didn't have anyone in the immediate neighborhood as close to her in age as Gwen was to me, so once Gwen and I were in school, Sister sort of hung around with Aunt Exer, Pop Pop, and Jeff Davis. As she writes:

From the time I was old enough to be trusted to walk the distance from our house to Leonie Wallen's store, I knew Jeff Davis loved me. Not that he said so—or even sought me out, for that matter. He was just always there over the years, he and N.M., and I.D. Preston, old men, sitting around at Leonie's, waiting for the mail every morning. And when I'd go in they'd talk and laugh and kid around with me about whatever was going on.

Then, when I was seventeen, preparing to leave Two-Mile for college, Jeff must have seen how sad I was that Momma—never a lover of cats—intended to turn two of my favorites out to God-only-knows-what. So, the day before I left for Eastern Kentucky University, here came Jeff. He hadn't told me he was coming and still said nothing special. He simply bundled both those cats—one underneath each arm—walked them down the road to his house, and gave them a home. And that was the end of that.

And a year later, when word was passed that Patsy Jaye Preston had come home from college engaged and would be marrying at the end of summer, again Jeff Davis came to the house. He walked up our driveway with the first gift to celebrate the occasion. He brought a box full of necessities from Leonie's store—two dish towels, two serving bowls, and a set of salt shakers.

The Jeff Davis tale is Sister's story, not mine, but I always felt protected by that extra layer between me and the world. Living on Two-Mile in the late forties and early fifties meant our parents did not have to be completely responsible for us, because every adult in the area watched out for every child. It was not at all unusual for one of those old men to take one or more of us children into the woods to gather (depending on the time of year) persimmons, papaws, hickory nuts, or black walnuts. Gwen, Sister, and I agree that as we were growing up we received about as much nurturing from men as from women—maybe more. The women were busy. And that's as close as I can come to characterizing the attitude of older males toward children during my years growing up on Two-Mile.

As for the connection between and among different generations that was common in that time and place, all I know is that it happened. It was not in any way sexual. And I never experienced anything approaching inappropriate touching or the kind of leering commentary that should be cause for alarm. As a child, I was alone with my uncle Burns—a ladies' man if there ever was one—when he was so dog drunk he didn't know who or where he was, but he never said or did anything sexually inappropriate. Gwen, Sister, and I also spent considerable time in the woods with my little dried-up Pop Pop, and I don't recall his ever touching any one of us, unless it was to steady us or help us gain our footing. I will not further belabor this point, but I just want to make clear that if you're looking for some sexual abuse story, you won't be hearing it from me. That was not my experience. We are not that kind of people.

Sister, Gwen, and I are in agreement that we would not trade our childhood years for anybody's. Though we did not have the material wealth and conveniences today's children take for granted, we had everything we needed—and more. Our growing-up years were full of love and laughter, and we never doubted that there was more where that came from. While the work was almost endless for our parents, we kids always had time to play, and Pop Pop took time to play along with us. I came along at just the right time, when Pop Pop's working days were almost over and his only responsibility was to care for his retarded daughter, Jo. He had a small blacksmith shop out between our house and his, and Sister, Gwen, and I spent countless hours watching him beat auger blades into submission. Sometimes he let us use his big bellows to fan the flames as he heated those augers.

On a summer's morning, we kids would get up, eat breakfast, go do whatever garden work our mothers deemed necessary, go to the post office, eat some lunch—my favorite was saltine crackers crumbled into a bowl of home-canned tomatoes, cooled in the fridge. Some folks preferred cornbread crumbled into milk for lunch or a snack, but I never cared for that combination. Give me the tomato-saltine combo every time. No gazpacho I've ever eaten compares with those canned tomatoes, salted and peppered up with a handful of crackers crunched into them. Don't think that taste can be replicated using store-bought stewed tomatoes either. I don't know whether it's the spices, the preservatives, or the process that causes it, but the taste of the store-bought is off. The first time I tasted tomato juice from the store, I deemed it far better than the home-canned stuff, but I long ago changed my mind about that.

Once lunch was over and our mothers got into their afternoon chores, we'd slip away and play house for a bit or catch crawdads in the creek for a while. Then we'd saunter down to Pop Pop's in an attempt to prevail upon him to take us to hunt for hillside treasures or to go on some other foray into the woods. Usually we'd find him in the swing on his porch, with Jo sitting in the faded green rocker right near him. She'd be cutting out something, careful not to allow any paper to fall on the porch. We'd beg a little and soon he would give in and lead us up around the hill back of his house or ours. Pop Pop would putter along, with Jo a foot or so behind him, wringing her hands up under her chin, while Gwen, Sister, and any other neighborhood kid up for the adventure fanned out in front, behind, and to either side. As I think on it, it is hard to believe my grandfather took so much time just doing nothing with us kids, but I don't recall his ever once shooing us away. Maybe some of it had to do with Jo, too; he was ever patient with her, and we did provide companionship for both of them.

My aunt Jo's life, such as it was, was a tragedy for both her and the family. She would have "spells" where she bit her fist, stomped her feet, turned in a circle, and sort of shook all over. And I might as well say it, every one of us kids mocked her. Though we all did it, Gwen and I probably did the best job of "making fun of Jo," because we were so often around her when she'd fly into one of her fits. If our mocking Jo seems at odds with our closeness to her and to Pop Pop, it was not. First of all, we did not do it in Jo's presence or in front of grown-ups; we knew better than that. The business of judging our treatment of Jo—and the whole family's treatment of Jo, for that matter—is another instance of looking at the past through today's lenses. I have spent more than thirty years teaching human development and psychology, and in my professional opinion, Jo was probably autistic—to what degree, we'll never know. I feel certain that she was never examined by anyone trained to diagnose her affliction. Yes, I think her condition was an affliction, and no, I do not think she was "differently" abled. Though we are now at a place where we are better able to determine what might be wrong with a person, we appear to have lost the ability to call it what it is. When a family member is like Jo, it affects every aspect of the life of each member of the family as well as the ways they relate to each other and to outsiders.

The greatest blessing Jo offered our family was that she may have been the reason Pop Pop was so patient with children. Moreover, I believe all of us dealt with her as well as we could have been expected to. I never once saw anyone hurt her in any way, and we all went out of our way to include her and to entertain her. We loved both Pop Pop and Jo, but we were kids, and mocking Jo was another of those behaviors we engaged in to entertain each other hoping we'd not be caught. At the time, it certainly never occurred to any of us that we were doing anything other than having a good time. Jo outlived Pop Pop by more than forty years. For all his fears she seemed as happy in the nursing home as she ever was at home. Making fun of Jo is like many of the other sneaky things we did when we were younger and are ashamed of now that we know better. But we grew up. Jo never did.

Though Momma had enjoyed living in West Virginia and was not thrilled about moving back to Two-Mile, she did look forward to coming back so she could be near her family—especially Grandma Emmy. In the spring of 1945 Momma writes, "I'll be home one of these days to do your spring house cleaning," and she speaks over and over in her letters of helping my grandmother raise her garden. All Grandma Emmy's girls worried about her working herself down, and each of them did what they could to take some of the burden off her.

Grandma Emmy had more than her share of troubles, beginning earlier with having to care for a paralyzed husband and raise nine children on land already just about worked out before she ever got ahold of it. Her daughters felt a responsibility to their mother for having sent them all through high school, which was not common with girls in those days. Both Momma and Aunt Amanda told me folks urged Grandma Emmy to pull those "big girls out of school to help you around the place." Aunt Amanda said that when she finished eighth grade there was no high school nearby. Grandma Emmy took sixteen-year-old Amanda to Paintsville to the head of Mayo Vocational School. There she arranged for room, board, and tuition by saying: "Now, I don't have any cash money, but I will give you garden vegetables in the summer and canned stuff and hog meat in the fall if you'll see to it that my Amanda gets her education." The deal was set, and my aunt never forgot it.

My grandmother valued a high school diploma for the job opportunities it opened, but education was important to my grandma Emmy in the sense that she valued being able to read above most everything else.

I never gathered that she saw reading as a chore, but rather something that brought infinite pleasure. Thus, it was important for her to get the real work—the incessant house and field work—out of the way so that the pleasures of the day could be enjoyed in one book or another. My grandmother read for entertainment rather than for information, but because she read everything she could get her hands on, she was very well informed for a person with a sixth-grade education. She had gone to school for as long as she was able, but when her daddy left her mother with five kids and nothing but the place she lived on to support the family, my grandmother was forced to drop out of school. To hear her tell it, she loved school but had no choice but to quit and care for the younger children and help her mother do the necessaries around the place. That marked her, though, for she was very proud that despite being put in practically the same position as her mother, she was able to see every one of her children through high school. What's more, all the girls made schoolteachers, even Aunt Gladys, who was sick unto death by the time she got her high school diploma.

Aunt Gladys died on May 16, 1934. And Grandma Emmy's packet of letters includes a registered letter dated May 22, 1934, from the Department of Education in Frankfort, Kentucky, to:

Mrs. Elijah Mollette
Mother of Gladys Mollette, Deceased
Boone's Camp, Kentucky

Dear Mrs. Mollette:

Enclosed you will find two dollars in currency in lieu of the legal fee submitted by your daughter. We are also enclosing the certificate submitted to this department.

The members of the department extend sympathy in your sad bereavement.

Very truly yours,
A.P. Taylor
Director of Certification

Enclosed is pink teaching certificate S1928 No. 4851, issued May 13, 1932, certifying that Gladys Mollette could teach in "the elementary schools of Martin County, first and eighth grade inclusive for period ending June 30, 1934."

I didn't realize that any of Grandma Emmy's male children taught school, but Billie Edyth Ward says Uncle Fred taught for a little while. It was hard for a man to support a family by teaching school, though, so Momma's brothers were among many who left it for the mines or moved north for factory jobs.

No, Grandma Emmy never saw education as a way to the good life—teachers hardly made a living wage in those days, just as they don't today. While she insisted her boys get a high school diploma before they went to the mines, the WPA, or some other job of work, her intent was that all her children be able to figure well enough to keep folks from cheating them and that they learn to read for the pure fun of it. I agree with my grandmother here, though I might state it differently. In my view, degrees and diplomas may well prepare me to make a living, but the information and habits attendant to an education add immeasurably to the making of a life.

The notebooks and letters found in my grandmother's trunk reveal that she, her husband, and each of her children were quite literate for the times and that every one of them loved books. In June 1944, Momma writes: "I never have gotten time to fix Stella's books up but I'll try to Sunday. Jay wants to buy Tom a batch of new ones." By October 1944, she was sending yet another batch: "We're going to send them some more books & Tom some cigarettes if we can get them next week." Again in December, one more load of books went from the coalfields to the country: "Hear from Stella real often. We sent them some more books this week." Then, in a January 1945 letter, Momma asks Grandma Emmy if Aunt Stella has yet picked up "those books we left with you." On February 16, 1945, Momma says: "Jay went & bought Tom a load of books last night. I'm going to send them today. I had some for Stella already. She wrote that he was out of anything to read." And in mid-March Momma reports: "I wrote Stella & sent her & Tom a bunch of books & she never did even write me whether she got them or not."

Though Momma's letters are the only ones making mention of sending books, it was not simply a one-way undertaking. The Lige Mollette family formed their own book exchange, and as far back as I can remember every member of the family sent books to every other member. They'd read anything from Zane Grey to F. Scott Fitzgerald, from the old-time country newspaper known as *The Grit* to the Bible, and everything in between. Momma passed along books to her mother and each of her sisters, and they passed theirs back to her. I also do not recall any reading material ever being off-limits in my house, though Momma didn't much approve of my reading *True Story* or *Confidential*. Still, from the time I was about thirteen, I was able to buy and read my own comics, magazines, and books.

In 1958, when I was a senior in high school, Coach Wendell Wallen took the Meade Memorial Red Devils to the Kentucky State Tournament. I was a cheerleader and we had put on a couple of bake sales to raise the money, so I got to go with the team and stay in the Phoenix Hotel in Lexington, Kentucky. It was my first trip downstate, where I finally saw the Kentucky of all our dreams—bluegrass, blood horses, bourbon—all that. Well, after our daylong trip on the school bus, we checked into the hotel, and the team and cheerleaders went down the street to Cottrell's Bakery for supper. The team had to eat whatever they were supposed to, but we cheerleaders had our own money, so we ordered from the menu. I don't recall anybody else's food choices, but I had a hamburger, which was served to me barely off the cow. I was ashamed to send it back—and I couldn't even eat the bun, because it was stained pink—so I ate my French fries, drank the Coke, and had two of their finest brownies.

The next day, we lost the first game to a team from downstate and had to go back to eastern Kentucky without a single win. As for the cheerleaders, we had considerable money left, so for our last meal at Cottrell's, we ordered the most expensive thing on the menu—the sixteen-inch T-bones. Of course we knew what "oz." stood for; we just read it wrong. When they brought those steaks, there was enough meat for a good workin' and they were blood rare. We looked at each other, then at the waitress and inquired as to whether she thought they might cook the meat—like, a lot more. Took 'em three tries, but once they got them sufficiently brown, we ate like field hands and headed home.

Before we got on the bus, however, I bought what looked like it might be a pretty good book from the gift shop at the Phoenix. Since I've always been prone to motion sickness, I take enough Dramamine to be able to read upside down on a Six Flags roller coaster. And so it was that I climbed on that school bus, full to bursting with Dramamine and T-bone and in possession of a little paperback called *Peyton Place*. Gotta tell you, I had never seen anything like that. If any teacher on the bus had had any idea what I was reading, that little book would have been confiscated and I'd have been in deep trouble. But it was March 1958, and nobody'd even heard of Grace Metalious, much less suspected that such stuff could be published and sold right out in public at the Phoenix Hotel in Lexington, Kentucky.

I agree with Grandma Emmy. Education is its own reward.

The Lifie Jay Preston four-room house—some might even call it a cabin—sat in a natural sycamore grove alongside a creek called Two-Mile. Every stroke of the hammer and push and pull of the saw that went into the building of that house was performed by my daddy or his daddy, my Pop Pop. I didn't have the opportunity to watch that house go up, because it was built before I was born. A rough timber bridge across the stream gave passage to and from that little house, and across the bridge lay a road that was blacktopped when I was four or five years old. For my first seventeen years I simply took for granted that I would spend my whole life within walking distance of that house, maybe even end my days in that very structure. Through a series of seemingly random events, it has not turned out that way, and I've not turned out the way I or any other members of my family had any reason to expect I would either. I crossed that little wooden bridge and took the winding county road that lay beyond it to find other highways, distant places, unfamiliar houses—a different life perhaps. That modest house was built to last at least a couple of generations, but it burned to the ground in 1955, taking with it every material possession my family owned. Pop Pop had died the summer before the house burned, so Daddy had to rebuild the new one himself.

As he was rebuilding, Daddy would come in from the mines around 4:30 or so in the afternoon and, still in his work clothes, he'd set to work on the new house. As the house neared completion, though, Daddy began changing out of his dirty mine clothes before he set to work so that he wouldn't get coal dust on the finish work. Sister and I—and sometimes Momma—would take him a cup of coffee and sit and watch as our daddy constructed the new house board by board. Occasionally Daddy would ask one of us to bring him something he needed that lay just beyond his reach. Now and then, if he needed help hoisting rafters or thick studs, one of the neighborhood men would come over and help him out for an hour or two. I don't think I ever heard Daddy explicitly ask for help, but if he needed it some neighbor just naturally appeared— the same way you could be sure folks would show up when somebody's corn came in all at once and he needed to get it in before it hardened. Then near dark, after we'd all assured ourselves and each other that this was indeed the most beautiful house south of Huntington, West Virginia, we would walk the two hundred yards or so down to Pop Pop's place and eat our supper. At that time we would have laughed to think we were eating fashionably late, since our eating habits, like everything else in our lives, were simply scheduled around work. Momma and Daddy— indeed, everybody I knew—learned early on to get the must-dos out of the way before the want-to-dos.

By our standards, Daddy made a good living, and my family was typical of the other families in our community; we were ordinary people. Statistically, the census figures from that time suggest that we were poor, but the story of my childhood is not about poverty, or helplessness, or hopelessness. Instead, it is a story of a very rich childhood. Two-Mile Creek was a community in the best sense of the word. Everybody worked hard most of the time to see that nobody went hungry, and if somebody got down sick, others pitched in and helped out. And the best thing about it is that, as far as I can recall, nobody kept score as to who did what and for whom. When things happened on Two-Mile—good or bad things—our responses were the same. We shook our heads, sighed, laughed, or maybe cried. Then with the help of the Lord and our neighbors, we went on living our lives. My family, friends, and neighbors would never have thought themselves to be community-minded, nor would they ever have engaged in the types of behaviors thought to be community service today. Instead, my people saw themselves as good neighbors, who gave naturally to each other even when their own needs were great.

When my family's house burned the first Saturday in December 1955, the fire wasn't even out before people in the community—our neighbors— began the country version of community service. Around ten in the morning, Momma had gone to town to pay bills and do some Christmas shopping, and by the time she returned at 2:30, the house was gone. Sister was just eight years old, so our up-the-road neighbor, Hollie Daniel, picked her up at school and took her to his house, where he and his wife, Rose, kept her occupied until Daddy got home. Sister recalls the Daniels feeding her supper, Cokes, and cookies and playing board games with her. She also says Hollie made her hide her eyes as they passed our house so she wouldn't see it burning.

I got home from school a little after 3:00 P.M. and sat over on the Holbrooks' porch with Momma and assorted neighbors just watching the fire burn itself out. From the time I took my place with my mother on the Holbrook front porch, I listened as Leonie Wallen came by and told Momma that the Wallens had plenty of room and would be glad if our family would come and stay with them until we "worked something out." Edna Ward sent Easter to make the same suggestion about staying over with them. Meanwhile, Aunt Exer didn't say a word. She just went in the house and made up a bed for Momma and Daddy, a pallet on the floor for Sister, and it was assumed that I could sleep with Gwen. Several other offers came in by way of children of families up and down the creek who sent word that they would be tickled to death for us to stay awhile with them. These invitations to bed and board four people were not simply a formality either. I do not doubt that we could have moved in and lived off just about any one of our neighbors, none of whom had any extra to go around. Those were not empty invitations, for we were indeed welcome to share in anything they had. As it turned out, those many offers of hospitality, though sincerely proffered, were unnecessary.

Daddy came home from work that day to find the still-smoking ruins of the house he had built twenty-some years earlier. As he pulled in the driveway, Momma and I, accompanied by several of the Holbrooks, straggled across the road to join him. He got out of the car, walked up to the smoldering remains of his home, slowly shook his head, said, "Aye, boys," and that was the extent of his expression about our tragedy. After walking around the place and seeing for himself that there was nothing left, he then walked the hundred yards down to Pop Pop's little house that had sat empty since his death the summer before. Other than cleaning out the refrigerator, nothing had been moved since Pop Pop lay a corpse there in July 1955. Daddy opened the door off the end porch (no, of course it wasn't locked), walked in, and—still in his dirty mine clothes—he began to move and straighten furniture in what became our home for the ten months it would take him to build back.

A scant fifteen minutes into his and Momma's commencing to clean up the gaum in Pop Pop's place, seemed like half the men on Two-Mile were there to help. They didn't offer; they simply set to work. There were women, too, of course, most of them bringing food they had cooked for supper that evening. They all said the same thing: "Just thought I'd bring over a little extra." Truth was that nobody who lived around us had much in the way of "extra," but they managed to find some anyway. That night, "extra" was primarily food and the barest necessities. Leonie Wallen sent brand-new dish towels that I know in reason she had put by to use herself, and Edna Ward sent several cans of home-canned tomatoes. Aunt Exer sent me a pair of Gwen's panties so I'd have clean underwear for school the next day, but since Gwen was about as overweight as I was underweight, I had to pin those pink suckers to keep them from falling down around my ankles. When the first bell rang to change classes the next day, old Gwen sidled up to me and inquired as to whether I was "keeping my drawers up." We snickered about my bloomer situation all day.

I doubt that there was one family within a mile of us who did not help clean or send food that evening, but it didn't end there. For weeks people kept bringing things to us, enough so that at some point, Momma—the mistress of overstatement—remarked that "everybody in the whole wide living world" was represented in her cutlery drawer. Moreover, I want to point out that this was not charity, not at all. Our family was as well-to-do as anybody on Two-Mile, and it might even be that some of those who gave to us were maybe not as well-off as we were, but not that night. That evening, and for a time thereafter, the Lifie Jay Preston family was truly needy, and everybody gave.

It didn't take long to ready the house that night. There was an over-abundance of help for Pop Pop's tiny place. Altogether the house probably didn't have five hundred square feet, but since Pop Pop had lived alone there taking care of Aunt Jo, they hadn't needed a great deal of space. With a little help from Daddy, Pop Pop had built the place himself while he was living with us in 1949. It consisted of a porch that fronted on Two-Mile Creek and led into a ten-by-ten living room. A fireplace took up the right wall of the living room, and just beyond the fireplace through the back wall was a door into the kitchen. A six-by-eight-foot kitchen sat directly behind the living room and was furnished with a gas cook stove, a refrigerator, the smallest pie safe I ever saw, and a wooden table (about the size of a card table) covered with red-and-white-checkered oilcloth. Pop Pop had only used two wooden chairs at that table, but we found four—chrome with red plastic seats and backs—that Daddy had stored there just six months before when we got our new yellow plastic and chrome dinette set.

All four of us sitting around that table made a pretty tight fit, but gather around it we did from the day after our old house burned until we moved out of Pop Pop's place in the fall of '56. Whatever else might have been going on—ball games, dates, church, all manner of commitments—every member of our family always came together for supper. Daddy was funny turned in that he didn't like to eat anyplace except his own table, and when he sat down to supper, all four of us sat down to supper. Though he never said it explicitly, that was a rule we did not break unless in extreme emergency.

In the summertime, from the time Daddy came in from the mines until dark, we'd work the garden at Grandma Emmy's around on Greasy. Even then, none of us ate until we all ate. Before she died, Grandma Emmy sometimes cooked our supper and we ate at her house before coming back to Two-Mile, but most often we'd just wait till we got back home and devour whatever Momma had cooked earlier and put in the oven so we could eat together. We'd squeeze around that table and laugh and talk and recap our days—even the sad ones, like those days after the fire, when Momma would almost always have a story about what she had missed since that particular day. I recall that we must not have had mashed potatoes for the three weeks after the fire, because Momma was cooking Christmas dinner when she realized we no longer had a potato masher—one more missing implement. That Christmas we solved the problem by taking our boiled potatoes whole from the bowl, adding butter and mashing them individually in our plates. We all declared them "just as good, if not better" than potatoes mashed the traditional way, but Momma picked up a new potato masher on her next trip to town.

My memory turns often to that time after the fire and the effect it had on Momma, Daddy, Sister, and me. Thinking back on it, I don't recall our having been any happier or sadder than at any other time in our lives. Even with Momma's reports of missing items, I don't remember any particular sadness over what we'd lost. That first day, we cried—all of us but Daddy. The next day, we were back in business. Daddy went to work; Sister and I went to school; and Momma went to town and bought new underwear for all of us and another set of work clothes for Daddy. When Daddy came home from the mines that first afternoon, he was carrying two pairs of printed cotton pajamas, pink for Sister, blue for me. In the same sack—from the company store, of course—rested a box of shiny red Christmas balls, two sets of tree lights, and a half dozen various ornaments—silver balls, reindeer, and a couple of Santas. We made no mention of the fact that he had not replaced the silver star that had always crowned the top of our tree. I don't know when Momma replaced that star, but a review of my pictures of our family's Christmas trees shows only two years with a tree-topper. For thirty-nine Christmases—between 1955 and my parent's deaths on November 11 and December 5, 1994—only 1980 and 1989 reveal an ornament at the top of the Preston Christmas tree.

We had no insurance, of course, so I know the loss of all he'd owned was a real setback for Daddy, but if it preyed on his mind he never let on. In truth, nothing about our lives and the way we went about living them changed that much. Yes, we lost our indoor plumbing, which meant an extra step or two were added to Momma's cooking and dishwashing, and the new task of carrying out the chamber pot in the morning fell to me. But I don't recall any excess whining on the part of any member of the family over any particular object that was missed. Since we ate a lot of mashed potatoes, we did replace the missed potato masher. Christmas came without the star, and as we found out we could have plenty of Christmas without a tree-topper, it was not replaced for several decades. Even then, the star's appearance was sporadic, and like many of Momma's choices, I cannot tell you why. That's the problem with trying to analyze and interpret stories to get some better handle on the truth. It cannot be done, not with any degree of certainty. All I can tell is what I remember or was told.

In this case, the fire had happened. We went on. Everybody in the community helped as much as we would let them, so that by spring the only real reminder of the fire was the scorched earth outlining where our house had been. By the time the blooming dogwood began to dot the spring-green hillside, the men on Two-Mile had helped us clean up the soot and ashes, and Daddy had laid the foundation for our new house —built squarely atop the memory of the one that burned. At the time the house burned, Daddy was working at David, so we could have moved into the coal camp up at Middle Creek, in Floyd County. We had another option, too, since the year before Daddy had bought out the heirs to Momma's home place at Three Forks of Greasy. Grandma Emmy's house still stood on that property, a house seat that had a good well on it, and we farmed two of the bottoms there. But we never even considered moving off Two-Mile.

Perhaps the major reason for our affinity to Two-Mile had to do with our neighbors. We loved and trusted them as family, and they returned the favor. Our families had known each other for several generations, and parents didn't have to worry about some of the problems that plague today's society.

As I grew up, I became less and less able to tell where I ended and the rest of the world began. As a Creeker—a term used to describe a rural Appalachian who lived outside town—I internalized very early the we/they boundaries that were clear between town and country. With every birthday I celebrated on Two-Mile, however, the lines between family and community grew fainter still.

I believe you would have to go back at least seven generations for me to claim kin with the Wallen family of Two-Mile, and throughout all those hours spent in their store, I never thought of them as family. But Leonie and Mitchell Wallen's son, Wendell, who is about six or seven years older than I am, became one of Kentucky's greatest high school basketball coaches. Let me say also that in Kentucky claiming that someone is a *great* basketball coach is not done lightly. We take our basketball very seriously, which makes Wendell Wallen—along with Donnis Butcher, who played for the New York Knickerbockers and, later, the Detroit Pistons—the most famous Two-Mile native ever. Wendell grew up across the road from me and I ran into him in his family's store, but he was just enough older than I was for me not to think of him as a friend. Still, when he got to be a well-known coach, I took as much pride in his success as I did in that of Russell Williamson, the famous coach of Inez High School, who is close blood kin to me.

During the years I lived in Kentucky, when my downstate friends decided to be critical of Wendell or his coaching, they soon learned that I am as quick to defend him as I would any other member of my family.

That "family first" attitude may not be inborn, but it was part of me so early that it stuck. What's more, I tend to see that feeling for family as one of the strengths of the heritage I passed along to my son.

My mother and father came from very different families—or families who looked for different things out of life. But one thing was constant and shared by both families—a tradition of laughter. My parents worked hard and enjoyed spending time at home swapping tales with their parents, brothers, and sisters, but they also went out looking for fun. Both loved music and could play by ear—a talent lost on me but inherited by Sister. I joined them, though, in an appreciation for all manner of singing and playing.

One of the homegrown sayings that has always rung true to me is that "Country music is three chords and God's honest truth." And for all those who poke fun at the overt sentimentality in this genre, I'd suggest that much of it is reflective of the hard life lived by those who like to listen to it. With its tales of love and loss, such music takes us out of ourselves while folding us more deeply into ourselves. At sixteen, I fancied Hank Williams and Faron Young. At sixty, I enjoy Patty Loveless and Dwight Yoakam. In between, I have been possessed by many artists, more songs, and just about every sort of music. The only types of music I really do not like are mariachi and Hawaiian . . . and jazz, I'm not overly fond of jazz either. I like lyrics.

Hillbilly music provided the score for all my growing-up years. Not country music either. I said "hillbilly" because that's what we called it. What folks call "country" today is more like early rock 'n' roll than the strain of hillbilly music my family listened to on Two-Mile in the fifties. There was some bluegrass, some folk, and just lots of plain old wailing hillbillies like Hank Williams, Kitty Wells, Lefty Frizzell, the Carter Family, Little Jimmy Dickens, and Carl Smith. Early on, when we stayed with Grandma Emmy, Daddy played guitar and sang, and sometimes Momma or Grandma Emmy sang hymns a cappella. By the time we moved back from West Virginia, though the Two-Mile house was hooked to power lines running down the main road, and Momma was able to use the radio Daddy had bought her. Pop Pop lived right across the road from us, and he loved his music as much as we did. We were all big fans of the Grand Ole Opry, which was sure to carry between our houses on a Saturday night. Sometimes it was hard to pull in a station, but I don't recall us ever turning off a program because of static. In fact, I don't recall us ever turning off the radio for any reason.

We lived our lives to background music, radio talk, or static in some form or another. When Daddy worked the David coal mines and had to get up at four in the morning, he often went to bed at dark, and the small white bedside radio lulled him to sleep. Though Momma got up earlier than Daddy, she stayed up later and would turn off Daddy's radio when the station signed off. Otherwise, she also went to sleep by the radio, and it sat there and fizzed until sign-on the next morning. Nobody in my family felt that a radio or TV playing in the background— or foreground, for that matter—was a distraction. We found most of the burdens in an average day to be lightened by music, and we appreciated the free entertainment. I don't get what all this need for silence in order to concentrate is all about. As I sit at my computer and write this piece of work, Patty Loveless singing "You'll Never Leave Harlan Alive" serenades me.

In April 1949, when WSIP-AM radio went on the air in Paintsville, Kentucky, my family saw it as real progress, and we were as involved in that station as country folks with full-time jobs and crops to raise could possibly be. WSIP had a format that included a little bit of everything, from the daily "Swap Shop," where folks called in to buy or sell whatever they wanted or no longer needed, to dawn-to-dusk preachers saving souls on Sunday. In between those poles was a range of entertainment options, including news—both local and national—and every category of music any Johnson Countian could request, and request we did. Once we got telephone service, we could call in to several shows and request songs be sent out to our nearest and dearest. Most of the requests were predictable: "June Ann wants 'Always Late' sent out to Rodney" or "Audrey requests Lefty Frizell's 'Mama and Daddy' for her parents, Mr. And Mrs. Kenneth Justice of Hager Hill."

And then there were the contests—contests to name new shows, for example. I recall Bill Barker had a show that came on around 3:30 P.M., just as we were getting home from school, and WSIP held a contest to submit names for it. He ended up calling the show "Platter Party" instead of our entry, which was "Willie's Wax Works," Momma's creative suggestion. Though a number of folks of all ages would be listening at my house, Momma had the wildest imagination. She had considerable range, my mother. One contest had to do with being able to place something geographically. Such a contest usually began with a five-dollar prize, say, which increased by about a dollar for each week the question went unanswered. We had to send in our name and phone number and hope they drew it out of the glass bowl and called us at a time when nobody else was using our eight-party telephone line.

In my memory, the longest one of those contests ever lasted was once when the prize money got to twenty-five dollars and my momma won it all. I honestly do not recall what the question was, but the answer was Tibet. Momma knew that answer almost from the beginning of the contest, but it took a lot of other folks answering incorrectly before they finally called our number. I think I was about nine years old then, and as usual our house was full of teenagers sitting around Momma's bedroom drinking Cokes and smoking while she ironed our clothes. Everybody talked, laughed, and listened to "Platter Party" but got real quiet when the phone rang. Momma turned down the radio, picked up the phone, nice-as-you-please, and answered without hesitation. After she won, we all jumped up and down, whooping and hollering, and the phone rang off the hook with folks offering congratulations. Everybody in the house had a drink of some sort in hand—RC, Coke, Pepsi, iced tea, maybe—but nobody lifted them high to toast the occasion. I don't know about everybody else, but I had never seen anybody make that toasting gesture. Television really changed things on Two-Mile, in that home folks picked up on a lot of the small stuff—things like the toast gesture—simply from watching the "stories" on TV.

Some of my favorite memories of family outings revolve around the weekly talent shows that used to be held at the old Royal Theater, located across from what is now the Johnson County Public Library in Paintsville. Strictly speaking, the talent show was not simply a contest, for interspersed among each week's contestants were several regulars, most of whom had at one time or another competed in this show and won. Sister and I could never be certain of going, because our attendance depended on the weather and what was on Daddy's agenda. Still, we went more often than not, and all four of us looked forward to it. Every Thursday afternoon Sister and I would pile out of the school bus and hit our front door on the run. Momma couldn't even tempt us to stop for a fresh cookie or brownie, as I headed directly to the kitchen, where two empty water buckets waited for my trip across the road to replenish the Preston drinking-water supply. Sister would feed the chickens and maybe set the table. As soon as we completed our after-school chores we moved on to our lessons, so that by the time Daddy returned from his day at the mine we'd be ready for a big night out.

After Daddy took his bath and we'd eaten supper and cleaned up the dishes, we were on our way. Our Royal Theater evening began with popcorn and a Pepsi apiece as we found our seats before the lights dimmed. Usually Momma and Daddy ran into folks they knew in the theater lobby, so Sister and I would saunter on down near the front and find four seats— five if Bonnie Butcher was with us—together on the aisle. Daddy and Momma soon joined us, with Daddy sitting in the end seat, then Momma, Sister, and me strung out along the row. As I progressed from a child to a teenager, I recall coveting that center seat, for I could pretend that I wasn't there with my family but maybe had a boyfriend who sang in the talent show. Such a possibility was unlikely for a number of reasons. First of all, if one member of our family went somewhere, all four of us went. What's more, to my recollection, none of the young men in the talent show ever showed the slightest interest in me.

I did have a huge crush on one Eugene Hall, I believe his name was, who was a spindly little fellow—a regular, who often led off the show with his rendition of a song called "Wondering." He sang it as if it were pronounced "*wandering*," and I surely sat there *wandering* about Eugene more often than not. Some of the greatest romances I never had were right there beside Baby Sister in row three or four of the Royal Theater, sometimes with Bonnie Butcher sitting on the other side of me, which stepped on my fantasies somewhat. An empty seat right next to me always stirred my imagination, but Bonnie accompanied us whenever she didn't have to work the night shift at the hospital. Once old Eugene launched into "Wandering," I could come close to forgetting there were others in the theater anyway.

From early on I have been able to lose myself in music, and I have to believe Momma and Daddy passed that along to me, for they were that way, too. Their passion for music had to be pretty powerful for them to stay out past ten o'clock on a work night, knowing that the clock would go off a scant five hours later. Daddy's work had no give to it, so there was no sleeping in, ever.

Sometimes we would not go to the talent show because the car had developed a problem and had to be worked on immediately, or Daddy was just too tired. No matter what illness was plaguing Momma at the time, she was always up for going, but every now and then Daddy would come home with the sick headache. When that happened, he wouldn't even be able to eat supper. He'd usually get out of the car, walk over toward the toilet, and throw up in the branch. Then he'd come on in the house, wash the coal dirt off himself, and go straight to bed, where he would sleep straight through to the next morning. I don't recall a time in my life when Daddy was free of the severe headaches that sometimes lasted for several days. If he was lucky, they would strike him on a Friday and he could go to bed for the weekend to wear them out. If, however, a headache came earlier in the week, he would go directly to bed, without a bite of supper, at the end of each day, but he never missed one day of work to deal with his headache, ever.

The talent shows were held on Thursday night, but if no headache intervened we always had a big Saturday night, too. One of our favorite Saturday night affairs was the jamboree held in a big room near El Pack's garage over in Stafford Bottom, with live hillbilly music usually preceding the talent show. I don't recall there being a Eugene Hall at the jamboree, so I must have been younger. Though Daddy never took his guitar and played in any of the jamboree shows, I recall folks asking him to "bring your git-fiddle next time, Lifie Jay, and we'll pick a little." Daddy would nod his head, seeming to agree, but despite Momma's urging, he never would. I don't recall Daddy ever picking guitar with anybody except Frank Ward's boys when they would come in from Ohio and Michigan, but earlier in his life he must have played with some of the jamboree boys, because they seemed to know him and to know he played music. Also, they called him "Lifie" Jay, which meant they had known him early on. By jamboree time in our history, everybody knew Daddy as Jay or E. Jay except folks who had known him before the West Virginia years.

Later still, when WSIP became a reality, we used to go over to the station on a Saturday night and watch through the glass as live country bands performed. Bonnie Butcher was almost always with us, and each of us had favorites we liked to see and hear. A singer named South Salyer was Momma and Daddy's favorite, but I was still loyal to Eugene Hall. I recall one time that Bonnie had met South Salyer when he visited somebody at the hospital, and she introduced him to us between sets. I don't know about Momma and Daddy, but I was certainly impressed—nearest I had ever come to meeting a star. This was many years before home girl Loretta Lynn made it big in Nashville.

The first time I heard "Your Cheatin' Heart" sung by Hank Williams, I was lying in the backseat of Daddy's old blue '49 Plymouth riding back from Fort Gay, West Virginia, where we'd gone to buy beer. Daddy, Momma, and Bonnie Butcher were crowded into the front seat, and Baby Sister and I were lying in the back. I think Sister might have been asleep, because she would have been no more than three or four years old. The gray felt seat smelled of cigarette smoke and coal dust and was rough against my cheek, and Sister's left foot was up under my right arm as ol' Hank said he was going to perform this new song for the first time. I wasn't the least bit uncomfortable lying there in my pink knit nylon sweater and periwinkle blue corduroy flare-tail skirt, my leg rubbing up against Sister's white rabbit fur coat. I know Sister was young then, for she hardly took up half the seat, all stretched out, with her head wedged between the worn felt armrest and the corner.

We used to do that a lot, go down to Fort Gay, West Virginia—just across the state line from Louisa, which was the closest place to buy alcohol. Daddy never was bad to drink, but the post-jamboree days often found us on the way to or from Fort Gay on a Saturday evening. Of course, if drinking were the real purpose of the trip, Daddy could have bought from any one of the ubiquitous bootleggers in Johnson County. Instead, we'd get all dressed up (that pink sweater and blue skirt was my favorite outfit till I outgrew it), pick up Bonnie, and drive to Fort Gay, with the Grand Ole Opry playing on the car radio. Once there, we'd pull into a drive-in, and the inhabitants of the front seat would have one beer apiece. Sister was always asleep by the time we got there, so Momma would order me a fountain Coke to sip on. Sometimes one of us would get a hamburger, hot dog, Squirrel peanuts, or a Hershey bar, but most often we just sat there and drank silently, listening as the Opry "Let 'er go, boys!"

Most of the shows—the jamboree, talent show, and WSIP Saturday nights—were modeled on the Opry in that they had serious songs and singers interspersed with comedy. There'd always be a Grandpa Jones or Minnie Pearl-like character who would run around, making a fool of himself for our entertainment. We loved the Carter Family, especially June Carter, who was the act-a-fool member of the group, so once she married Johnny Cash and changed her persona, it took us awhile to accept her as a serious singer. Though such comedic characters were based on traditional hillbilly stereotypes, we never took offense. We knew we weren't like that, and watching somebody act a fool between serious songs that often dealt with very real problems took us out of ourselves.

After we got a television set, we spent most Saturday nights at home watching whatever show was on WSAZ-TV, the one channel we got, out of Huntington, West Virginia. Saturday nights meant Sid Caesar, wrestling, and *Your Hit Parade,* but playing in the background—always, even with the TV on—was WSIP on the small brown radio that sat on the kitchen counter and was never turned off. On such Saturday nights, Daddy often went to bed by nine o'clock, leaving Sister, Momma, and me, with whoever else happened to be there, to watch TV without him. In his bedroom with the door closed, Daddy allowed the Grand Ole Opry emanating from his bedside radio to sing him to sleep.

Once we got the drive-in theatre in Johnson County, I don't recall our ever going to Fort Gay again. Instead, we'd often go see live entertainment at the drive-in. The drive-in concession stand had a flat roof, and groups would sing and play standing on top of that roof. Some folks took blankets, got out of their car, and sat near the concession stand to hear better. Daddy said the sound was just fine with our car windows rolled down, which meant that Sister and I couldn't get out and run and play like some kids did.

In December 1955, Daddy's guitar was destroyed with the rest of our belongings when our house burned. I don't think anybody much missed it, because—post-TV—Daddy seldom played in the wintertime anyway. Then, in the summer of '56, Daddy was so taken up with building back our house that we didn't spend much time sitting in the yard. By the next summer, I was sixteen and gave no thought to my family as anything but a hindrance I had to put up with. Hence, I never missed Daddy's playing. I don't even recall anybody ever saying anything about Daddy's guitar after that, and I certainly never thought about it. After the house burned, Momma and Daddy stayed home more, at least Daddy did. Momma joined the church and usually went to services on Sunday and sometimes Wednesday nights, while Daddy took to his bed and the Opry.

In the summer of 1964, when my son was little more than a year old, we moved back to eastern Kentucky, and I asked Daddy why he never played his guitar anymore. Typical of Daddy, he said, "Ain't got time anymore," but Momma said he'd never replaced his old guitar that burned. I thought he might take it up again if he had a guitar, so for Christmas 1964 we bought him a new guitar. As far as I know, he never picked that guitar even once.

Songs of Life

I have two fathers. The first, one Elipha Jay "Life" Preston, was born on March 12, 1917, down on Bob's Branch, a tributary of the Levisa Fork of the Big Sandy River—and now lies buried on the top of a ridge that rolls right down to that river. He was an eastern Kentuckian, both by birth and by inclination. He loved the place, never wanted to live anywhere else, and his body now lies within walking distance of his birthplace. He was my daddy—my beloved "Daddy"—and I never called him anything else. Oh, now and then, I'd call him "Paw," just funnin' him. While I never used the appellation "Father" in my life, I do have a father—a father created by none other than my little provincial daddy, who never wanted to live anywhere outside the hills of Johnson County, about as far east as you can go in Kentucky without tripping over the West Virginia state line. That father is inside my head, and he won't be gone even when I am put to rest beside Daddy on that hilltop graveyard. It is the part of me that taught my boy who he was and is and the kind of people he came from.

We are first, last, and always working people—people whose jobs may not have been what we might have chosen, if we'd ever thought we had a choice to make. But the father I carry around with me will not allow me to rest until I have given whatever task I have taken on everything I can give it. If I inherited anything from my family—Momma and Daddy, both—it is a legacy of work. Perhaps the place my daddy is most alive, most present, is in the tools he left behind—the rust-pocked T square measuring ninety degrees off the edge of the bookcase facing my desk, and the carpenter's level, its bead still balancing true, that hangs on Sister's office wall. Daddy was about his carpentry, his work—about *work*, period, truth be told. He was proud of his work, however menial someone else might have considered his contribution to be, and he judged Momma's brothers as plain sorry, less because of their drinking habits than because of what he thought was their bone-laziness. According to Daddy, Momma's brothers thought they were too smart to dig ditches, while Daddy believed that a man who did not work for pay at any available job was pretty close to worthless. No work was beneath a man who needed a job, and the fact that Daddy got up, went off to the mines every morning, and put in a full day was a source of pride to him. That idea lay at the base of Daddy's respect for himself. He always said he might not know much, but he knew he could work.

Much of the time, I agree with those who suggest that defining and classifying folks by their jobs is insulting, especially to those whose jobs are not considered prestigious. My daddy's work—both as a coal miner and later as a house builder—was integral to his image of himself. While he appreciated the role of the union in getting eight-hour days, decent money, and benefits for miners, Daddy never believed he needed the UMWA (United Mine Workers Association) for lay-off protection. Though the duties that made up his days might have been interchangeable with any number of day laborers, my daddy was convinced that he would not be replaced capriciously, because he worked harder at his assignment than most others were willing to.

I'm sure that if he'd been asked whether he preferred to work or not work, Daddy would have laughed at the question. What common man of his time would choose the pure grunt labor of the jobs he held to the sitting around that constituted our definition of relaxation? A man would have to be a fool to work if he didn't need the money; everybody knows that. It is commonly accepted that though professional people may derive pleasure from their jobs, blue-collar workers make their contribution to society simply to make a poor man's dollar. I am not suggesting that my daddy ever once woke in the morning with a strong desire to go to the mines and do his job. At the same time, I don't think it ever occurred to him to go in late or take a day off for no good reason.

I admire the combination of heart and backbone that made my daddy get up every morning at 4:30. An hour later, he'd drive himself and four other miners over winding mountain roads through all kinds of weather conditions to work the early shift at the mine. At 4:00 P.M. he reversed the process, hauling his carload back to Two-Mile and Greasy so that they could come home, clean up, and work in the garden or around the place before going to bed early in order to repeat the whole business the very next day.

Day after day after day of nothing but backbreaking labor and sameness wore many a man down, but once the circumstance was set, the choice of attitude was left to the individual, and there my daddy had them. The mine could set his hours. They could tell him what to do— and when and how to do it. But they had no control over how he would feel about it, so he did his work and paid close attention to it, as well as to much of what went on around him. In that watchful mode, he gathered little stories to bring home to share with us. While now and then he would bring a sweet treat for us in the corner of his lunch bucket, his stories were the real treat, frequent and funny. Even the sad ones had a funny spin on them. Daddy was always quick to laugh. It was his greatest strength. He often said that he had everything he'd ever thought of to want, and I think he genuinely believed that.

My daddy could build anything. Not only that, he could also fix anything that was broken or had quit for any reason. He did most of what he termed his "Jake-leg" work on weekends or evenings in fall or spring, when it was too late in the season for gathering or too early for grubbing. He'd come home from work in the afternoons around 4:30, wash the coal dust off him—Daddy never was one to use a bath house—eat a bite of supper, take his cup of coffee with him, and go off to construct or to repair. Sometimes the implement that was to be repaired or untangled was small enough so he could sit in a chair and pass the time with the rest of us while he worked at his leisure. Most times, however, he would work on the broken object just wherever it came to rest when it ran aground—inside the house, on the driveway, or in the backyard.

Since he drove—and hauled riders—twenty-some miles to and from the David coal mines five days a week, many of the repairs were car-oriented, and it seemed as if Daddy always had some kind of little car problem. Hollie Daniel, who lived about a half a mile up the creek from us, did the big car repairs, but Daddy didn't take the car to Hollie until he had determined that it would require a part that could not be put on without some equipment we didn't own. One Saturday when I was about nine years old, my daddy taught me a lesson in perseverance that went unnoticed for just a lot of life. One of the Pack boys had broken his power saw, decided he probably needed a new one anyway, and traded the old one to Daddy for some combination of carpentry tools—and maybe a pocket knife or two. Daddy was always trading off one thing or another with other fellows on Two-Mile or around on Greasy; trading off provided a regular pastime for a lot of the men. On this particular Saturday morning, Daddy had carried that saw across the backyard from the can house, where he'd kept it for a week or so, backed up behind other more pressing jobs essential to our day-to-day lives. Unlike essentials such as a broken refrigerator or a flat tire, scheduling the power saw repair had some give to it.

That Saturday morning, I watched Daddy break down his new power saw as I was throwing feed to the chickens, and he was putting it back together when Momma called us for lunch. After we had finished eating, Sister and I went to the can house for a couple of Mason jars so we could meet Gwen to catch crawdads in the creek out front. We tarried to watch as Daddy tried for the first time to start up the repaired saw. "Goddammit," he said, when he couldn't get a rise out of the thing by the third try. Just to be certain, he tried her one more time, then began—piece by piece—to break it down again. He was reassembling that saw as Sister went inside for a nap and Gwen and I shifted our attention from the apprehension of fractious crawdads to playing house over on the bank below the hog lot. This time he tried only twice to get the saw going before silently beginning to take it apart.

Late that afternoon, as Gwen and I began to turn out our final set of dirt cakes, Daddy once more tried in vain to fire up his saw. As I passed him to go help Momma cook supper, he slowly shook his head and muttered to himself, "Now, I'm not to be outdone." Daddy's project once again lay in pieces as I called him in to supper, and I don't recall his day's work being mentioned at the table, but he was at it again before Momma got all the dishes transferred from table to dishpan. I don't know what all my daddy did to that saw or even how many times he fooled with it, but he was putting it together again an hour or so later as I folded my dish towel and hung it to dry on the side of the drain board. Around ten that night, I was getting into my pajamas when I caught the first low whine from Daddy's all-Saturday project, but it was not by any means the last time I heard its keening. I don't believe he got another saw until after our house burned five or six years later. While the fire took everything else we had, that old saw survived by being in the trunk of Momma's car, and Daddy used it to rebuild the new house. My daddy was not to be outdone.

Along with just about everybody else, I always considered Momma to be a lot smarter than Daddy, because she read more, was a gatherer of facts and philosophies, and she never forgot a thing. In part that was our view because we were taught to believe that if smart counted, effort counted more. Daddy always said that being smart was secondary to the willingness to work at something until you figured it out. Daddy also did not believe a really smart person would ever show out, for to do so would be to put folks on notice that they had to watch out for you, making it less likely that you'd ever get what you were after. In Daddy's view, a worker could always get ahead by not worrying about what the other fellow was doing and just privately going about minding his own business and doing his own job. He really looked down on folks who thought they were somebody and couldn't keep from telling you about it.

Daddy had a cousin, Johnny K., who had gone away to Michigan to work the steel mills, married well, and made good in his father-in-law's construction business. He'd come driving his big old Chrysler home of a summer, stay for two or three days, and buy his mother a new refrigerator or bottled gas stove before he headed back north. He was maybe ten years older than Daddy, but they'd both grown up over on the head of Bob's Branch, so he always made sure to come by and see us when he was home. Johnny K. had two or three kids, though we never saw them; we never saw hide nor hair of his wife either. We understood that Johnny K. did bring his wife home one time right after the war, because Pop Pop remembered having seen her. He said she was a spindly little thing—quiet—not at all like big old, backslapping Johnny K.

Daddy was never one to talk about money—never said we had it, never said we didn't—but Momma would tell me from time to time when the family financial fortunes were particularly bad or good. One spring, when I was about thirteen years old, Momma confided that Daddy'd been able to get a lot of overtime the year before and had made nearly five thousand dollars. In the early fifties, that must have been considerably more money than folks in our community made—Momma always knew such things. She was clearly proud of that figure—wouldn't have bothered to tell me otherwise—and it sounded like about all the money in the world to me. I kept it to myself, of course, and I might well have forgotten all about it had it not been for the Johnny K. incident. A few months after Momma had imparted this wage information to me, I walked back across the road from an early evening water-fetching trip to find Johnny K. sitting in the yard with Daddy. As I stood at the well box drawing the second bucket of water, I had seen him pull in on the driveway and had only just edged my two-bucket load past his big black Chrysler, which was barely pulled off the road. Johnny K. never would pull his car all the way into our driveway—out of concern, he said, for whether "that little bridge will hold it." He made a point of saying that every time he came to see us, and nobody ever pointed out that the boy who brought our winter's coal routinely drove his fully loaded half-ton pickup across that "little bridge" without incident.

By the time I got my cargo in the house, poured me a glass of tea, and joined Daddy, Momma, Betty Holbrook, and Johnny K. in the yard, our guest from the north was into a full-tilt bragging fest. The four of them were sitting in those heavy, arch-backed, aluminum lawn chairs—the ones with the ninety-degree bent-back pipe supports—that Daddy had painted pink, and Sister was piddling around over on the rope swing about fifteen feet away. I spread out the old yellow towel I'd brought from inside there on the ground and plopped down on it. As I took the first sip of Momma's supersweet tea, cooled by the lone cube of ice (ice was not easy to come by in that long-ago Kentucky summer, so we rationed it very carefully), Johnny K. launched into a new story. He began, "You know, Lifie Jay, I give Uncle Sam more than five thousand dollars in income taxes this year," and he paused to allow this bit of information to sink in. Without missing a beat, Daddy slowly shook his head, said, "Aye, boys. Don't reckon you could loan a feller a couple bucks, could you?" We all laughed, and Johnny K. continued with his tale.

Incidentally, my daddy could hardly speak without cussing, so if I am to quote him I will use some words not acceptable in polite company. Be forewarned that in conversation Daddy referred to virtually every male, friend or not, as a "sumbitch." He did not differentiate, and I have heard him refer to both his brothers, whom he loved mightily, as "sumbitches." Indeed, if Sister or I had been a boy, I am sure he would have used that term about us. He also used the term "bousard," a word he'd heard some fellow miner use for "bastard," interchangeably with "sumbitch." In neither case was Daddy questioning the parentage of the one so designated, nor was he using the term in a derogatory fashion. That was just the way Daddy talked, and I grew up perceiving this as ordinary language. In those days, to call a man a son-of-a-bitch would get you a fight, but people seemed to know Daddy didn't mean anything by it, and I never heard anybody call him out for it. Daddy's use of profanity did not elicit the usual response, in part because my father was so imaginative in his swearing and everybody knew he did not intend to blackguard anybody. My daddy was constantly profane, never vulgar, for I do not think he had a leer in him.

Much of today's discourse strikes me as far more coarse than colorful—and lacks range, for that matter. I can be offended by some men's use of virtually any four-letter word or sexual innuendo, yet not be offended by hearing others use the vilest of terms. For me, the difference has to do with intent—the expression or attitude accompanying the words. Like, did the sumbitch smirk as he said his piece?

Whenever Daddy took us to the coal camp up near Middle Creek, he would drive by his past week's jobs and point out whatever he had been working on since we were last there—a roof patch on a house, maybe, a water line rerouted, some steps or a new building near one of the tipples. Daddy would discuss how big or small a job it had been, what problems he'd solved doing the work, and who had said what about it. He had two coworkers, Goble and Joby Puckett, who were friends of his, and, best I can recall, they were both hard workers who did not appreciate slackers. Daddy would report that this fellow or that one "got all red around the ass" because Joby had tried to get a little work out of him. Daddy was of the opinion that a man was either "worth a damn" or not, and he deemed the Puckett boys "worth a damn." The three of them shared the opinion that folks who didn't put their whole heart into their job might as well steal. "He ain't got a good day's work in him; sumbitch'd steal shit from a blind tumblebug" was Daddy's pronouncement about loafers. Daddy—and Goble and Joby, too, I suppose—worked as hard as they could all day, every day, and considered that to be their "full day's work for a full day's pay."

At some point, one of Daddy's bosses, an engineer, gave the men a plan for a set of steps that twisted their way up and around the hill between the tipple and the shop. Daddy said the three of them spent the better part of two days trying to follow the boss's plan. On the third day, Daddy had a plan of his own and, as he said, he "got tired of it [trying to follow the instructions] and just built the damned thing." He said this set of steps was within sight of the office up the hill, so the boss could have stopped the construction at any point during the day. Both Goble and Joby cautioned that they'd likely have to tear the whole thing out and rebuild it, but they went along with Daddy's plan. Just before quit time, the boss yelled down, "Preston!" then jerked his head to indicate that Daddy should walk up to his office. Daddy said, "I figured the sumbitch was going to ask me when I reckoned they made me the boss." Instead, the engineer asked Daddy to explain, "How in the hell did you do that?" Daddy said he couldn't explain it; he just did it. At that point, the boss admitted he had watched the men work on that project for three days but had no idea how to draw up a plan that would solve the problem. On one of our company store trips to the coal camp, Daddy showed us the steps and the crooks and turns that gave them a problem. He then remarked that the boss praised Daddy's "good eye." After that day, the story was never mentioned again, and Daddy would not have approved of any of us bringing it up. He was proud of doing a good job but would have been embarrassed if any of us had told anybody.

Over the years he worked different mines, Daddy was offered a bossing job or two but refused to take one, because he didn't see himself as one who could get work out of anybody but himself. Momma never understood why he resisted such opportunities and perennially made the case for bossing. In a letter to Grandma Emmy postmarked January 8, 1940-something (the year was illegible), Momma wrote of Daddy's being offered "the carpenter boss's job at Big Sandy—ten miles below here & the best house in the camp." He did not take that job or any other position of responsibility, ever. Even when he had his own construction company, Daddy was reluctant to see himself as anybody's supervisor. He hired men he knew to be hard workers and competent builders, then worked alongside them, the only goal being to complete the structure. His position was that if you got good, hard-working men in the first place, no "bossing" was necessary.

Throughout the West Virginia years, Daddy's eyes were forever turned toward Two-Mile, and when he was offered the job at Princess Elkhorn Mine at David, it was considered a blessing for our whole family. Princess Elkhorn was a union mine, which meant the money was good and it was close enough to Two-Mile so we could live at home.

I don't know what his earlier policy might have been, but from the time he went to work on Middle Creek (David) for Princess Elkhorn Coal Company, Daddy hardly ever picked up his check the day it was issued. The miners didn't get a pay stub with their money. Instead, a few days before payday they received a statement that reflected how many hours of work the miner had put in and the hourly wage for this. There was also a section for what was taken out of the payday. This section showed any purchases from the company store, visits to the company doctor, or any other outstanding expenses that went against the payday. Now and again somebody would ask Daddy, "How many hours of overtime was on your last statement?" They were much more likely to ask it that way rather than ask how much overtime he'd put in.

As I recall, the mine paid after 5:00 P.M. on Friday evening, about an hour or so after Daddy's shift, so he usually waited to pick up his money on Monday. While in those days Momma and Daddy didn't have a savings account, Daddy tried to keep enough cash on hand to take care of unexpected emergencies. About once every month, all four of us would clean ourselves up and go up to David to pick up Daddy's paycheck.

Though we said we were going to get Daddy's money, the real purpose of the trip was to shop the company store—and to catch up on what Daddy had been working on lately. After I became a teenager, I always pleaded to stay home, but that never happened. Once I saw that I couldn't beg my way out of going, however, I enjoyed these little Saturday outings; we all did. What's more, I don't believe Daddy and Momma ever made that trip alone. If they went, Sister and I went, too.

With today's two-career family and round-the-clock work schedules, it is commonly thought that time and effort spent at work takes away from time invested in relationships with family and friends. While Daddy and Momma were seldom idle, I never felt that either of them neglected me or spent too little time with me. From my earliest memories, all four of us spent Saturday together, whether it was spent working at the house or in the garden, going to town for supplies, or going to David for Daddy's paycheck. As a teenager, I hated this practice, for it meant I could not spend Saturday—and a great many evenings—with my friends.

Daddy was funny turned when it came to his family. If one of us went somewhere, we all went. That was true for the company store trips, the movies, the country music jamboree, and just about any other form of relaxation, right down to sitting in the yard. While such a practice was not a favorite of mine when I was a teenager, I have no doubt that is why I grew up so close to the other three members of my family. No matter how whiny I might have been about being required to stick so close, it was left to me to get over it, because my attitude would not make one bit of difference in our activities.

After Grandma Emmy died, Daddy bought the Mollette home place from Momma's brothers and sisters. By the time he was laid off at David in 1962, Daddy had built a spec house about five hundred yards across Greasy Creek, above Grandma Emmy's. When he sold that house, he built and sold another one, then another, and folks began contracting with him to build them a house. As Daddy put it, he "went out on the road" as a builder. Then around 1965, Daddy bought the Sant Preston Branch, a hollow nearer to town than to Two-Mile. He scooped out that gully, built himself a house at the mouth of the branch, and began stringing houses, one by one, up his newly created hollow. He christened this project Preston Estates, and though you'd never hear him admit it, my daddy was inordinately proud of himself. In what could now accurately be called his "building business"—a.k.a. Preston Construction—Daddy had been joined by four or five ol' boys who worked as hard as he did. When he went out on the road, the first to join his building crew was Capp Walters, a former coal miner and lifelong resident of Two-Mile. Capp worked with Daddy from the first house he built through the end of his building business, and they worked together as well as Daddy and the Puckett boys from David.

Despite the fact that he was down sick for the better part of two decades, my daddy never gave up the dream of going back into the building business, and the last summer of his life he spoke to me of his and Capp's plans to "go back out on the road." Though he was never able to return to business, in the dementia that characterized his last months Daddy still "worked" alongside Capp and Spud and the others who had shared with him the best days of his life. It comforts Sister and me to know that even Alzheimer's was unable to eradicate Daddy's good humor, his work ethic, and his time "out on the road."

Daddy's good eye manifested itself at least one other time that we know about. When my son was about five years old, he—accompanied by Sister and her husband—had meandered up the branch so that Daddy could walk back home with them and show them the houses he and his crew had been building. As they passed by one of the houses under construction, Daddy called out to one of the men to check the pitch on the roof. The man assured Daddy that the pitch was perfect, and all those walking with Daddy said it looked fine to them. Daddy thought, however, that the pitch might be a "little off" and asked that the workers measure it. Sure enough, the pitch was a little off, and they had to tear it out and redo. My daddy had a good eye.

Daddy also had a history of "doing for" people, but most of the stories of his doing we found out about by accident. He simply did and never said anything about it. Some stories folks told us after Daddy was dead, but now and then I got in on a secret simply by overhearing something I shouldn't.

Sometime in the early nineties, I was on one of my monthly trips home to see to Momma and Daddy. By that time, both my parents were very fragile and had caregivers staying with them. Since Daddy required daily visits to the doctor's office to use the breathing machine he needed to treat his black lung disease, Momma usually accompanied him, with the caregiver driving. When I was home I would take Daddy to the doctor's office to give Momma and the caregiver the opportunity to stay home. On this particular day, I had gone out and warmed up Daddy's old Mustang, got him bundled in his flannel jacket and hat and into the car, and fussed with him about wearing his seatbelt. I backed the car out of the driveway and changed gears from reverse to drive when it died on me. Then, try as I might, I could not get the Mustang to start again. Daddy said, "Just leave 'er right here and get your Maw to call [old so-and-so]. He'll take care of it and we'll just take the big car." I so instructed the caregiver, installed Daddy and me in the Cadillac, and went on to the doctor.

When we returned, the Mustang was fixed and in the carport. As soon as I got Daddy into the house, he told me to go back over to town, gas up the Cadillac, and pay old so-and-so for the repair. I drove back to town marveling to myself at how we got some fellow to make a house call at nine in the morning, that he did it so quickly, and that he had apparently not insisted on immediate payment before returning to the service station. Fifteen minutes later, I pulled up to the gas pumps of what had been Doug's Service Station. Old so-and-so was the present owner, and when he came out to gas up the Cadillac, he asked, "How's Lifie Jay?" I said Daddy was about the same, explained that I was there to get gas and take care of the Mustang's repair, and told him how much I appreciated his coming out to the house to take care of Daddy's car. After he'd finished filling the gas tank, I gave him my credit card and told him to put the repair charges on there, too. When old so-and-so brought the credit card slip for me to sign, I noticed there was no charge for anything but gasoline. When I questioned him about this he said, "Aye, wasn't much to be done."

"But," I argued, "I need to pay you for coming out to the house."

"Lifie Jay's done a thing or two for me," he said, turned, and went back into his service station.

The concept of neighborliness and the behaviors that constituted such a concept anchored our value system on Two-Mile. Moreover, that neighborliness did not extend merely to those who lived within sight of the house. In 1953, Kentucky Route 40 between Paintsville and Inez wound its narrow way down Two-Mile, bisecting the distance between my house and Gwen Holbrook's. Traffic was limited and foot travel was the norm, so unless we saw an oncoming car, we tended to walk on the blacktop. One day, Momma, Sister, and I had been over to Aunt Exer's and were walking back across the road to our house. I walked in front, carrying two buckets of water, with Momma following closely behind me holding six-year-old Sister's hand. Heading east on the south side of the road, our backs to eastbound traffic, we talked back and forth with Aunt Exer, Bud, and Gwen, who were sitting up on their porch about thirty feet above the road. I passed the stand of tiger lilies that grew about ten feet west of our driveway, with Momma and Sister walking maybe five feet behind me. As we strolled along, passing the time of day with our neighbors, Elster Sizemore's taxi picked off Sister, tore her loose from Momma's hand, and landed her fat little bottom right smack-dab in that stand of tiger lilies. Though the Holbrooks saw the car coming, they didn't think to warn us, because the road was clear in all directions and we were way off to the side. At the time it was not that funny.

Just about as soon as Sister's hind end landed in the lily patch, Momma grabbed her up, sat Gwen and me in the backseat of our old Plymouth, and took out for the hospital. Sister was lying in the front seat with her head in Momma's lap, of course.

Momma drove like a wild woman—she never was much for slow driving even on a regular day—and we made it to the hospital in record time. Elster and Ernestine Sizemore, fully remorseful, got there about ten minutes behind us. Sister wasn't bad hurt—just a little cut in the outer corner of her left eye. She got an eye patch, drank a cup of orange juice, and was hardly even shaken. By the time we got back home it was clear that the biggest damage was that the event had scared the fool out of half of Two-Mile.

About an hour after we got home from the hospital, Daddy got in from the mines to find a house full. There was a gaggle of Holbrooks, Wards, and Wallens with Sister all cagged-up in the bed enjoying being the center of attention. Momma babied that girl till she was thirty—not that I care, of course. It's true that Daddy might have been accustomed to some assortment of the aforementioned neighbors being there at the house when he got home, but pulling into his own driveway and finding himself parked behind one of maybe three taxis in Johnson County was a first. Though technically the taxi driver was a Two-Mile resident, in that he received his mail at the local post office, you couldn't say he was close in kin or companionship to any of us.

Elster Sizemore lived—with his much younger wife, Ernestine—about a mile up the creek from us near the head of Two-Mile, right about the base of Two-Mile Hill. We didn't know Elster and Ernestine very well— just saw them over at the post office from time to time. Word of mouth held that Elster owned his own taxi, which he drove over in town. Not much of a living could be made driving a taxi in Paintsville, Kentucky (population 4,500), in 1953, but it was rumored that one or more of the three or four cab drivers might have supplemented their income by selling a little whiskey out of their taxis. I'm not implying that Elster bootlegged out of his taxi, because we sure never did know that much about him. I'm not sure who Elster's people were, but he did live near— and was supposedly affiliated with—the John Earl Cantrell family. The Cantrells were known to be bootleggers, and John Earl had been sent to the pen at least once for selling whiskey, but I still couldn't say with certainty that Elster had a thing to do with that.

Well, it turned out that one of the reasons Elster was hovering so close up might have had more to do with self-preservation than concern for Baby Sister's welfare. Though Elster himself was a grown man nearing forty, apparently Ernestine—who was at the wheel when the taxi ran down Sister—was barely sixteen and just learning to drive. Still, the situation would not have been so troublesome for the Sizemores had Ernestine managed to avail herself of a learner's permit prior to her unfortunate encounter with Sister's tail end. All this information revealed itself in one form or another over the course of that extended afternoon.

Later that evening, I lurked just inside the back screen door and heard Elster explaining to Daddy just what was at stake. The two men were standing between the back door and the can house, and Elster first asked Daddy if he'd like "a little drink of whiskey." Daddy declined, saying, "Nah, buddy. Not tonight, I reckon." Then Elster Sizemore promised my daddy everything but his first-born son not to report the accident to the police. I also recall exactly what Daddy said then: "Aye, bud, don't worry about it." And he continued to repeat that phrase as Elster offered to pay the emergency room bill, buy Sister some new clothes to replace the ones she was wearing, and give the Prestons free taxi service anytime to anywhere. Daddy continued to refuse each offer, until finally he just said, "Hell, it coulda happened to anybody. Go on to the house. That girl's fine. It's took care of." And that was the end of that.

Though nobody ever knew about it, my daddy kept a diary of sorts—a history, if you will—by writing down what he spent, and where. He used no words, just dates and numbers, but in those figures he kept a running tab of his world. When he died, there they were—those tiny, blue-lined notebooks full of penciled-in dates and numbers. You'd think a man who'd do that was stingy, trying to keep count of his money. But not my daddy. I think he was trying to keep count of his time more than his money and he was just better with figures than with words. Those figures he left us tell stories about Daddy, stories about my family and what we valued, and when.

No, Daddy wasn't tightfisted with his money, not one bit. He was constantly doing some little something for somebody—nearly always something that cost him money as well as time. In truth, he was one of the most generous people I've ever known, always picking up the check before anybody else could grab it. Until he died, he continued to try to help out Sister and me financially—long after such help was good for us. After his death, his old desk yielded a drawerful of second mortgages folks had never paid off. Some of those papers were on houses he had built thirty years before he died. He'd penciled in on each mortgage how much and when if there'd been any payment. But for every one of those marked paid-in-full and duly dated, there were two with no mark on them at all, and another with payments that gradually got smaller and finally ended.

Sister and I did nothing about those pieces of paper, because we wanted to carry out Daddy's wishes, and we figured if he'd intended to get the money out of those folks he'd have done so—but I kept those papers, every one of them. Who, after all, can throw away a father's diary, so meticulously kept? He was my daddy—tied to me by blood and time, and love that translated into figures penciled into notebooks that will survive the both of us—and I hope his legacy of generosity will endure.

Daddy was typical of a number of eastern Kentuckians; he loved his home and his family, and if he could have made it so, he'd have continued the patch-off tradition right on into the thirtieth century. While Momma encouraged Sister and me to go off and live away, Daddy was just the opposite. It was only in the last years of her life, when she thought Sister and I needed to come home and take care of her and Daddy, that Momma got upset about our living at a distance, but Daddy never came to terms with our being gone from home. He genuinely believed the old "blood's thicker than water" dictum, and if Sister or I had married men able to take up carpentry work, Daddy would have given them everything he had to get them started and on their way to making a living. He'd 'a put them out on the road in a minute.

There are probably a lot of things I don't know about my daddy, but I know he belonged to eastern Kentucky with all that was in him. He spent time working in West Virginia, but like many native Appalachians, there was not a moment spent away that he was not longing for home. And it wasn't that he didn't want to see other places—indeed, he managed to visit all the lower forty-eight states—but I don't believe he would have moved anywhere else so long as he had any alternative way to stay at home. Even downstate Kentucky was a foreign country to my daddy. As he said often, "[Eastern Kentucky] is the prettiest place they is." And that's the way he said it, too, using "they" for "there," though he knew the difference.

Momma and Daddy were married for fifty-eight years, separated only when Daddy couldn't find work at home and had to go over to West Virginia. From the time he got on at David around 1950 until Momma had to be hospitalized for a few days in 1986, I don't believe they spent one night apart. During my lifetime, my father always used "they" for "there," "h[y]erd" for "heard," "hoss-peetal" for "hospital," and "seegretts" for "cigarettes." Meanwhile, though her hill-country accent was almost as thick as Daddy's, Momma's grammar was damn near flawless. I don't think I ever heard my mother make a grammatical error, and she was quick to correct Sister and me if we did, but I never once heard her correct my father.

My parents were very different from each other, and they each brought various strengths to their union, but I learned from watching them that although loving somebody is important, respect and kindness are a significant part of the mix of marriage. Over the years, I heard Daddy and Momma disagree on a number of issues, but they were united in believing that the man makes a living and the woman makes a home. That made my daddy the worst kind of chauvinist—the kind who protects his women and in so doing infantilizes and cripples them. He protected my mother right into her grave.

I do not doubt that Daddy would willingly have died for Momma, Sister, or me. I think that's why he pleaded with the army to reexamine him so he could join the service. The very fact that he knew he was asking to be sent overseas with an ocean between him and the home and family he loved speaks to the seriousness of his commitment to his country and to the protection of his family.

I believe Daddy was proud of Sister's and my willingness to work, but I also know in reason that he was relieved both times I married. Relieved! Daddy honestly believed I needed a man to stand between me and the world, because in his view, a husband's primary role was to furnish protective custody of his wife and children. Everything I believe I know about men I learned from my daddy, and I suppose I have him to thank—or blame—for the fact that I believe that as a group men have been judged harshly. See, Daddy was terribly chauvinistic, but he was that way out of his sense of duty to protect his girls from the world's dangers. What's more, if he'd had his way, Sister and I would have lived next door and our children would have moved in right on the other side of us.

My daddy never sired a boy, which living in that place at that time cast a poor light on his manhood. I know what that had to mean to him, though he never let on. Considering the way Sister and I turned out, both fully employed every day of our postcollege lives, I also know he could not have felt very good about our lack of success as wives and mothers either. It never occurred to me, however, to doubt Daddy's love for either of us. Clearly, he loved us—and Momma—unconditionally. Both Sister and I gave his surname to our sons as middle names, which carried on the Preston line as best we could. In all honesty, I never thought a lot about my daddy and the son thing, though when I was a young girl, some neighbor or another would bring it up in a teasing way.

Then, in the spring of '94, Momma got herself in the hospital, and I got one of those "Sister, we got trouble" phone calls that signaled an immediate trip home. We already had two dependable women alternating shifts to care for Momma and Daddy, but Sister went on ahead to stay at the hospital with Momma. Arriving late that night, I picked up a car at the Lexington airport and drove directly to the hospital, where Momma didn't seem all that bad off but was talking out of her head, as they say. I relieved Sister on the night shift to sit with Momma. Over the course of the night Momma's head seemed to clear some, so when the doctor came by the next morning he said she could go home that afternoon. Then he told us he wasn't nearly as concerned about Momma as about Daddy. It seems Daddy had been forgetting things—like where home was and who he was. In the doctor's opinion, this periodic forgetfulness, in addition to his being practically blind, caused Daddy to be incapable of driving. He said he had talked to Momma and Daddy about it but couldn't persuade Daddy to surrender his car keys. The next step was abundantly clear to any thinking being: Daddy had to be prevented from driving again. What's more, he never would listen to Sister—she was the baby—so I had to be the one to take his car keys. Such a moment has to be seen in the light of my daddy's history with cars.

In the early thirtie, cars were a rarity in Johnson County, but Pop Pop bought one for his baby boy, which gave Daddy a lot of freedom before he had a lick of sense about what to do with it. Daddy admitted that he all but quit school right then, choosing instead to use his new wheels to chauffeur local folks from place to place. After an extended period of nonattendence, Daddy returned to school and was told to report to the principal's office to account for his absences. He ignored this command. He left without seeing the principal and never went back to school. After that, Daddy did pick-up day labor and carpentry work with Pop Pop until he went to work in the mines in the early forties, but he continued to hire out to those needing a ride.

The fact that he always owned a car was one thing that set Daddy apart from many of the young men of his day. Over the years, however many financial setbacks our family might have suffered, he always managed to keep a car. Though he took a bus to West Virginia, once he got work he came home and got his car, and that car only returned to Kentucky two or three times until we came home to Two-Mile to live in '46. Most of our travel back and forth between Kentucky and West Virginia during the war involved catching the train in Welch, riding to Kermit, and then taking the bus from Kermit to the mouth of Greasy and walking the half mile or so to Grandma Emmy's house. Meanwhile, Daddy's hand-polished Plymouth sat collecting coal dust, pulled in beside the coal pile at the edge of the yard of Aunt Polly Blevins's boardinghouse on Pitch Holler in Hemphill, West Virginia. There was no gas for the two-hundred-mile round trip, and if there had been, it's doubtful that the little Plymouth would have been up to the monthly trip to Kentucky. Still, Daddy had reason for wanting his wheels in the coal camp.

Every Sunday, we would dress up—memories and pictures show Daddy in a suit and tie—and Daddy would drive us into Welch, where we'd have Sunday dinner at the Blue Swan Café. Afterward, we would drive out to the country around Welch, sometimes to construction sites or other mining camps, sometimes to more rural spots, where Daddy would park and we'd sit in the car and watch the people. This people-watching proclivity did not change when we moved back to Kentucky. Daddy's favorite Sunday afternoon activity involved piling the four of us into whatever Plymouth he owned at the time and driving to Flat Gap, Oil Springs, or beyond. Occasionally we'd stop along the road somewhere for Sister and me to wade the creek or take each other's picture standing in the highway, sitting on the bumper, or leaning on a road sign.

Sometimes we'd wander as far as Broke Leg Falls, down past Salyersville, where a one-hundred-foot waterfall rushed down the mountain face into a ravine. I don't know why it was called Broke Leg except, maybe, that was the name of the creek, and I suppose somebody or another must have broken his leg there in some far off time. I just know it was a long, long way to drive, and we didn't go there often. It remained one of Daddy's favorite places, though, and along with Hungry Mother State Park over in Virginia, was Daddy's standard comment on any of Sister's or my far-flung travels. When Sister and her husband, Michael, came home with stories of a summer spent riding trains through Europe and Scandinavia, Daddy'd say, "Well, you coulda stayed home and gone with your Maw and me to Broke Leg Falls and Hungry Mother Park."

In her later years, the sole topic that competed with health concerns in Momma's conversation was her itemized recounting of their travels.

Though Momma loved to tell in minute detail about their several car trips all over the North American continent, each time Daddy was asked about them, he'd say, "Never saw nothin' to beat Broke Leg Falls or Hungry Mother Park." He was teasing, of course, for such was my daddy's way. We knew he was impressed with the Grand Canyon, as well as the canyons of Wall Street. He drove one Cadillac or another to both, for he wanted to see it all. Then, however, he wanted to come home, home to the hills of eastern Kentucky. Broke Leg Falls and Hungry Mother Park were representative of the land he loved. Daddy was part of those old green forests, with their virgin timber and rushing waters that bubbled and frothed unexpectedly out of the rocky soil. And always, his car of the moment was an extension of his body, enabling him to go and see whatever he had a mind to go see.

French philosopher Jean-Paul Sartre said something along the lines of freedom being what you do with what's been done to you. Despite his never breaking the traces and just taking off, my daddy was a free man in that he did everything he did because he wanted to. I don't think he ever once felt trapped by his life's circumstances. Neither his exhausting job nor his burdensome family broke his spirit, for he always knew he could run if he wanted to. He had a car and he could use it. Instead of using his wheels to get away from us, however, Daddy included us in everything that was important to him, much of which began and ended within a day's driving distance of Two-Mile. If our Sunday drive was bounded by Johnson County and we didn't stop by to pass the time with some relative who was sitting in his yard, we'd circle back around to Paintsville. There, Daddy would park in one of those diagonal parking places in front of the courthouse across from G.C. Murphy's five-and-dime, and we'd sit for a couple of hours to watch the people. In those days, the stores were not open on Sunday, so it was always easy to get a good parking space. The best parking spots were close to—but not directly in front of—the corner restaurant, which was open on Sundays.

We brought along books—and sometimes Bonnie Butcher, Bud, or Gwen Holbrook—and we passed the afternoon sitting around in the car. Sometimes Momma would send me into the restaurant to get a Coke for us to share, and now and then some peanuts, but I don't recall much eating going on. When I was maybe nine, I recall reading "'Twas the Night before Christmas" to my three-year-old sister so many times that every line of it is still embossed on my memory more than fifty years hence. Now and then, somebody we knew would come by, perhaps Uncle Burns newly freed from his confinement in the courthouse jail due to another overspirited Friday or Saturday night, or some other soul just passing the time of day walking around the block.

It always began the same way. Sunday dinner over, Daddy would say to Momma, "Want to take a run over around the block?" Momma would respond, "Ki-i-i-ds?" and Sister and I would scurry for our coats, books, and paper dolls, as I appealed to "ask Gwen?" Sometimes we could ask somebody to go with us, and sometimes we couldn't. The final decision rested with Daddy, and the request had to be made anew each Sunday. What's more, this trip was never taken for granted, despite the fact that it occurred with weekly regularity whenever the weather was mild enough so we could sit comfortably in coats and mittens. These excursions were not boring either, for a variety of activities took place during those afternoons, as well as disagreements, conversation, and laughter.

When I was about eleven, I got one of those one-foot-square weaving looms for Christmas, and while sitting on the courthouse square watching the people, I made red pot holders for half of Two-Mile. Though we didn't dress up for our Sunday afternoon outings, we were not in our everyday clothes either. I recall practically ruining a nearly new pair of black patent Mary-Janes in a grab-and-struggle with Sister over a bottle of dime-store bubble mixture. Sister may have been six years my junior, but she was a strong little booger, and Momma never did discipline her properly, even when she ruined my paper doll Betty Grable's famous legs by bending her at the knees. To this day Sister and I have issues, many of which began in the backseat of the deep blue '49 Plymouth as we Prestons spent one more Sunday afternoon of togetherness.

Daddy's car, then, was more than a simple possession. It was a sign of his success and a symbol of his freedom. After the doctor told me I had to take his car keys, I drove that big white-on-white Cadillac with spoke wheels and Continental kit back to the last house Daddy built for himself in the subdivision that bore his name. As I pulled in on the driveway, he was sitting in a frayed, green-striped, nylon lawn chair on the front porch, smoking his cigarette. I went directly into the house, got myself a Diet Pepsi, poured Daddy a fresh cup of coffee, and returned to the porch to sit on the steps. First, I told Daddy that the doctor had said Momma could come home, so Sister would bring her on home as soon as they could get her released. Then I told my daddy—the man who had been responsible for taking care of himself and the three women in his life for as far back as I could remember—that he could no longer drive his car.

If I had it to do over, I'd have had my son, Brett Preston, deliver this bit of news to his grandpa. Still, like most things that have broken my heart, I was right in the middle of it before I had any idea. Even Daddy's death—Momma's too, for that matter—didn't hit me as hard as that one conversation. Daddy still had periods of being himself, and he was nearly blind by then, but he knew exactly what I was saying. He could no longer take care of Momma. He couldn't even take care of himself. And he wasn't going anywhere . . . ever again.

Daddy's achievements surrounded him on that porch. We were sitting on land he loved, in a house he built, within thirty feet of his latest Cadillac when it hit me: If a man like my daddy has to hear this kind of news, he should hear it from a son.

There's a new road going through the River Narrows now, going past Sant Preston Branch, bisecting the two subdivisions Daddy developed. The state is taking a couple of sections along the edge of his land, cutting off the rock cliff across from his new house, taming the curve of Kentucky Route 40, and moving the road closer to Daddy's living room. As the construction has progressed these past three years, a number of folks have said things like, "It's a good thing poor old Jay isn't here to see what the road's doing to his property." I answer, "Yeah, well . . ." because that's what Daddy would say.

Truth is, Sister and I—and Gwen and Wallace too—believe Daddy would be tickled to death if he could see what's happening to his place. If he'd lived to see this, he'd have sat right there in his front yard—in all the dust and the noise—and watched those workers blow that hillside all to hell. At the end of the day, once the workers went home at quit time, Daddy'd have moseyed over to see what they'd accomplished that day. He'd have gone over—not to opine about it to anybody—just to look close at it and figure out for himself how they'd go about accomplishing such a feat. In any sort of construction, Daddy loved to look at what had been done and try to sight it out for himself. As a family, we were just as likely to drive to construction sites as to natural settings, for our daddy was about as impressed with the wonders of man as he was with the wonders of nature. During the construction of Dewey Dam, up near Prestonsburg, Sister and I roamed the environs of that site for many more hours than either of us ever spent later on enjoying the lake created by it.

The really notable thing about the River Narrows project is that it's right there, right in Daddy's doorway—all the digging, and blasting, and clearing away, and straightening up. Not only would it have provided him constant entertainment, Daddy could have watched all that and would not even have needed his driver's license.

We lost Daddy four or five years before the breath went out of him, lying in his rented hospital bed there in the master bedroom of the first house he built on Sant Preston Branch. Earlier we'd brought him and Momma home to die and replicated as nearly as possible the situation they'd lived in for the past twenty years, but they were both too sick to lie in their own beds. While Daddy was too bad off to know much of anything, Momma was at herself enough to throw a fit about the two hospital beds that replaced her white-with-gold-trim, queen-sized bed we put into storage. That was just like Momma, too, that throwing a fit. You'd think somebody old and sick would plead or maybe just ask nicely for her own bed, but that was not my momma's way. She, by God, knew what was what, and we shouldn't question it. For all that was or may have been wrong with her, my momma's everlasting stubbornness killed her.

I think my mother would be alive to this day if it hadn't been for her resolute denial of Daddy's condition. While it's true that Daddy's mind came and went for three or four years, the last couple of years of his life he was gone more often than not. Momma would call me home and say we had to "do something," but she never allowed us to reach the logical conclusion. That being that Daddy—or she and Daddy—had to be moved to an extended-care facility. After a lifetime of being right more often than not, Momma was so accustomed to being the final arbiter of all questions that she was not open to suggestion. The implication of being asked to "do something" was that my opinion would be taken into consideration, but that was not Momma's way. Admittedly there's enough of her in me to make me just as intractable, which meant that on this subject we quickly reached an impasse. While Sister is somewhat more malleable, she suffers from being the baby of the Preston family, which meant her opinion counted for less than anybody's.

For my whole life, my mother hid her own wishes behind Daddy's position in our little family constellation, and that very spot ended up killing her. Ostensibly, Daddy was always the one in control in that his word was law and he always had final say, but anybody with a lick of sense could see that Daddy always relied on Momma's judgment of just about everything. Once Momma weighed in, Daddy would then decide on an issue, and though he didn't often disagree with Momma, when he did there was no argument. Period. I don't recall my mother ever telling me what she thought about anything without couching it in terms of Daddy's opinion. She'd say, "Your daddy thinks" this, or "Your daddy was so ashamed of" that. And frankly, this method was very effective in shaping my behavior, since I'd do almost anything to keep from shaming my daddy. The problem was that once Daddy lost his ability to make coherent judgments, our family dynamic just went all to hell; the center would not hold.

Whenever I would suggest that they move to an extended-care facility, perhaps one with different levels of care for her and Daddy, she'd say, "That would kill your daddy. He wants to be right here at home."

I would point out—often with Sister sitting there backing me up— that "Momma, Daddy doesn't know where he is anyway. He's all the time saying, 'Grace, let's go to the house.' He doesn't know me and Sister and sometimes not even you. Now, you know that, Momma."

"He's just having a bad day," she'd respond. "He's just fine when we're here by ourselves. Having those girls [the two caregivers] in the house upsets him. You know he never did like for anybody to be in the house but family. If you were just around here to see him when the girls aren't around, you'd see he's fine."

Momma and I—and sometimes Sister—had this conversation dozens of times over the last two years of her life. Right up to the end, she persisted in believing that Daddy's mind would return to him if Sister or I would just come home and take the place of the caregivers. Momma had such confidence in her ability to know what was proper, what was perfect, that the only person she ever listened to was Daddy. Once she had convinced him of the accuracy of her judgment, she relied on Daddy's power to carry it out, especially within the family. The problem was that she never learned to listen to Sister's ideas or mine; she simply presented whatever conclusion she had reached as Daddy's and expected us to agree to it. Most of the time Sister and I did indeed go along with what our daddy suggested, not simply because we loved him, but also because he had an unerring common sense that we had learned to respect.

My daddy, Lifie Jay Preston, was as clear a thinker as I've ever met—just cut right through the BS to the heart of things. Sister or I would tell him some big-eyed tale about what we'd seen or heard or planned, embellishing as we went along, of course. He would respond with an "mm-hmm" or two. When we finished puffing it all up for him, he'd give us one of those fish-eyed looks, kind of shake his head, and say, "Now, you're th' doctor." Sister and I have grown fond of saying that same thing to our adult children—and to each other, on occasion—when their projects seem bigger than their proofs. When we say that, our kids just roll their eyes, because they know we would not recommend going forward, which, in their view, means we just don't understand.

The truth is that Sister and I respected our daddy's opinion, but we also respected Momma's input into Daddy's decisions. Daddy was the executive branch of our family, but we never doubted that every piece of legislation was drafted by Momma. The only person she ever relied upon was Daddy, and once he lost his ability to conceive and consider, their checks-and-balances system was over. Though our family dynamic was always powered by Momma, she could not get her head around the idea that she had to make decisions and carry them out without Daddy in the next room or without Daddy's judgment made explicit in her every word. For all her illnesses, real or imagined, the loss of Daddy's protective custody killed Momma.

My mother's story—a story of a woman born fifteen years into the twentieth century, dying before the sun rose on the twenty-first—is in some ways a cautionary tale, for it tells of a woman who never once put herself, her desires, or her needs above her family's. She shared that habit, I think, with most rural, hill-country women of that day. Not until the generation after mine were female children allowed—no, *encouraged*—to develop the virtue of selfishness necessary to gain independence. That my mother missed out on that saddens me more than I can say. Then again, the same could be said for Momma's sisters. Though two of them were widowed before middle age, they had been so instilled with the virtue of female selflessness that they spent their whole lives doing for others rather than asking themselves what they might like to do. Still, Momma seems to me to have been most nearly the victim of the times, since she was the only one to have been so utterly taken care of—by Daddy, of course.

Though Momma did teach for a brief time, just before and after she married Daddy, she was the only one of Grandma Emmy's girls who never had to be responsible for financially supporting herself. None of her sisters kept the kind of meticulous house, made (sewed) clothes and draperies, or raised and put up vegetables as well as Momma did. Though it must be said that Aunt Lizzie was a better cook, I'd put Momma's baked goods up against anybody's. I take after my mother in just about every way but can't hold a candle to her in any area domestic.

Much as we favored one another, my mother's road to reality was hardly ever wide enough for me to travel. While our noses might be pointed in the same direction, our meaning-making instruments were tuned to such divergent frequencies that as far back as I can remember, the two of us could look straight at the same thing and call it something different. Still, I always trusted her intelligence. Her ability to tell *what* was acute and unerring; her explanations of *why*, however, lost me every time.

My mother was a very special person, one of the most enigmatic characters I have ever known. Perhaps all of us think our mothers are special simply because they gave birth to us and mothered us into existence, but Momma—in all her complexities—Lord, she was a piece of work. Momma was a Freewill Baptist who lived her early years at Three Forks of Greasy Creek, married Daddy, and moved to Two-Mile Creek, where she spent most of her life. With the exception of the six years when she lived off and on in a coal camp at Hemphill, West Virginia, my mother spent nearly eight decades in Johnson County, Kentucky. Though she lived out her life on Two-Mile Creek, my momma was not your typical hill-country woman.

In the fifties on Two-Mile, most of our neighbor women adopted an appearance far older than their years. They did not wear slacks or shorts, and their dresses covered their upper arms as well as most of their calves. They wore no makeup, pulled their graying hair back in a twist, and covered their heads with sunbonnets when they worked the garden. Most of my friends' mothers did not drive, and nobody's mother smoked cigarettes. In contrast, Momma smoked two packs of cigarettes every day, her lips and fingertips gleamed bright red, her hairstyle reflected perms and peroxide, and her red short-shorts were outrageous enough to cause Grandma Emmy to forbid her to wear them when she came to work the garden at Greasy. She died in a pale blue silk chiffon gown and negligee typical of those she wore every night of her married life.

Momma was smart, hard-working, hypochondriacal, good-hearted, judgmental, fun-loving, beautiful, and believed with all her being that if a person worked hard enough she could achieve perfection. If she had put a priority on those qualities, I believe my mother would have owned up to each attribute, but not in that sequence. The order is mine. On her list, Momma would have put "beautiful" first, always first. For all her life, she kept her person as physically attractive as was humanly possible.

I suppose Momma would list "hard-working" second on her list of important qualities. Consider her schedule on a typical Kentucky August Tuesday in the early fifties. After arising at four o'clock; stirring up a dried beef, eggs, biscuits, and sawmill gravy breakfast for Daddy; getting him off to work; making their bed; and straightening the house, she'd wake Sister and me. While we ate, she made our beds, fed the cats and dogs, and while we cleaned ourselves up, she washed breakfast dishes. She would then drive us around to Greasy to pick white half-runner beans at sunrise, be canning those half-runners by 10:00 A.M., and spend the afternoon ironing the clothes she'd washed and starched on Monday.

By the time Daddy returned from the mines around 4:00 P.M., Momma would have supper cooking on the stove, and she, Sister, and I would be as freshly cleaned and pressed as yesterday's wash hanging in the closet. Daddy never came home to a messy house or a wife with a hair out of place, never. This was accomplished in the days when we didn't even have water in the house and all the water for cooking, canning, and bathing was heated on a big black coal cook stove. While Daddy washed the coal dust off him, Momma put supper on the table and the four of us sat down to eat before the August heat and humidity took the starch out of our clothes. Daddy's khaki pants and shirt were starched, creased, and fresh for him to wear that evening and to the mines the next day, as were Momma's, Sister's, and my shorts and shirts. None of us ever wore the same clothes two days in a row, not even Daddy. He and Momma looked down on women who were too lazy to keep their families in fresh clothes.

These habits did not begin on Two-Mile, for on June 10, 1944, Momma writes: "I cleaned the house Monday & washed the biggest washing Tuesday & ironed all day Wednesday & yesterday, too." On November 2 of that same year, she says: "I've washed and ironed all week." Then, in a letter written August 2, 1945, she tells her mother: "I washed yesterday, had 20 dresses (counting 2 pinafores) & a skirt & blouse for Linda & me. Don't guess I'll ever get them ironed." She'd quote Grandma Emmy that "you can always tell trash because it stinks," and she was as meticulous about starching and ironing Daddy's work clothes as she was about Sister's and my ruffled pinafores. Daddy's daily homecoming was an important occasion, and his three girls were always ready to celebrate it.

I also do not recall ever seeing my mother's hair unkempt in the evening. Usually she washed, pin-curled (using an ink pen to wind each curl, because that was the only way to pin-curl properly), and covered her hair with a silky scarf before she woke Sister and me for breakfast and our trip to the garden. Just before she put supper on, then, Momma would take a sponge bath, put on fresh clothes, dab on cologne, and comb out her hair. Momma also frequently commented on women who "let themselves go" and tried to make certain Sister and I did not fall into that category. There can be no doubt that our sixties-era adoption of jeans and sweatshirts for every place but church gave her pause, but Momma never accepted it. Throughout the late sixties and early seventies our mother's customary Christmas gift to each of us was an elaborate dressing gown. In no case could these garments be called bathrobes, though Sister and I certainly used them as such, for they would have been appropriate to any salon. These gowns, which Momma designed, cut out, and sewed herself, were heavy satin or velvet, trimmed in silk braid or sequins. Sister and I have teased each other for years that our lifestyle has yet to live up to Momma's Christmas gowns. For Momma, those dressing gowns were part of the trappings of success in the image she had drawn from books and TV, and she was determined to drag Sister and me into that image. By the late sixties, Daddy was doing well in the building business, and as soon as supper was over, Momma would put on a similar dressing gown among the many she made for herself. They would settle down to watch TV in their columned house with the Cadillac in the garage.

My parents' success was built on hard work, and it was every bit as dependent on Momma's work as on Daddy's. In fact, Momma may have been more responsible for their achievements than Daddy. For her, it was all about things being perfect—never "perfect-minus-X"—no matter how hard she had to work. She was going to, by dog, get it just right if it hare-lipped Santa Claus—and killed all four of us, for that matter. In Momma's view, there was no excuse for sloppiness, ever.

Recently, Gwen Holbrook said she was commenting on a neighbor's new outfit when the woman remarked that she'd had it for several years; Gwen just hadn't seen it. Gwen said, "Why, I see you all the time. How could I not have seen that dress?" The woman replied, "I don't know. I don't wear my good clothes around the house. Do you?" Gwen laughed, "No. Actually I don't know anybody who wears good clothes all the time," to which the neighbor replied, "Grace always did." Gwen reported that conversation to me, and we agreed that Momma accepted no excuses for looking sloppy, and I told her Sister's flood story.

At the time of the '87 flood, I had moved to Montana, and Sister was living in downtown Frankfort, Kentucky. Sister had a ten-year-old son and a seven-year-old daughter, and in addition to owning and operating her own business, she and her husband, Michael, owned several pieces of rental property in the Frankfort flood plain. As the Kentucky River rose, Sister and Michael spent the first night emptying their own basement, then turned their attention to helping their tenants move their belongings to higher ground. According to Sister, she had been working for thirty-six hours, with maybe five hours of sleep, when a CNN reporter caught up with her on the porch of one of their rental houses. She answered his questions, finished the job, went home to bed, and thought no more of it. Six hours later, around 7:00 A.M., she was wakened by the bedside phone and Momma, whose opening line was, "What in the name of God happened to your hair?"

Sister also recalls Momma's need for perfection, as she says: "One of the most striking things about our mother was that she always seemed to know what was 'appropriate,' even though we were miles from anyone else who [might have agreed or cared]. She knew we needed to have linen dusters, and black patent Mary-Janes, and white hats and gloves, when the nearest ones existed only in her mind!" Momma subscribed to several magazines, and you can bet that if *Redbook* or *Good Housekeeping* declared the "correct" way to do something or another, the Prestons of Two-Mile Creek set about behaving properly. Our family was always in keeping with the latest standards, and though Daddy didn't always go along with the program, he made certain Sister and I were in compliance. "Mind your maw," was all he had to say to keep us in line.

A little more than two decades ago I accompanied my husband, Arthur, to a conference of university presidents, where the "spouses' meeting" was a euphemism for a training session of first ladies. Best I could tell, the first session was devoted to candles—where to display them, when to display them, where and when to light them . . . Well, you get the picture. Imagine my surprise when I found that—like most rituals dealing with separating wheat from chaff, as it were—simple ownership of a candle had its own set of picky rules devised for the express purpose of determining who was who. By this time in my life, I had already owned a candle or two, mistakenly assuming that you put a match to them when the room got dark and you didn't want to turn on a light. Well, during the course of this session it came out that there were precise rules for when it was okay to turn on the electric lights, too. The outcome of this three-hour discussion convinced me that there were women in that room who would not turn on a switch or light a candle before 6:00 P.M. even if the house were black as a pot.

I distinctly recall that upon learning this particular rule, I gave thanks to the Power that nobody ever told this to my mother. Because, let me tell you, if Momma had come upon this piece of news, the little Preston family would have had to curse the darkness. Momma wanted everything perfect, and she damned well brooked no opposition to whatever decree she was adhering to either. She was especially not open to the argument that what we were being asked to do made no sense. Reasonable had little to do with what you should say, how you should dress, or otherwise conduct yourself. The problem was that Momma read whatever she could get her hands on, so in terms of fashion or behavior she was forever way out ahead of the pack.

The pack, however, was very clearly where I wanted to hide. Let's just say I was trying hard to fit in, while Momma prided herself on being different. With a little age on me, I could better appreciate my mother's emphasis on standards, but as an adolescent, life was not easy. Sister agrees that "Other parents might let their children do any number of things, but for us it was not an option. Why, Daddy wouldn't think of it!" Momma never took credit for such proclamations either, choosing

to invoke Daddy's name because she knew it would ensure our coopera-
tion. And Daddy never let her down, tacitly agreeing to Momma's every
decree. In Sister's view, "Other families might make excuses for not making a big deal out of holidays, might decide it was too inconvenient, too
much work, but we never would. Things had to be just so . . . because
they must be perfect."

On Two-Mile, we had patterned linoleum rugs on every floor in the
house, and Momma had definite ideas about which patterns were kitchen
patterns and which ones were appropriate for bedroom or living room.
Momma was also the one who decided when one rug or another needed
to be replaced. Unlike some folks who would simply move their rugs
around, always putting the new one in the living room, rotating the others, and cutting up the throw-out one—usually the one in the kitchen—
for doormats, the floor of the toilet, or the can house, Momma would
never put a living room rug in the bedroom or rotate a bedroom rug
into the kitchen. That rule meant that over the years we got rid of a
pickup load of perfectly good linoleum, since Momma was far more likely
to get tired of a rug than we were to wear it out. The rugs didn't go to
waste, though, for Grandma Emmy inherited our castoffs, and she didn't
even have a designated living room, so she used them wherever a worn-
out one needed replacement.
    Picking out a new rug was an occasion in itself, a family affair, with
everybody's opinion considered before Momma made the final decision.
Usually we bought the rugs at Hardware Charlie's over in town, but
every now and then we'd buy one from the company store up at David.
That was a bit more complex, because it entailed hiring somebody with
a truck to go fetch the rug, while Hardware Charlie delivered. Sometimes it would take two or three visits, with Momma pondering the
attributes of the rug with the palest fuchsia seashell patterns, which
would go with the fringe on the front bedroom curtains, versus the one
with pink cabbage roses, a perfect match for the peacock outlined in
the middle of the chenille spread. Meanwhile, Sister and I clambered
over a roomful of rolled-up linoleum, each with about a foot of its edge
unrolled, giving just the slightest taste of the beauty it promised. And
Daddy, only slightly embarrassed, stood on the fringes, periodically suggesting it was time to "Make up your mind, Buddy, 'cause we got to go

to th' house." Though he was always hurrying Momma on to the house, he didn't mean it.

I never doubted that Daddy was proud of Momma, of her persnickety ways, of her knowledge, of her taste. If Momma got tired of a rug, however much wear might be left in it, Daddy was proud of being able to buy her what she wanted. In some ways, too, Momma had a reason to get tired of her rugs earlier than most. Though it was her own choice, she spent a good bit of time up real close to those seashell and cabbage rose prints. See, Momma insisted on using paste wax—the kind that must be buffed and shined—for example, rather than liquid wax, the splash-and-spread stuff. Liquid wax could be applied with a mop, then left to dry and shine itself, while paste wax put you on your knees in a prayer-ful position—if not a prayerful mood—both for application and shine. We had two bedrooms, a living room, kitchen, and—after 1951—a half bath, and my mother waxed every inch of them once a week. Sometimes the kitchen got it two or three times a week. In this one task—not the waxing, but the shining—Momma called on me to help. This meant I spent what seemed like forever on my knees coaxing a shine that I swear you couldn't tell from anybody else's on the creek, all of whom were liquid wax devotees. I spent endless hours attempting to educate my mother as to the qualities of liquid wax—just in the kitchen, for Godsake—alas, to no avail. In retrospect, I don't think the paste wax thing was one bit about wax. Momma also baked a lot of cakes, yet she never had a box of cake mix in her kitchen. Somewhere she picked up the idea that the easy way to do a job—any job—was inferior to the hard way. Getting perfect is about almost anything but easy.

And I guess I have to say here that though I respected Momma and tried to please her, I always thought myself to be more like Daddy. Probably because he was easier to please, but also because I was taught to be that way. There were no male children in my family; I was the elder child, so I was as close as Daddy was going to get to a boy. Hence, though I kept my behavior within the cultural boundaries of our society, I took on more of Daddy's characteristics than Momma's. I did none of this knowingly, of course; it just happened.

I believe, however, that I learned virtually all of my social behaviors from my mother. She was extremely outgoing, loved people—individually and in crowds—and the more relationships she had, the happier she was. I do not recall her ever wanting to be alone. Though my daddy was quite content to interact with any and all who came around, he would have been just as happy if he never saw anybody other than his immediate family. Momma remembered every fact, every date, every piece of action, behavior, or material with which she'd ever come in contact. I swear she did. What's more, if someone got anything—a fact, date, or idea—wrong, she'd take them on about it. Over the fifty-plus years I knew her, I could count on my fingers the number of times my mother was wrong about something. By contrast, I don't believe I ever heard my daddy take exception with anybody. He simply would not state an opinion one way or another. If you asked him what he thought, he'd say, "Aye, boys," and shake his head. If pressed, he'd do no more than shake his head and refuse to answer. At the same time, I hardly ever saw him change his mind about anything.

I cannot imagine what I might have done with my life if I'd somehow been given a different mother. Though I still do not agree with Momma's position on any number of issues, I am certain of one thing: She was never wrong about me, and she never hesitated to tell me in the most irritating way.

Most of my knowledge of my family's history was told to me on front porches or in graveyards—most of the straightforward, public information, that is. The other, the secrets, the things hardly ever brought up, especially in the presence of outsiders, well, that I learned from Momma or Grandma Emmy, and I never learned one bit of it in any heart-to-heart conversation. It was passed along to me, bit by tiny bit, as we worked alongside each other shelling peas or stringing beans, or—especially in Momma's case—while she was ironing. I'd sit at the kitchen table, eating some freshly baked cookies or brownies and doing my homework, while Momma, at her ironing board, discussed whatever came to her mind to talk about.

From the time I was a tiny girl, it seemed to me that my mother spent an inordinate amount of time ironing. Once I started school, though, I don't recall spending much of that ironing story time alone with Momma—or just with her and Sister. Usually there was a crowd. Greta Preston, Lois Ann Colvin, Roma Lou Ward, Bonnie, or Betty, or Bud Holbrook—any or all—were almost always present for the ironing talks, and during such times I was usually not even in the kitchen but lurking and listening just out of sight. Momma never said she liked to iron, quite the contrary, but she ironed every piece of cloth that made it through the wringer washer. Since she had grown up in a house with no electricity, she was fond of pointing out the miracle of an electric iron. Grandma Emmy had two irons; one sat on the hearth at the edge of the front room fireplace, another on the kitchen cook stove. Each iron was placed near the heat source necessary for its use, where my grandma warmed them in order to dewrinkle her ankle-length rayon or wool serge dresses. I don't know why she had two irons, for they were identical—maybe one had belonged to her mother. Those flatirons were smaller than electric ones—about three-quarters the size of Momma's, I'd say. This size differential meant it took longer for the person ironing to cover the same amount of fabric, and sometimes the iron had to be returned to the heat source in the middle of a garment. Those flatirons did not hold their heat for all that long, so the job grew exponentially. Let's just say that you had to care just an awful lot about linen to go to that much trouble.

An aside here: I think one interesting thing about social class markers is that they have a way of hanging on, even when they no longer make much sense. Whenever people tell me about how much more comfortable natural fabrics are—sweat evaporation and all that—I wonder whose discomfort and whose sweat they're talking about. I remain convinced that the preference for polyester-free cloth is rooted in the days when rich folks squandered all those (wo)man-hours behind a washboard or an iron so the privileged could strut around in white linen. You want my opinion? Anybody—male or female—who wears linen ought to be required by law to do it up himself.

I'll have to admit, though, that my mother and grandmother tucked a passel of information into the wrinkles in my brain while they were pressing the wrinkles out of some piece of cloth. Whenever Grandma Emmy ironed, she would reminisce about her youth, when she wore starched white waists (blouses), and she stressed the difficulty of keeping those waists perfect. I never doubted, though, that the time spent keeping clean and pressed was well spent. Grandma Emmy sometimes let me help her iron, but not until she had used the poker to lift the iron from the fireplace and placed it upon the front edge of the hearth. Only after she had wrapped the handle in two pot holders, consisting of several layers of rags, did she allow me to grasp the handle and apply it to the garment waiting on the ironing board. I only recall this happening once, for I remember few times when Grandma Emmy carried her ironing board into the front room. Both Momma and Grandma Emmy did most of their ironing in the kitchen, but I've seen Momma iron in most every room of the house.

Grandma Emmy used the fireplace iron only when she had a fire going in the front room and needed something ironed between meals, and she didn't want to fire up the kitchen stove for another hour or so. Ironing in the kitchen was easier, and I doubt I saw my grandmother use the fireplace iron more than three times in my life. Her operational efficiency was extraordinary, but she was never enamored of the ironing thing the way Momma seemed to be. Whenever Momma spoke of ironing her sheets, Grandma Emmy would shake her head, set her mouth, and say, "Takes a pure fool." Still, for all the time she put in behind the ironing board, Momma never allowed me to help. She might get a hired girl to help her or even let one of the teenagers hanging around the house iron a piece or two, but I don't think I had an electric iron in my hand until I went to college. Momma never allowed me to work with her the way Grandma Emmy did. On Two-Mile, I did more of the outside "boy" tasks than the inside "girl" chores.

Momma and Daddy were united in the belief that a woman should not work outside the home, especially if that woman had a good husband and a child. A good husband was one who didn't drink, gamble, or fool around, but mostly, the "good" label had to do with who was able and willing to put food on the table. In their view, a woman who worked outside the home for any reason was neglecting her primary responsibility, to cook the food that the man bought and to keep him in clean, pressed, and mended clothes so he could go out and earn more.

When, at age nineteen, I married Brett Dorse Scott, he was teaching school and working in the butcher shop of the A&P grocery—a job that required a white shirt and tie three evenings a week, plus Saturday. Since my mother had always been the sole mistress of the iron in the Preston household, I entered that marriage without having ever even pressed a skirt. I received an iron and ironing board as a wedding shower gift, and since for nineteen years I'd seen Momma spend at least two afternoons a week ironing everything she could get her hands on, I figured I could catch on to it. Just a week into the marriage, however, my first attempt at ironing one of my husband's white shirts pretty much ended the honeymoon. That iron got put away somewhere, and the Scotts' laundry bill sometimes rivaled our golf expenses, ironing—like typing and driving—was something I simply could not master. Since I tried not to focus on my new husband's addiction to golf, he never called attention to my failings at most of life's domestic tasks. We kept that ironing equipment through many moves, but I recall some embarrassment once, when I was unable to unearth the iron for some weekend guest who felt the need to put a fresh crease in her husband's slacks. I finally bought— and continue to operate—my first iron about a year ago after using one in a hotel room to get a stubborn wrinkle out of a linen skirt. I found the iron to be both easier and superior to my brought-along steamer, which for more than twenty years I had rated just below handheld hair dryers as a flat-out blessing from the Lord. Not to get all Freudian here, but I have lately taken up ironing with a vengeance, to the point where I now almost enjoy putting a slick finish on fabric. Too bad for the dry cleaners, but I know Momma would be proud. I guess she had to be gone for me to give her the satisfaction of seeing me do something she approved of.

Clearly my mother was the proverbial Russian judge when it came to approval, yet for all my formal education in the vagaries of the human condition, I never got over trying to get her to change her mind about my choice of pursuits. I'd drag my accomplishments home like a cat with some freshly killed field mouse, always sure that this time Momma and Daddy would be impressed. Somewhere in the mid-seventies—during the height of my ALS ("arrogant little snot") period—Momma was on me big-time about the importance of shaping up and shoring up my dead-but-for-the-funeral marriage. In her view, this could be accomplished by leaving my job and taking up wifing full time. My response was to point out that through some combination of consulting, university teaching, and administration, I had earned enough money in the year just past to put me in the top one or two percent of American female wage earners. I then pointed out that I had managed to make this money working and traveling on several continents. (Yes, I know how egotistical that sounds, but behaving badly cannot be simply recast and thus erased, and this sort of behavior was fairly typical of my I-am-a-citizen-of-the-world time.) Think my momma was impressed? She fixed those green eyes on me and said, "Well, Linda! Barbara Walters is making a million dollars a year."

To say that Momma took her health seriously is a massive understatement, she was forever sick with something. I was born five years into her marriage, and I was—and still am—very much like her, so it was natural that I would also be sickly. Between the time I was born and the time we moved back home when I was six years old, I had measles, scarlet fever, and recurring bouts with illnesses serious enough for Daddy to have the company doctor make a house call to see me. Practically every letter Momma wrote to Grandma Emmy includes a litany of complaints about my health, Daddy's health, and her own health. In one sentence she would be telling how I "ate like a pig," was "fat as a bear," "mean as a snake," or "happy as a coon." And the very next sentence would have me "cross" due to teething, being sick with a cold, or having the flu. The same was true of her description of Daddy's health.

The following is from a letter was written in January 1942, when the three of us were living in one eight-by-ten-foot room on the top floor of a coal camp boardinghouse. That we were sharing the most primitive of facilities with six or seven other coal miners brought not a peep from Momma about the living conditions. The health digest, however, was very definitely reported: "We're all okay except for colds. Linda first had one & now she's better & Jay & I both have one. I think we're both better & I reckon Linda has a tooth at last. She's feeling good again now. She was pretty cross here for a few days."

As for her own condition, Momma would juxtapose her report of all the work she was doing or had just completed with the state of her physical condition, then reassure Grandma Emmy, "Don't worry. I'll be fine." In the oldest letter, postmarked sometime in 1941, Momma writes Grandma Emmy: "I haven't been feeling so well for the past week. Jay took me down to see the Doctor one day last week & you would be surprised at the things I have wrong. (Ha) He gave me a whole load of medicine & it makes me feel worse instead of better."

One of the advantages of living in a coal camp was accessibility of medical care, such as it was. Peggy Ward Crutchfield says of the company doctor: "The fee for the doctor was $2.00 per month (deducted from the paycheck) and this included any medicine you needed. The doctor always carried a little black bag with rows of pills in bottles so you never had to have a prescription filled. He put the pills in a very small envelope and wrote directions for use on the outside."

When we returned from West Virginia, Momma had a batch of those small packets containing an array of what she referred to as her "medication." She kept these in a drawer of a small kitchen cabinet. While searching for a spoon one day, Uncle John opened the medicine repository rather than the adjacent knife and fork drawer. "Lord God, Grace. You're a pure dope fiend," he declared. Momma was unamused. She needed her medication. I want to make clear that although my mother's cabinets held ample medication for as far back as I can remember, I do not believe she ever abused any of those drugs. Momma was always more into holding than using. I believe she kept those packets and bottles for two reasons: One, in the event that she got really bad off and needed some potion, it was right there and she wouldn't have to suffer; and two, I believe the very presence of so much medicine reinforced her vision of herself as a sick woman. In regard to her many illnesses, Momma never felt she got her just respect from anybody. I think she was reassured by telling herself that if a doctor had prescribed all that medicine . . . well, she must be as sick as she believed herself to be. When we cleaned out the house after Momma's death, we found prescription medicine dating back to the late fifties. My mother was a holder, not a user.

One of the reasons nobody took Momma's many complaints of illness seriously is because in the very same letter where she declares that Grandma Emmy would be surprised at the things the doctor found wrong with her, she went on to say: "I have been washing today & scrubbing & this afternoon I had to walk to the shaft store to get some scrip & since supper I've been down." Early on, Daddy's way of jollying Momma out of her sick was to tease her about it. In one letter she writes: "Jay is tormenting me to death. He said tell you I'd had a back-set." After some discussion of the rainy weather and Daddy's work, Momma continues: "I'm just about the homesickest person you ever saw. Don't be at all surprised if you see us coming in pretty soon. I'd give anything to be there on the fourth. Well, I guess I'd better stop here, as I don't feel so good & I am tired, too."

When we lived in West Virginia, I believe Daddy attributed most of

Momma's sick to homesickness, but it was not so easy to explain away once we returned to Two-Mile. In the top margin of the third (last) page of this same letter, Daddy wrote: "Say Boy Grayce isn't sick she just thinks she is. That old lonesome train bawls out going through an she bawls louder than it does." However much my mother thought herself desperately ill, I do not recall a time in West Virginia or the early years on Two-Mile that Daddy could not tease her out of it. Once he made her laugh, she'd forget about being sick and tease him right back. Momma's sick became a long-running private joke in our family as we competed to see who could make Momma laugh and get over herself.

My earliest memories of my mother and father are of their laughter. Momma could be so much fun, and she and Daddy genuinely seemed to enjoy their time together. Whatever was on her mind, however, Momma always had to chronicle her latest ache and pain before she could get on to anything else. In the event that a discussion began with and remained concerned with another topic, however, Momma would bring it around to her physical condition, or tack it on at the end. This was the case in conversation and is a theme that runs through virtually every message she wrote. In a letter postmarked October 27, 1943, Momma writes Grandma Emmy how worried she is over Tom Fletcher (Aunt Stella's husband) and Maggie Mollette (Uncle John's wife), both of whom had been diagnosed with TB. Momma did love both these folks like family, remaining close to Maggie even after she had divorced Uncle John. Then she says: "Jay never has let me write and tell you but now that I am better I'm going to write. I have had that cough again ever since I had that cold—like I had last summer & my legs have been swollen until I could hardly stand on them for nearly two weeks. I don't know what causes it. They just swell and turn blue spotted but they're better now & don't swell to amount to anything." Note how she says she is "better" but reports her condition as if it is ongoing. Then, "Jay said you had too much to worry about for me to tell you before. He worries about my coughing so but it is just about the same as the cough I had when I was there." Again she attributes her own feelings to Daddy.

With Momma's vast range of symptoms, it was always hard to tell what might be really wrong with her. In May 1942, Momma writes: "We are all O.K. I'm having an awful lot of trouble with my arm. It keeps me awake at night & hurts most of the time. I get to thinking sometimes that I'm going to be paralyzed." After assuring Grandma Emmy that "Linda is fine. She gets fatter all the time," she continues: "I washed Monday and I have been ironing off and on ever since. I had a lot of mending to do & I've just ironed along as I could stand it. I'm nearly through now. My arm and shoulder hurts so I can just do so much." Then, after discussing the approaching Decoration Day, pointing out that "Dad will be dead three years Sunday," and declaring how much she would like to be home, she says: "Aunt Polly had us over to dinner Sunday. Had chicken and dumplings & everything & I never tasted the chicken, ate one bite of dumplings & filled up on home raised lettuce & kale or mustard or something." Where I come from, refusing to "take nourishment" is a sure sign the person is bad off.

On January 28, 1943, Momma reports that she is listening to Lacon (some preacher) on the radio and Linda is running around in pajamas and bedroom shoes. She says:

Linda is some better. We thought we were going to lose her for a week but her thrash is some better. She has a new eyetooth & one stomach tooth. That just leaves one stomach tooth and one eyetooth to cut. She has a little cold.

I send my washing to the laundry now & have it brought back damp & I iron it. I wash mine & Linda's underclothes, sweaters, & things. It sure helps to have it done. Since she's been sick I haven't got to do very much of anything.

I washed my curtains & Jay helped me stretch them & washed my kitchen curtains Monday & I ironed them & have them all clean & up. They'll bring my laundry today & I'll be plenty busy ironing the rest of the week.

She then pleads with Grandma Emmy to visit and says, "You may not be coming to see me long for I don't think I'll live anytime . . ."

Here is a woman sick unto death, who cooked, kept house, cared for a sick and teething two year old, and washed and stretched her curtains. Stretched her curtains? For those too young to know what a job that was, let me remind you that the washing was done with big tubs of water heated on the stove, and clothes were rubbed clean on a washboard propped up inside of one tub. Some folks never washed their curtains, or they bought curtains that could be washed and ironed without stretching them. Curtain stretchers were used to give shape to organdy or lace curtains after they were washed and starched. Peggy Ward Crutchfield recalls that curtain stretchers "were made of a wooden frame with little nails (I recall ours had pins instead of nails) spaced about a half inch apart all the way around. Every time Mother washed curtains, we spent a bunch of time putting those things on stretchers. They ended up with little tiny curves between the nails but always looked great as soon as they were up. You could put several pieces on the same stretcher (over top of each other)."

Momma used curtain stretchers until I was out of high school, and I recall the washing and stretching of curtains as one laborious task. Doing up organdy curtains is not exactly a chore I would be engaging in if I thought I did not have long to live—or if I felt even slightly sick, for that matter. Just thinking about it could give me a sinking spell. Still, Momma finishes the letter on an upbeat note, saying she has a "million things to do." In a letter postmarked March 22, 1943: "Just a line to tell you that I am sick. My head has never stopped hurting for about 13 days & nights. The Dr. said last week I had Typhoid Fever but Jay went after him yesterday & he came & said I had Toxemia poison. You know that's what Stella Mae [Uncle Fred's oldest girl, who died at age fifteen] had. I've been awfully sick & I don't feel any better today."

I'll have to admit that Momma's "Typhoid Fever" assertion was a new one on me. I honestly thought I had heard her claim every malady known to man, but typhoid fever? She goes on:

I've vomited so much & taken so much medicine I don't know half the time what I'm doing. Jay is doing the work & waiting on me & tending to Linda & working, too. Mrs. Kelly [a next-door neighbor] comes in & looks after us every little while. You can't hire anybody to stay now.

Jay wanted to bring me home when I first got sick & we were having this Dr. here & now I'm not able to be moved. The Dr. said if I didn't get better he would have to take me to the hospital & feed me through my veins.

I hadn't intended letting you know for Jay said not to worry you but I am so sick today I'm afraid & I thought I'd write & tell you.

Here Momma is notifying her mother of her imminent death, but then she says: "Don't worry about me. Jay will let you know. The baby is fine. My neighbors come in pretty often. The Dr. said my blood had poison in it & he can't find out where it's coming from. He's giving me enough medicine. He thinks it's from my stomach." In the lower right-hand corner of the envelope, Momma wrote: "Please deliver at once."

By April 1943, however, Momma had survived and even made a trip to Kentucky. On Saturday before Easter, a couple of weeks after the visit home, she wrote of moving into the rest of the house we had been sharing with another miner:

> I'm going to write a line while my kitchen floor gets dry enough to wax. We've moved into the kitchen and little back room we were telling you about. We have both porches now & our kitchen looks like it did at home [on Two-Mile].
>
> We're trying to houseclean & I'll swear I have worked till I'm half dead, & we have just gotten started.
>
> Jay is working today. Linda is fine & as fat as a pig.
>
> I'm more homesick than I ever have been. I don't feel like I've been home for I didn't realize I was even down there.

Momma was always claiming not to have experienced one thing or another because she was so bad off she was "out of her head" and therefore did not realize where she was. She continues:

> I have nearly all of my medicine taken and I'm losing weight right on. My hair has come out until I'm nearly bald. I look so funny I laugh every time I look in the mirror.
>
> I wish you could have been here & heard the Good Friday services on the radio yesterday. I was ironing and listened to them.

Three letters from June, July, and August 1943 indicate that Momma and I spent much of July and August with Grandma Emmy, for each message says something about letting my grandmother know we made it back to West Virginia. Momma wouldn't leave Daddy in May and June, because the union called the miners out on strike. Though Daddy was always a union man and didn't believe in scabbing, he was among a number of union members who refused to strike during wartime. On June 26, 1943, Momma says: "It's over now, I reckon, until November. I couldn't leave as long as they were out [on strike] here." She goes on to say that we will be in the next week for the Fourth of July in order to see Daddy's sister Irene's family, who are at Pop Pop and Grandma Alk's through Independence Day. Momma promises she and I will stay for at least a month this time and ends the letter by saying Monday is her (twenty-eighth) birthday and she is feeling "awfully old."

After the Fourth of July weekend, Daddy went back to West Virginia and returned to fetch us in early August. On August 9 Momma writes: "I believe we had a very good trip. Jay stood up from Inez to Kermit for the bus was crowded but we got a seat on the train & made it fine & got a taxi down. Jay had the house fixed so pretty it made me want to cry. He'd done everything to it." After assuring Grandma Emmy that "Linda is fine, asks every day when she can go back to Grannie's, had a runny nose Tuesday but is O.K.," Momma says, "My cold gets worse all the time & I'm coughing my head off. I washed Wednesday & ironed all day yesterday & got nearly done. I am going to finish today and scrub and wax."

In September 1943, Momma reports that: "We're all alright. I've been sick for over two weeks I'm better now." She then talks about the weather, asks for news of Uncle Burns and Aunt Lizzie's son Gene Ray, and signs off, "Love to All." Then, beneath her signature she adds, "Mrs. Kelly said she was going to write you about me & I told her you didn't care." I can only guess that Grandma Emmy had been after my mother about what she termed Momma's "foolishness." While the family mostly dealt with Momma's sick by teasing her or ignoring it, on occasion Grandma Emmy would take her to task about taking on as she did. This may have been Momma's way of responding to that.

Earlier I quoted from a letter from Momma's oldest sister, Lizzie, chiding Momma a little for taking to her birthing bed longer than her counterparts, but Aunt Lizzie was by no means the only family member to tease Momma about her illnesses. Over the course of my mother's life, I recall, among others, Grandma Emmy, Daddy, and Uncle Burns all attempting to tease Momma out of her sick—sometimes more sharply than others. We seldom dealt with the sick issue directly, for Momma never used her illnesses to get out of work. She never ceased taking care of every task a day could hold but seemed unable to focus on any aspect of her life as important as her health—her ill health. I do not recall my mother ever failing to get out of bed and do whatever chores were on the agenda for the day—cooking, cleaning, working the garden, canning. Apparently this had long been the case, for in a January 1945 letter she says: "Can't say that Jay and I are doing any good about getting better.

It's sort of like running a race to see which one can cough the longest & loudest. (Ha)" She then speaks of one of the chores she plans to do despite her illness: "I want to stretch some curtains today maybe. Jay put the stretchers up last night. I just have to do as little as I can get by with now. That bronchitis keeps me winded & I cough up so much blood. Jay's scared I'll burst that lung out again. Oh well, maybe it will hold." And in March 1945, she says: "I have a pretty nasty cold & cough but I am working as usual. I'm trying to houseclean a little jig. I washed the bedroom curtains, dyed them blue, washed the windows & put the curtains back up, waxed my bedroom suite, Linda's bed & the floor & scrubbed & waxed the kitchen, went to the store & cooked, washed dishes & scrubbed one porch. So you see I'm not too bad off."

Momma would go on at length about how bad off she was and in the next breath bravely point out that she was perfectly okay. Early in 1945, Momma begins referring in her letters to our plans to move back home and speaks of getting the Two-Mile house ready for us. Her letters promise that she will soon be home to help Grandma Emmy work, and her references to illness, though always included, are shorter. In April 1945, she pens quite a lengthy letter describing a strenuous return trip to West Virginia, but near the end, almost as an afterthought, she writes: "My head never has let up since I came back."

Never in my memory did Momma attempt to get out of any scheduled task and in her drive for perfection even seemed to go out of her way to make more work for herself. Once she had performed her necessary chores, however, she was down. Even then, she wouldn't go to bed; she was sick right out in the middle of everything. On a typical Two-Mile weekday afternoon, Momma would be standing at the drain board stirring up cornbread when the sick would overcome her. With the tablespoon still standing in the cornbread bowl, she'd stagger out beyond the can house next to the branch. There she'd throw up whatever little thing she had eaten that day—usually half a biscuit and five cups of coffee— and shake (like a dog) with dry heaves for a few minutes. Then she would stumble her way back into the kitchen, wash her hands, and resume stirring her bread. Sometimes, walking across the living room or kitchen, Momma'd just collapse, grabbing the edge of whatever was close to break her fall. Most often, however, her collapse was merely partial. Momma's shoulders would droop, her upper body sagging inward, as if headed for the fetal position, but as she bent at the waist, her knees would lock, preventing a fall.

I realize this sounds callous, but during such a collapse, nobody in the family paid this behavior any attention. We continued whatever we were doing, never even questioning her as to what was wrong. Nothing was wrong. That was standard operation in my family. If we'd paid attention every time my mother took bad sick, we never would have had time to get any work done.

Having toiled all day, Momma would get a big supper (incidentally, we "got" supper or breakfast, we didn't "cook" it), put it on the table, then sit with us and not eat a bite. Oh, maybe she would take out a small portion of potatoes or beans and pick at that while the rest of us ate. This is a woman who, despite her many illnesses, never once allowed me or Sister to cook or bake anything for supper—not even to finish stirring the cornbread while she was out throwing up—not once. So there we'd sit at the table—Daddy, Sister, me, and sometimes Uncle Burns—digging into our soup beans, fried potatoes, and pork chops, while Momma, shoulders slumped, chin down, chest caved back into herself, could hardly summon the energy to lift her fork. This posture never lasted very far into supper, however, for we completely ignored her. Daddy, Uncle Burns, Sister, or I would start with a story—always a funny story—and by about the third big laugh, Momma (still not eating, of course) would join in, and we'd all enjoy our supper. Daddy's stories from the mines would start out with some whimsical distortion of a word he'd heard that day; maybe he'd tell something about the fellow who was always going to quit the mines and go to "Michington," where the big jobs were. My family never called the state of Michigan anything else. As I deplaned in Grand Rapids just a few months ago, I smiled as I thought, *Well, hellooo Michington.*

Once we got Momma over her sick, we always had the biggest time at the supper table, and Momma joined right in with funny stories of her own. By the time she cleared the table she was fine, as were we all. My family has always enjoyed spending time together, from the years when there were only us four until just before Momma and Daddy died, and there were nine of us crowded around the table. I remain convinced that nobody catches each other's jokes or plays on words the way my family does. Most of those jokes are on us, and stories of Momma and her sick are a part of that. Being in just about every way my mother's daughter, tales of my own sick are occasion for much family merriment. You see, I can identify with what my mother went through in all her fear for her physical condition.

Since I inherited Momma's every tendency toward sick, I can go from robust to failing in about half a minute. I'm one who expects G. Reaper to appear at my door imminently—my mailbox flag's perpetually up for that fellow. Never able to put my finger on precisely what might be wrong with me, I wake every day of my life convinced that I will probably not live to get out of bed. All the while, I am confident that the degree of my illness is so extreme that nothing can be done; I am a sick woman, and nobody can expect me to go on. Then I get out of bed and get on with my work and my life. Just like my mother before me. I have a life to live and work to do; I just don't waste my energy collapsing. Every day I try to deal with my own sick the same way we handled Momma's—I ignore it. Momma's sick behavior made such an impression on me that to this day if I thought I was having a stroke at the table, I promise I'd absent myself as graciously as possible, denying any problem, and pass quietly into the hands of my Maker in the nearest restroom.

SONGS OF SISTER, SISTER

It would be difficult, if not impossible, to document the rapidity of social change in the forties and fifties in my eastern Kentucky community, but one way of looking at it might be to compare my growing-up experiences with those of my sister. Except for the six-year difference in our age, Sister and I are a great deal alike. We are the only children of Life and Grace Preston. I was born near the beginning of the forties (1941), she near the end (1947). We grew up in the same house(s) on Two-Mile, attended Meade Memorial High School (and were both valedictorians—1958 and 1964, respectively) from first through twelfth grade, and share a communal history with many of the same people. While Sister and I harbor common memories of our youth on Two-Mile, our experiences of it differ. I believe the reasons for this have something to do with national cultural shifts, but maybe more to do with the effects of radio and television on our community.

On February 8, 1947, nearly six years after I was born on a feather bed in the upper room of my grandmother's house at Three Forks of Greasy, Sister was delivered by the same physician in the Paintsville Clinic. While coal oil lamps illuminated my birthplace, Sister had access to the latest technology available in Paintsville, Kentucky. Though I was a low-birth-weight baby and was always referred to as "sickly," Sister—robust from the beginning—weighed in at nearly nine pounds.

On that cold February 9, Grandma Emmy and I were sitting before the fireplace in her front room, just about twelve feet from the room where I was born, when Daddy's car pulled up on the bank out front. Grandma Emmy was sitting in her high-backed wooden rocker, and she had my cane-bottomed chair pulled up close so she could help untangle the laces on one of my new brown pebble-leather oxfords. Daddy had bought these "big girl" shoes from the company store at the coal camp over near Ragland, West Virginia, where he had worked off and on since we'd moved home from Hemphill to wait for Sister. I did not yet know how to tie a bow, so when my right shoe had managed to untie itself, I'd made a mess of a knot. Daddy's car pulled up out front, and by the time he burst in the door announcing, "It's a girl!" I was dancing up and down with my right shoe untied. "How's Grace?" Grandma Emmy asked. "Just fine," he said, as he bent to hug me then tie my shoelace, "and the baby's a big 'un."

Daddy was bareheaded, wearing a heavy denim jacket with the tan corduroy collar turned up to cover his ears. He took off his jacket, laid it on Grandma Emmy's freshly made bed, took my hand, and the three of us walked back to the kitchen so my grandmother could fry some bacon and eggs and foam up some sorghum for his breakfast. It was daylight but dark, being early February, so my grandmother carried the lighted oil lamp to guide us as we made our way through the dining room. Before she began to cook, Grandma Emmy poured a cup of black coffee for Daddy and one for herself from the coffeepot that sat on the cooling stove. Daddy fetched the coal bucket from the corner beside the kitchen door, inserted a short stove poker into the burner pocket, lifted one of the iron burners on the coal cook stove, and dumped in the few remaining lumps of coal. Then he sat at the red-and-white-checked oil-cloth-covered table, drinking his lukewarm coffee as he recited the specifics of Sister's entry into the world. Grandma Emmy spooned out some dry coffee, poured several dippers full of water into the coffeepot, and took two eggs from the glass bowl she kept in the pie safe. She then set the two eggs alongside a gallon jug of sorghum on the white-topped metal table that functioned as a sideboard, picked up the bowl of biscuits and bacon left over from the morning's breakfast and put it in the oven. While the stove warmed, Grandma Emmy sat with us and sipped her coffee as she caught up on what Daddy had heard during his time at the hospital and his stop at my paternal grandparents' house on his way here.

In our part of the country in the forties and fifties, when someone said, "What do you know?" it was not unusual for them to expect breaking news—at least "breaking" to them, for there was no telephone, radio, television, or local daily newspaper. Folks on the main road had electricity and others had battery-operated radios, but my grandmother had neither. Grandma Emmy took *The Grit*. When she finished it she often passed it along to neighbors, who in turn passed whatever publications they "took" to my grandmother. News, however, was carried person to person and provided entertainment and enlightenment.

Not much had changed in Grandma Emmy's house in the nearly six years between my birth and Sister's—indeed, between Momma's birth (nearly thirty-two years earlier) and Sister's. Momma was my grandmother's ninth child, all of whom were born in the same upper room. What's more, I don't even know why the two rooms on the front of that house were differentiated by calling them "upper" and "front." Both faced the road, and I never heard anyone designate the front room as the "lower" room.

Though I am sure I do not recall a number of experiences that took place in my early years, the morning after Sister was born remains vivid for me, in part because of how delighted both Grandma Emmy and Daddy seemed at her birth. In light of what I know today, their clear joy in Sister's appearance seems strange for several reasons. Since Momma was not well, she had been advised against having more children, which made this baby Daddy's last chance for a son. At twelve days from being six years old, I had no idea what a blow it had to be when Sister turned out to be a girl. My age protected me from knowledge of a number of issues faced by my family. I also did not know, for example, that since we had moved back to Kentucky the spring before, Daddy had been unable to find steady work near home. This meant he would come home after his Friday shift at the Ragland mines, arriving after midnight on Friday. Then he had to turn right around and go back late each Sunday afternoon. In light of this information, Sister's birth should have been inconvenient, if not outright disappointing, but I do not believe it was. I don't think anybody thought of babies—any babies—as anything other than a blessing, and nothing I ever heard or even intuited from anybody in my community suggested anything else. Best I can figure, then, Sister was loved from the get-go. She agrees with this assessment and says she had to leave home before she encountered a world where people did not necessarily love her. Though my own early experience was not so gratifying, I believe she had every reason to feel that way, for I was there from the beginning and I tell you that was the case.

Though we had the same mother and father, Sister and I experienced them quite differently. Maybe it was because my birth was more difficult, or because they were younger, or because they were never sure I was going to be okay, but I never felt that Momma and Daddy enjoyed me very much. From the inordinate anxiety over my health the first ten years or so of my life to their excessive concern with my reputation as a teenager, both my parents seemed perpetually worried about me. Best I could tell, they never worried one day about Sister, and for all my life I have thought that "difference" they made between Sister and me had to do with some essential distinction between the two of us. Now, however, for the first time, it occurs to me that the times had something to do with it.

From the beginning, Sister's life has been very different from mine. Whereas I was born, all four-or-so pounds of me, by the light of the fire and coal oil lamps in my grandma Emmy's log house, Sister entered the world at more than eight pounds at the Paintsville Clinic—born in town! Although technically she was from the same genes and the same environment, the timing of her birth put her in a whole different world and in another variation of the family I knew. Although our common memories suggest that Sister and I may well have looked out on the same vista, let me tell you that we saw very different things. Sister's earliest memories do not include the morning ice-on-the-water-bucket, slop-jar-to-the-toilet rituals that were so much a part of the mornings of my early years. By the time my sister reached puberty and could take over such chores, they were no longer necessary, since Daddy had installed indoor plumbing and central heating in our house. It is for that reason, I believe, that my sister has far more nostalgia for the old days than do I. Her memories coincide with mine when it comes to the holidays, celebrations, exploring in the woods, crawdad catching, and the like, but her recollection of friendship patterns, interactions with teachers, and romantic entanglements with boys are way different from mine. You see, Sister fit in.

Sister was lucky. She was not just smarter than I was, she was also pretty and popular. How can I say this so it is clear, yet not indelicate? Like my much-envied classmates Esther Wells and Ronalta Mae Pelphrey before her, Sister was a full-figured girl. So much so, that when she was eleven years old, she wore a 32DD bra (think suspension bridge here), while at seventeen, my charms were quite well contained in a fully padded 32AA. If you think this did not bother me at the time, let me tell you, I have issues—major issues—in regard to the entire body image area. For many years, I would not change clothes in front of my own baby sister and, believe me, modesty had little to do with it. When I later studied phenomenology, I was struck by the idea that each individual's subjective world is shaped by the configuration of his or her body. I believe the reason that concept resonated for me began with watching the difference in the treatment accorded me in contrast to my sister by the world we grew up in. You might say that the fact that the good Lord didn't see fit to give me breasts till I was thirty meant my stock didn't peak till well after I'd sold. I should also mention here that in addition to getting the big bazooms gene, my sister also had/has the world's most gorgeous hair—dark, glossy, exceedingly thick, and straight as a stick. For all her life, Sister has had wash-and-go hair. Meanwhile, without the assistance of five products and three electrical appliances to wrestle my crowning glory into submission every morning of my life, I cannot face the world at all. As I think about it, it's a wonder I didn't kill her.

Since Sister was pretty and popular in high school, she had many young men paying her attention. I do not recall her ever appearing as needy of male companionship as I was every day of my adolescence. What's more, I know in reason that she never spent the inordinate amount of time worrying or daydreaming about love and coupling that I did. Although in high school she dated far more than I had, there was no question of her dropping out of school to get married. Perhaps because I had gone to college, or maybe the times had just changed, it was always a given that Sister would go on to school. She was also class valedictorian and received many scholarship offers. Unlike me, she chose to leave the hills for college and has not lived in any part of Appalachia since she left at age seventeen.

Sister is so much younger than I am that you'd think she would be able to profit from my wise counsel, but if you thought that you'd be wrong. I do not recall her ever taking one piece of advice from me . . . never, not once. Take, for instance, marriage. I married Brett Dorse Scott after my sophomore year in college, when I was nineteen years old. To this day, my wedding day—August 7, 1960—remains the most nearly perfect day of my life. I knew exactly what I wanted, and closing that particular deal was about as close to the pinnacle of success as I ever expected to get. It was a good marriage to a good man, and it took me nearly a decade to realize it was not his fault or mine that there were hardly any interests the two of us had in common. The major problem with that marriage was simply that we had married before either of us became fully formed adults; then we proceeded to develop in very different ways. Upon reflection, the first indication that I was beginning to believe I'd married too young was in the way I responded to Sister's first marriage.

Six years after I went off to Pikeville College because I couldn't persuade Billy Daniel to marry me, Sister broke half a dozen hearts by heading downstate to make her scholarly mark. Sister was going to be an artist, and she had the brains to know she needed some letters after her name to support her until she could develop her talent and catch a break. Her goals could not have been more different from mine; the last thing she wanted was to marry. But Sister was seventeen years old, and before her eighteenth birthday she met Gary Harp and fell in love. When she came home for Christmas in 1964, she was engaged, with plans to marry the next summer.

My baby sister's eighteenth birthday found me with a husband and a two-year-old son, living in Pikeville, Kentucky, working as a claims representative for Social Security. I had been married—happily, I swear—for nearly five years to a man I loved, who loved me back. My husband and I made good money and had a sweet little house on a hillside above the railroad tracks on the north side of town. If anybody had asked me—

under hypnosis, even—if I was happy, I'd have had to say *yes*. I had to be happy. I had far more of what I'd wanted out of life than I ever could have expected; what's more, I had it well before I might have hoped.

When Sister decided to marry, however, I was convinced that she was ruining her life. Though I had no reason to oppose it—Gary was a great guy—I decided that was one wedding I was going to stop. Considering that Sister was far more independent and headstrong than I'd ever been, my dedication to preventing her nuptials seems laughable at best. Still, with absolutely no grounds for opposing their union, I mounted an enthusiastic campaign. Once Sister came home for the summer, I spent every weekend back on Two-Mile in an attempt to persuade her to at least postpone marriage until she finished college. Sister, being Sister, just laughed at my pleas. She was just as certain of her desire to marry as I had been of mine five years earlier, and, if anything, my appeals made her even more determined. I used every argument I could think of, finally making my whole family mad by flat out saying, "For Godsake, just sleep with him. Don't ruin your life by taking up with somebody when you're eighteen years old!" This was 1965 in eastern Kentucky, and it might well be that there were indeed females having sexual intercourse without benefit of wedlock, but they were most certainly not doing so with conscious intent. We didn't come from that kind of people, and, frankly, that I would make such a suggestion to my baby sister shocked even me. You can see how desperate I was. Didn't do a bit of good anyway. Just made everybody wonder if I'd lost my mind. Far as I can recall, not one person thought to ask me if I were so all-fired happily married why I would oppose Sister finding her happiness in the same direction. And you can bet that's a question that did not occur to me for decades after that.

On August 22, 1965, in a wedding to a dot like my own barely five years earlier, Pat Preston married Gary Harp in Thealka Freewill Baptist Church. She even wore my wedding dress—or her version of it. My French lace dress originally had a high collar, which covered every centimeter of my long skinny neck. Though from the waist down we were the same size, Sister had to have some darts taken out of the bodice. Then she solved the upper body size problem by having the high collar cut out of the dress, exposing her throat and collarbones.

As I think on Sister's first wedding, it was—then and now—a model for my interaction with everyone I love. Seems to me I've been learning every damn thing that counts the hard—and worse, painfully slow—way. Then I run around jumping up and down yelling "Warning! WARNING!" to everybody else heading toward the edge of the cliff. Sister was the first of my loved ones to reject my advice, but I have found that I am remarkably more effective now that I have become more subtle—and have all those big-time letters after my name.

That August, then, our troubles culminated with my bursting into tears at Sister's wedding rehearsal—yes, the rehearsal. The next day I caused such a holy show at the wedding itself that those attending were trapped inside the church for what seemed like many extra minutes. Brett Dorse—who as head usher was supposed to return to the church and escort the mother of the bride out, thereby releasing everyone else from their pews—was so busy outside ministering unto his hysterical dolt of a wife that the crowd stayed put. Yes, everybody sat entrapped in the church house till usher Roger Burton saved the day by going in after Momma. Standing at the altar as matron of honor, I was suckin' air as soon as Beverly Ann Short launched into "Oh Promise Me" and crying out big 'n loud by the time the Reverend Chick Hall said, "We are gathered together." Let's just say it was not my finest hour, okay?

But that was merely the first of many times Sister rejected my sagacious guidance. I will refrain from recounting the numerous minor examples and go directly to decisions of the life-altering kind. Sister had her first child, Ryen, in August 1977, barely one month before my son left home for a Massachusetts prep school, which seemed to me a sign that I was meant to help her raise her boy. I'll have to admit that both her children have turned out well, despite my moving to Idaho when Sister's daughter, Amanda (born April 1980), was three months old. I attempted to advise more than a few times, but being that far away I suspect she handled the kids pretty much according to her own judgment.

Sometime in 1981, Sister decided she wanted to work part time and took a job with a head-hunting firm. It appeared to be just the right job for a young mother, since she was paid on commission, could work at her own convenience, and didn't have to dress up to go to work. As it turned out, Sister was very good at this job, and in her first year she made more than twice as much money as I was making as an associate professor of psychology with a decade of experience behind me.

In September 1982, Sister and her family spent a week with us in Idaho, and we took them all around Idaho and to the Oregon coast. Early in the visit, Sister told me she liked head-hunting so much she thought she might quit and set up her own firm, which she could run out of her house. I thought that was the most ridiculous thing I'd ever heard, and since we spent many long hours in the car together, I had opportunity to give her the full benefit of my experience. I pointed out what I understood to be the many disadvantages of self-employment and what I saw to be few advantages. After seven days of my superior advice, Sister returned to Kentucky, resigned her job, and set up her own business. I was right when I warned her that she would not make the kind of money she would have made working for somebody else. In her first year of self-employment, Sister more than tripled her previous year's income. Then the business took off, expanded, and twenty years later, she still runs most of it out of her house. Today, in addition to head-hunting and business consulting, she also owns a number of apartment buildings and has been extremely successful at all of it, often making more money in a month than I make in any given year or two. The fact that she has succeeded despite my best advice has not been lost on me, but it has not kept me from regularly sharing my opinion with her on matters large and small.

Am I jealous of her financial success? Sort of. I certainly wish I had more money, but I'm doing pretty much what I want to do with my life. Moreover, since I have never had my sister's ability or willingness to take economic risks, it's a comfort knowing she will be financially able to support me in my old age.

Now, given all the things I outlined above, you'd think Baby Sister wouldn't have ended up marrying her cousin. After all, she left for the Bluegrass country at age seventeen, had an active social life, was briefly married and divorced, and did not remarry until she was twenty-five. By the time she met Michael Greer, Sister had been gone from home for eight years, picked up her first college degree, even lived out of state for a time. Now, for a girl as pretty as my sister, the suitor selection pool never was exactly small, and she didn't even meet Michael in eastern Kentucky.

Summer of 1971 found Sister living about sixty miles northwest of me in Frankfort and working for the Kentucky Department of Human Resources at the state school and hospital. I was living in Richmond, Kentucky, while teaching and finishing up my dissertation at the University of Kentucky in Lexington. Sister and I talked by phone at least every other day and often spent Saturdays together in Lexington—twenty-five miles to my north, her east. We'd have lunch, go shopping or to a movie—any excuse to hang out together. In our bell-bottom jeans and shrink tops, we'd sit at one of the tiny front tables at Alfalfa—Lexington's first attempt at an alternative restaurant—order hoppin' Johns or some other veggie-heavy treat, and discuss politics, music, life, and philosophy. The sixties were still alive and well in central Kentucky, which means we took our independence, our opinions—indeed, ourselves—most seriously then. I was into my citizen-of-the-world period, and Sister was not far behind me as we discussed world problems, family gossip, and an assortment of issues and ideas. Like most women of that day, Sister and I were just beginning to see ourselves in terms of gender, so we spoke often of our new opportunities as women and what the new "women's lib" meant to us. Though we engaged in many self-absorbed, family-referenced conversations, updating each other on our respective Momma situations, I do not recall either of us ever once referring to our Appalachian heritage. I suppose if we'd been asked how that background had shaped us, we'd have said it hadn't. After all, everybody comes from someplace, and we just happened to be from 120 miles east of where we sat.

One Saturday, Sister told me she would probably be seeing more of me because she had signed up to take a Tuesday evening graduate class at Eastern Kentucky University. We had spoken many times of her desire to go to grad school, and we agreed this was an opportunity for her to begin that process. That she could also see more of me was a real plus. On Tuesdays, Sister got off work at 4:30, grabbed a sandwich somewhere between Frankfort and Richmond, went to class from six to eight-thirty, and usually ended the evening with a Pepsi at my house before driving home. Though initially she drove alone, Sister found that three of her classmates also lived in Frankfort, so they began carpooling. None of the carpoolers were in a hurry, so they agreed to drop by our place, too. I met them all, thought they were interesting, and welcomed the little Tuesday night diversion. One of Sister's carpool buddies was a guy from Lexington—Michael Greer. Next thing I know, she's going to marry this Michael Greer person. Turns out Mr. Greer has eastern Kentucky connections. Turns out the Greers and the Prestons have family connections. If you think I can let this pass without teasing Sister—and Michael—about it, well, not a chance.

Okay, so she didn't really marry her cousin, though the family connection's close enough for me to have just a grain of truth in my story, and a grain of truth is all my people have ever needed to make light of a situation. One of my favorite ways of tormenting Sister is to suggest she has been perpetuating Appalachian stereotypes by marrying a close family member.

One aside here: I cannot emphasize enough how much my people laugh about everything, so if you are looking for serious you're in the wrong store. The more painful or frustrating the situation, the more likely we'll make some sort of joke about it, and that joke will become a story—an oft-repeated story—and will spread in one form or another throughout the family and the community. Though we spend a lot of time going to graveyards, we honor the dead by telling stories all the way there and back, which means that gales of laughter trail in the wind from the tops of those ridges.

One of my favorites among the graveyard stories involves a burial involving Michael. Just to clarify here, Michael's family and our family are related because Michael's mother's half-sister, Needie, married Mack, my great-aunt Hettie's boy. That may not sound all that close, but we make more of kin in the hills. When Mack died in the late seventies, Michael was a pallbearer. Unfortunately, Mack did not choose to be buried near his parents—and mine—in the Ward Preston graveyard. Though that graveyard can be a pistol to get to in rain or snow—even in good weather if you don't have four-wheel drive—the ambulance can drive all the way to the gate. Instead of resting near his grandfather Asbury, Mack chose to be buried about as far down on Bob's Branch as you can go without paws and claws. As Mack's funeral train drove ever farther into the head of Bob's Branch, a spitty little rain got serious. Then the pavement ran out, then the gravel, and finally the ambulance pulled off the road next to a bank steeper than a mule's rump.

According to Michael, despite the grade of the hillside, he stepped up and shouldered his responsibility, just praying for all six of the pallbearers to stay upright until they reached the ridge-top tent swaying in the wind above them. Sister, in her black faille funeral hat, was just starting up the hill about twenty-five feet back of her husband in the trail of mourners following the coffin when she saw Michael begin to slide backward down the slippery hillside. Since he was supporting the casket's back left corner, as Michael lost purchase on the muddy path, the coffin dipped precariously, and both he and Sister thought it would surely land on top of him. Thank goodness, two strong fellows jumped in and averted that disaster. Michael righted himself, but by this time, for all their love of Mack, both Sister and Michael were working hard not to laugh. Sister swears that by the time Michael got his feet under him, she'd hunched her shoulders and tucked her head so far down into her coat that she couldn't see one step in front of her. According to Michael, she "looked like a damned mushroom creeping up the bank." That story has become a staple in our trek to the Bob's Branch hilltop every Decoration Day thereafter.

Tears, Tombs, and Reunion Tunes

I t is end of May in eastern Kentucky—the Friday before Decoration Day. The trees are leafed out so full that from the road I cannot be sure which hillsides have been logged. As I passed the home place this morning, I noticed that the stand of tiger lilies clinging to the bank of the main road is already in bloom. In my growing-up years I took those lilies for granted, but I've learned a lot since I left Two-Mile more than forty years ago. I've grown to appreciate those unexpected spots of beauty that come upon me unexpectedly—things I never noticed when I lived here but value so highly now.

I am sitting on the couch before the picture window in Bob and Jane Allen's modern living room on Tomahawk. Jane is in an easy chair pulled up close enough so we can share some pictures and genealogical records. My tape recorder whirrs softly on the coffee table as Bob sits on the raised hearth across the room and tries to answer my questions about our family.

I telephoned the Allens sometime in March, explaining to Jane that I was going to extend *Creeker* backward a generation or two and wondered if she and Bob would be willing to help me. Though I had not seen either of them in more than four decades, Jane issued the kind of blanket invitation I had known to expect when I called. It went something like: "I don't know if we can help, but come anytime and we'll try."

Bob is Stella Allen's youngest boy, the grandson of my great-aunt Louanna Cline (1867–1913), who was Grandma Emmy's oldest sister. Bob Allen is not merely part of my extended family; he was close to my parents when they were first married and forever a bit special to me. Had I been a boy, Momma and Daddy had planned on naming me after Bob—Robert Allen Preston—which always made me think of myself as merely one remove from being Bob Allen's namesake.

The namesake thing would not have mattered, though, in the welcome Jane extended me, for there are not many degrees of separation dividing us hill folk, blood tie or no. While I don't much appreciate the old joke about the hillbilly family tree being shaped like a wreath, I am struck by how very reflective that metaphor is of our kinship patterns and the ways we trace our common history. Indeed, on this very morning, I have found out that Jane Allen is part Preston. This information surfaced as we discussed Bob's spending a full day last week clearing off one of the old Preston graveyards over in Paintsville. Since a cursory examination of the tombstones reveals that the last soul buried in that particular graveyard died fifty years ago, it's not as if eighty-one-year-old Bob had any formal responsibility for cleaning off that cemetery. But he was there because he's a product of this family—of this community—and our people don't disrespect the dead by letting the briars take the burial ground.

And now Bob Allen folds himself, elbow upon knee, before the fireplace because he does not want to offend me with his cigarette smoke. It matters not that we are in his house, or that I practically invited myself to visit, or even that my reason for going there is so that he can do me a favor. His choosing to go out of his way to make me comfortable is as welcoming as the cake and cookies Jane Allen baked in anticipation of my visit. They want me to feel at home because I am Lifie Jay and Grace's girl, Emmy's granddaughter, and I belong to this family. What's more, they have no expectation that I will do anything for them in return. In a world where even personal relationships have become just more networking, this old-fashioned welcome seems worth noting.

Bob and Jane Allen are my people. They are consummate Appalachians, the kind of folks never seen in the documentaries of gaunt, sad-eyed hill folk standing before ramshackle cabins. Nor are they represented by portrayals of Appalachia inhabited by the weary disadvantaged and the fat cats who've taken advantage of them. They are an Appalachian success story in that they have chosen to stay in eastern Kentucky, to bring up their children there, and to live by a set of values that is characteristic of my people—the same set of values passed along to Gwen Holbrook, and Sister, and me. Maybe the reason Decoration Day is so special to us is that it provides for the yearly renewal of our particular brand of commitment to carrying the past into the future.

Every human being has a pass-along passion; that's what sitting, singing, and porch swinging on a summer's evening is about—pass-along. Grandma Emmy, Pop Pop, Keenis Holbrook—all the old ones—passed down to my generation a culture as rich as sweet potato pie and as colorful as a crazy quilt. I don't come from the kind of people who pass-along by setting words to paper, so my heritage has been largely ignored by folks who come from the East reaching down to help us. Those folks dropped in on us, then returned to their offices in universities or federal agencies and wrote of the everlasting cycle of poverty and hardship in the hills and hollows. It's hard to find a smile in the entire recorded history of rural Appalachian people. But the helplessness and hopelessness song, we got that one—over and over we got it, as if we were all the same. That story is out there, and it is most certainly a part of Appalachia. But it is not the whole story, not by a long shot. If there is one point I want to make here, it is to separate my rural Appalachian people—we of the creeks and hollows—from those rural Appalachians we have so long seen reflected in pictures of sad-eyed hill-country folk on ramshackle porches.

This rural Appalachian story—the one I inhabited growing up and the one that is with me every single day, whatever my zip code of the moment may be—is one of hard work and hope. It rings with the pleasure taken from doing a good job and sitting at a supper table laden with food you've raised, with people you love around you laughing at shared stories of your day. That Appalachia is a spirit, a sensibility, a way of seeing the world that was passed along to me and that will be a part of my family long after I am gone. It is the voice of Grandma Emmy, and Pop Pop, and all my great-aunts Ward, and even poor old sorry Uncle Burns—people who endured hardships, all, but you'll find no sad-eyed snapshots of them. My people—kin by blood or spirit—made choices, and once in a while they cried over mistakes, but more than anything else, they made do and endured.

From the coal camp boardinghouse, through the remodeled house on Two-Mile after Daddy had installed electricity and indoor plumbing, to Pop Pop's tiny house that had neither, where we retreated after the fire burned away everything we had, everywhere my family lived was filled with laughter. Maybe some of that laughter was to cover pain; I don't know. What I do know is that the legacy I carry includes the recognition that life is about working hard to take care of myself, doing my part in helping out folks when they need it, and working at whatever is necessary with a lightness of heart that makes even the worst of life's experiences tolerable. I was taught that it's up to me to make the best of what comes my way, but that whatever path I take, I will always belong to a family and a place that marked me early and well. Like everybody else, my people believed that if we had a lot more money—or even just a little—we'd be better off. While, objectively, that might have been the case, nobody I knew was sitting around feeling sorry for himself just waiting for some financial windfall.

Without exception, all of us believed we had some hand in shaping our future. So while we were waiting for the powerful hand of God to spread His Grace—or take out His fury—on us, we were busily making the best of our lives. We were grubbing new ground, turning the earth, putting in crops, quilting rag quilts, and laying in our application for any job that happened to be available, whether we were qualified for it or not. Though we had faith that God would provide, we were pretty sure that He expected us to help Him along a little. "The Lord helps those who help themselves," we told each other. Thus, we worked as hard as we could to assist the Great I Am in putting food on our table and clothes on our backs. We had faith that by keeping everlastingly at it we could manage to stave off at least some of the injustice of finding ourselves at the mercy of everything from nature's floods to mine lay-offs. We also had enough faith in our own ability to work that if some-body would give us a job, we'd do them a good one, whatever the learn-ing curve. I wish I could say that we had as much faith in using education as a means of gaining some control over an unpredictable world, but that would be a lie.

Some things about home were wrongheaded, at least as I see it. As my friend Gwen Holbrook says, "Linda, we had a great life, but let's not act like it was a perfect life." Thus, it's a less-than-perfect song we sing to our kids and grandbabies, those who never got to know Grandma Emmy, who never joyfully anticipated Miner's Vacation (the first two weeks in July, when the mines closed down so all miners could take their annual holiday at the same time), who never even had a chance to smell the rich essence of freshly turned earth. Just as the aroma of newly plowed ground often has more than a hint of the barnyard in it, the memories unearthed here are not without their unpleasant characteristics.

During the past decade, several folks have come from the East to help us in still another way; they put what they purport to be *ordinary* Ap-palachian hill folk on videotape. In these documentaries, outsiders nearly always choose to show folks who perpetuate the stereotypical helpless hillbilly, the victim of a society speeded up and rolling right over him. Such a picture is painted to show the good intentions of the filmmaker by implying that the importance of this piece of art is to shed light on a century of social injustices. After all, we are to infer, these poor folks cannot help themselves, since everybody from unscrupulous coal opera-tors to homegrown politicos take advantage of them. Okay. Right! That's the truth, too; but it ain't the whole truth. My uncle Burns was sorry as whale spit, down drunk too often to keep a regular job for more than six months. Still, during the times he was out of work living off some family member, his sober hours were spent working in the garden, white-washing the shed, or doing some kind of substantive work around the house while waiting for his next employment opportunity to present it-self. The expectation was always that he was *between* jobs. That he would never be able to get work, or that any one among us would not be ex-pected to spend our days in some sort of productive activity, was simply unacceptable. As for the focus of those documentaries, let me suggest that when I see a man my age who, best I can tell, never got his butt about doing much of anything except impregnating his wife way too many times, I do not see him as typical of *my* people. When, in addition, the whole damn clan for three or four generations seems content to do nothing other than supplement their welfare checks by digging a little "sang" (ginseng) now and then, I will tell you that is not representative of my people either. We simply do not fit into this acknowledged image of Appalachia.

And of the images of Appalachia, how many do we seriously want to change, and how many really need to be changed because they're wrong? People seem to think that stereotypes are always a horrible thing, but the stereotypical Appalachian allegiance to family is certainly grounded in fact and is still pretty true of my own family. I'm proud of that stereotype and proud of being from just such a family. And while I don't like the perception of all Appalachians as latter-day Hatfields and McCoys, it may just be that's one of those things that tends to come from exceptionally strong kinship and family loyalty.

In the early fifties, Arville Johnson—a distant cousin of Daddy's—moved to Two-Mile and set up a little grocery store about a quarter mile down the creek from our house. Arville had teenage kids, and his store soon became a hangout for young folks. I longed to amble down to Arville's, drink a peanut-filled Pepsi, and become one of the gang. But I never walked into Arville Johnson's store—not once. Daddy liked Arville Johnson, thought him an honest, hardworking man, but he would not trade with him, for in order to buy from Arville we had to pass by Mitchell and Leona Wallen's store. Daddy said, "Mitch has give me credit good times and bad and I'll be damned if any of my family's gonna walk right past his store to spend money on something he's selling." However much I begged to be allowed to go there, Daddy was adamant that no member of our family could buy so much as a candy bar from Arville. So the loyalty I recall is not simply to blood kin; it is about being loyal to self, to community—to the sense of kinship that inspires us to honor those long dead at least once a year. Decoration Day is about going home—home to remind ourselves who we are, who we were, and who we will become.

There are few terms in the English language as evocative as the single word "home." For me, it ranks right up there with "family" and "Christmas" on my all-time list of favorites. Though I have lived in a variety of places, the home I hold in my head and heart has never migrated. Apparently this idea of home was transferred whole to my son, who did not grow up there but admits to an inexplicable affinity for eastern Kentucky. My family, the Prestons, is of a specific place and of a particular people, and that will not—indeed, cannot—change.

For all my fond allusions to home and family, however, I am reminded at least a couple of times a year of some of the ways my family of origin was wanting. I am not throwing off on anybody or dogging my parents here, just pointing out that however fine it was to have spent my first nineteen years on Two-Mile Creek as Lifie Jay Preston's little girl, there were also disadvantages. My little family numbered among its imperfections the fact that there just never were enough of us. My mother was not a robust woman and did not bear children easily, so I cannot really blame her for the size of our family, which is . . . well, small. Now, nobody needs to tell me the advantages of having a small family. I am well aware that if I'd had another half dozen siblings, I might never have had access to some of the opportunities that enabled me to get to where I could contemplate—and write about—our family. I understand that. Still, in a place where large families were the norm, my family had no sons and only two daughters: Sister and me. That was it.

Even before Momma and Daddy died, our nuclear family reunions, however well attended, could not be termed crowded. Sister had two kids; I had one and married into three more. But you get the picture; we have not been prolific, and our heirs—such as they are—are not numerous. And though they're of an age to, not one of Lifie Jay's or Grace's grandchildren has yet gone forth and multiplied either. There are several logical remedies for Sister's and my annual urge to get back to where we began. We could look to Daddy's family, or Momma's—must be some reunion possibilities there. Well, Daddy came from a family of three boys and two girls, and the only one who produced more than two kids per family was Uncle Mitchell—the oldest one. At some point, without anybody noticing, my daddy's siblings must have scrambled on the Zero Population Growth ship and managed to ride that sucker right to the end of the line. What's more, every last one of the Preston aunts and uncles moved away from the hills—or into town (same thing)—except Daddy. Though Sister and I are in touch with several of those cousins, they've moved as far afield as we have and never were particularly close either to us or to their heritage. Such is progress, I suppose, but what about Momma's side of the family?

My mother was the youngest of a family of nine, but they also scattered and were not particularly fruitful either, narrowing that opportunity for big coming-home functions. In truth, I think my aunt Lizzie was a perfect kind of family reunion figure, one about whom heirs could cluster—and she could cook, too. But Aunt Lizzie died several years ago, and all her children have died or moved away, so there's nobody to issue the call for gathering every so often—or at least to issue that call and welcome anybody outside their own nuclear group. That leaves Sister and me with a coming-home feeling and no damn where to take it. Into this alienating situation, let me just offer up a small prayer of thanks for the Holbrooks! They are, in fact, our family. Daddy's mother, Alka Ward Preston, was the older sister of Aunt Exer Ward, who married Keenis Holbrook and produced this particular family. But blood is among the least of the reasons we are close to the Holbrook clan. They are much closer than second cousins to Sister and me, which is why we try to show up for their annual reunion whenever we can fit it into our way-too-busy lives.

When I was six years old, Grandma Alk died, and her youngest sister, Aunt Exer, moved into the home place directly across the road from us. Over my growing-up years, the Holbrooks became a great deal more than simply another branch on our family tree. While their youngest daughter, Gwen, was becoming my best friend, Gwen's older siblings—Betty, Bud, and Bonnie—were being mentored by my mother, and Aunt Exer was filling the role of Grandma Alk for Sister. Among other things, my sister, the consummate gardener, learned to plant and nurture flowers from watching Aunt Exer as she went about living her life on Two-Mile in the late forties and early fifties. In recent years, Gwen has often mentioned how much Sister seems to have turned out like Aunt Exer in the way she does for people. Baby Sister lives out what she sees as her religious commitment to community and the world by carrying in food, pulling weeds, or mowing yards for folks who aren't able to do it for themselves. In a like manner, Gwen's sister Betty grew to be more like my spirited momma— good women, both, but with maybe a little more rock 'n' roll in their soul than was common in women of that generation.

As I think on it, I'd have to say that the mentoring business took, although the word "mentoring" itself gives me a problem. I have trouble with forms of labeling relationships that cannot be adequately characterized by one somewhat abstract, impersonal word. I'd say that Momma loved Bud, and Betty, and Bon—all three—and they loved her back. The sterility of the "mentor" word does not begin to describe that relationship, nor does it come close to explaining the allegiance Baby Sister feels toward my aunt Exer either.

Today, most of the Holbrook heirs have gone from the hills, too. They've become city folks, just like some of the rest of us, but in one way they've been luckier than Sister and me. They have one of their own—my buddy Gwen—who has moved back to the home place there on Two-Mile and calls them home at least once a year for the Holbrook family reunion. And here I must point out that Sister and I are lucky in that although we don't have a trace of Holbrook blood in our veins, we're just full of Ward—among other things. Year after year, then, Sister and I get invited back to partake of the food, fun, and fellowship of all who can get back for the gathering of Holbrooks. And go, we do. Tenuous connection or no, the last weekend in May, Sister and I—husbands in tow—head for that welcome-back mountain range, first glimpsed as we top a little rise on the Mountain Parkway somewhere in the western edge of Powell County. Anybody from home can pinpoint the place, for our heart takes a lap around the old chest cavity as we look toward those hills. Our mountains are welcoming, their nesting quality friendlier than those daunting ranges west of the Mississippi. As we make our way back to one more homecoming, the initial view of that mountain scene reminds us of all we've brought along with us that is of little or no value to anybody except the folks we are hoping to see.

We have school pictures of our kids—even if we've brought those kids along with us, but especially if they couldn't make it—and newspaper clippings of our family's accomplishments since we last were home. If we aren't traveling from too far away, we are also likely to have a pot of cabbage rolls or dumplings—or whatever dish we fancy we make better than most—scotched into the corner of the backseat floor. For us expatriates, Decoration Day lasts for two or three days, since we must make time for visits to the living and the dead on all sides of the family.

It is Saturday before Decoration Day 2002, and we are headed once again to the old burial grounds up on Greasy and around on Bob's Branch. Used to be Daddy would be driving the first car and my family and Sister's would be in two or three cars trailing out behind him. We couldn't all ride together, because the flowers—fresh and plenty—take up too much space. Then in '94 Momma and Daddy died on us, and for the past eight years it's just been Sister and hers in one car, me and mine in the other. Today, my husband, Arthur, drives our green Jeep Cherokee, and Sister and Michael follow us in the little white car she just bought to replace her green Cherokee. But this time there's another car in our little motorcade. It's just more family, of course. I mean, who else would we be taking to the graveyards?

That third car holds three Californians—two from San Diego, one from Los Angeles. And they're family, all right—close family—but family I didn't used to know I had. Shortly after Christmas 2001, I received a call from a woman who said, "I am Barbara Mollette [she pronounced the word 'M'lette,' not our common 'Mol-it' inflection], your uncle Fred's daughter. After my mother died, when I was five years old, my father abandoned me and I never saw him again. You list his other children in your book, but not me. Why not?" Why not, indeed? So much for all my family-togetherness business. So much for thinking I know much of anything about who did what and to whom, especially when it came about before I entered the picture. And this Barbara person—well, she was no base-born child either. Uncle Fred was married to her momma, and Leon—who was raised by Grandma Emmy—was her older brother. After hanging up the phone, I called Sister and asked, "Did you know Leon had a sister named Barbara? Did you ever hear of this woman?" I knew my baby sister's answer before I even asked. Sister's six years younger than I am and never spent much time alone with Grandma Emmy. She was not even born during the summers Momma and I stayed up at the home place on Three Forks of Greasy while Daddy worked the mines over in West Virginia. I knew in reason that if I had not heard of this Barbara M'lette—Uncle Fred's girl by his first wife, Alma, who died of TB—then Sister most certainly was not aware of her.

Though I never claimed to know all there was to know about my family, I was pretty sure I knew all my first cousins. As I said, the big-family tradition stopped for both the Prestons and the Mollettes with Momma's and Daddy's generation, which makes for considerably less fun and family on Decoration Day and Christmas. But here we are, a new cousin found on this Decoration Day—and some cousin she is, too. We could not deny her even if we wanted to, this Barbara. Take away her dark hair, and she's a dead ringer for my bone-thin Momma, right down to the skinniness; I don't dare ask about her health. Barbara, her husband, Al, and their daughter, Diana, who has those Cline green eyes that both Momma and I got straight from Grandma Emmy, flew in from California last night ready for their first Decoration Day in Kentucky—our annual "tears, tombs, and reunions" tour. At least I hope they're ready, because all this history, all this family—living and dead—compressed into three days is a bit overwhelming even for those of us accustomed to it.

I have long been told that I favor Momma, especially in the face, but this new cousin—this Barbara from California—is a much more faithful copy than am I. Her hair is almost exactly the shade of dark auburn brown as Uncle Fred's, but the absence of gray makes me wonder how natural that is. Then again, some of Momma's people are slow to gray; Grandma Emmy hardly had a gray hair when she died, and Aunt Stella's deep auburn hair was never sprinkled with much gray either. I believe Aunt Lizzie's hair was a little lighter brown than Aunt Stella's, and I don't know when or if she ever turned gray.

The first time my husband met Aunt Lizzie, she was well into her eighties, and she and Aunt Amanda came by on Christmas Day. After they left, Arthur remarked that he understood why everybody was so taken with Aunt Lizzie, for we'd laughed at her self-deprecating stories all afternoon. He could not believe her energy and said he was surprised that a woman her age "didn't have a gray hair in her head." I explained that her hair had thinned and she was wearing a wig more the shade of Aunt Stella's hair—and Uncle Fred's Barbara—than Aunt Lizzie's natural color, at least as I recalled it.

One of my favorite pictures of Momma, taken with her two sisters that day, shows the three Mollette girls smiling broadly in Momma's fancy French Provincial living room. Each had been successful in her own way, and even Grandma Emmy, who could be the East German judge where her kids were concerned, would have had to admit her three girls had come a long way from that hardscrabble existence at Three Forks of Greasy. That Christmas Day picture shows Momma as a blond, but who knows what her natural hair color might have been? She bleached and permed her own hair, off and on, for thirty years. Then, Gwen Holbrook moved her beauty shop into a trailer down on Bob's Branch and kept my pretty Momma a blond to the grave.

There's a certain symmetry to the fact that Gwen Holbrook Williamson—the little girl for whom my mother bought a dress so she and I could dress alike in first grade—set Momma's hair and applied her makeup the final time on November 11, 1994, at Preston Funeral Home. At the visitation the next night, Aunt Eula Preston, whose opinion Momma cared about more than just about anybody's, remarked that "Grace would have loved this." That remark meant a lot to Sister and me. It made us feel we had finally done right by Momma. The funeral thing is big in eastern Kentucky, sort of like the grave visiting, and in truth, religion is only part of it.

While Sister and I may tease each other about our commitment to replacing Aunts Winnie and Millie, adding our big hats and hind ends to funeral processions marching into the twenty-first century, I suspect we will be there. Attending funerals and reunions and trekking to the top of the hill on Decoration Day is about honoring those folks on whose bones we made our own. We take our children and grandchildren to our burial grounds to make certain that succeeding generations know that these folks counted. They mattered to us, and who they were and what they did will continue to be valued by their descendants. We know they're gone. We are sad that they're gone. But we will honor them with the best funeral we can afford—whether or not we can afford it. Then we will drag ourselves and our children and grandchildren to remote graves and tell stories on those who rest there. In so doing, we make certain that what our forebears did, both good and bad, is remembered by generations of descendants whose lives did not overlap theirs. My people believe it is important to remember where we have been and what we owe those responsible for getting us here.

It is just this sort of tradition of belonging to a place and a people that Uncle Fred took from his daughter, Barbara. Today, we hope to let her fill out that phantom limb she's missing. We may not be able to take away the itch, but after our journey, perhaps she will understand the futility of trying to scratch it. We are going to introduce Barbara, Al, and Diana to our shared roots at Three Forks of Greasy, where both she and I began. Barbara has already endured the trip to the florist in Paintsville for the blankets of white roses, then the journey to the top of a ridge in Bob's Branch to lay those blankets on Momma's and Daddy's graves. Along with Arthur and Michael, the three of them watch as I take a hard look at the two white rose blankets, placing the larger one on Momma's grave. I put the slightly smaller blanket on Daddy and explain that the larger of the two must cover Momma because she would care; he wouldn't. We also spread red roses at Momma's feet and Daddy's, place flowers on the graves of Pop Pop, Grandma Alk, Uncle Keenis, Aunt Exer, Uncle Mitchell, and Aunt Jo. Finally, we place a single rose on the grave of each of the babies Pop Pop and Grandma Alk lost in childhood. The first one died in 1903, the last in 1913.

We tell our newly found cousins about why we chose a bench rather than a headstone for Momma and Daddy, then we take them on a little tour, trying to bring them up to date on who's up here and what their connection is to us. We talk about our little dried-up Pop Pop, who taught us everything we know about being woodsmen. When coming upon a persimmon tree, we'd pick up the odoriferous fruit, rub the ground off it on our shirttail, and make as if to eat it. Pop Pop would always caution us to sniff it good first in order to tell if it was ripe.

"If it doesn't have a high smell to it, it's too green to eat," he would warn. "You'll suck sorrow if you bite into it."

He was right, of course, about green persimmons and just a whole lot of other things he advised us about over the years. Pop Pop died when I was in high school, and you wouldn't believe what a hole that opened up in my life. Though I was a typical adolescent—right there in the center of my world, interested only in myself, my teenage friends, and basketball—Pop Pop and I talked every day. I'd get off the school bus at Leonie's store, run inside to see if any mail had come, and head up the road one hundred yards to my house. Along the way I'd pass Pop Pop's place, where in all but the worst weather he and Jo would be sitting on the side porch.

"Hidie, hidie!" I'd call out.

"What d'ye say here now?" he'd reply as I turned into our pea gravel driveway.

After I'd changed from my school clothes, gathered eggs from the hen house, and gone across to Holbrooks and drawn a couple of buckets of water, I'd head down to Pop Pop's to join him, Jo, and Sister. I'd step up on the porch . . .

"What d'ye say here now?" he'd repeat. That was Pop Pop's typical greeting and required no reply, so I'd drop down on the top step and recap my day. Though one of the characteristics of adolescence is reluctance to communicate with parents and grandparents, as a teenager, I was in the habit of telling Pop Pop everything I could recall from my day. I'd sit there and spill it all out while he whittled on a stick and nodded. Pop Pop was not very talkative, but he'd add a pithy comment now and then, sometimes a "suck sorrow" warning. When they put Pop Pop in the ground up on this old hill, I lost the best sounding board a girl ever had. He wasn't one to say much, but even then I never doubted his wisdom.

And then there's Jo. Yes, she's buried here, too—right within sight of Pop Pop. From the time Grandma Alk died, I don't think my poor little granddaddy had one peaceful day free of worrying about Jo. Then Pop Pop died so suddenly that Jo's future was anything but settled for the next I-don't-know-how-many years. After Grandma Alk died, Pop Pop tried to settle Jo with Auntie Irene's family, then with Aunt Exer's, but she was a disruptive force in every household. Finally, Pop Pop built the little house beside us and brought Jo home to live with him. From that day, unless one of them was in the toilet we hardly ever saw one of them without the other. Pop Pop would be puttering around, doing whatever he was doing, and Jo would be within an arm's length of her daddy. If Pop Pop had to go to town he'd sometimes leave Jo with Aunt Exer, where she would sit over on the Holbrook porch wringing her hands until he came for her. Sometimes he would give me or Gwen a dime to sit with Jo while he went across the road to Leonie's store, but for the most part Jo and Pop Pop were inseparable.

After supper, if he didn't have any big project to work on, Daddy was in the habit of taking whatever needed fixing and going down to sit with Pop Pop and Jo while he worked on his undertaking. One July evening, Daddy came back from Pop Pop's and said Pop Pop was sick and that I should go down and spend the night in case Pop Pop needed somebody. As far as I could tell, Pop Pop was not bad off that night, and he ate the breakfast Momma brought him early the next morning. Then in the afternoon, Aunt Ellie Johnson came to stay with him and Jo, and that night, Uncle Mitchell brought Doc Hall to see him. When the most important doctor in Paintsville made a house call, we took it as an indication of the seriousness of the situation. Pop Pop was down, and we knew it. We sat up with him that night and the next, but he didn't linger. I know the adults probably had some sense of how sick Pop Pop was, but from my perspective, one day he had no health problems, then he took to his bed, and less than a week later he died.

The grief for Pop Pop was exacerbated by the whole family's inability to deal with the Jo problem, and the fight over Jo began the moment the first spade full of dirt hit Pop Pop's coffin. We weren't off the hill before Daddy said Jo would be moving in with us. Momma said, "No, she won't."

Daddy loved his baby sister and said, *By God, it was his house and he'd take her.* Momma said *no, never, no way.* Daddy said if Momma refused to let her move in with us, he'd just move out and keep her next door in Pop Pop's little house. Momma pointed out that he'd have to quit his job at the mines and stay with Jo full-time and that his first responsibility was to his own girls.

Neither of my parents were argumentative people, and I honestly do not remember ever hearing them argue about anything else, but some version of the Jo argument went on in my house for years. I don't think Daddy ever got over his guilt about not being able to care for Jo.

For a couple of years after Pop Pop died, we went through the same pattern of shifting Jo from place to place that had occurred after Grandma Alk's death, with both Aunt Irene and Aunt Exer trying and failing to care for her. Without Pop Pop, Jo wandered at night; she was strong, willful, wouldn't mind anybody, and if not watched every minute was a danger to herself and others. Finally, it became clear that the family would have to put her in a nursing home, but not until after Momma and Daddy had war over it just about daily. Jo Imogene Preston (12/12/24–6/19/97) outlived every sibling except her oldest brother, who died six months later, and she was never able to do one single thing for herself or anyone else.

Daddy, Momma, and Uncle Mitchell visited her monthly, bought her necessities and trinkets, and worried about her forever. I stand looking down at her headstone thinking about the Lord working in mysterious ways and biting back the comment "What on earth could He have been thinking?" But Jo has come full circle now. She is right back where she began—her grandparents, daddy, mother, and two brothers scattered out around her, protecting her from the outside world, just as they tried to in life.

We clean up our mess, take trash to the trash barrel at the gate, and continue our journey.

As we head out to Three Forks of Greasy, Barbara rides with Sister, Diana with me, and Arthur goes with Barbara's husband, Al. Clearly these Californians are not familiar with graveside visiting and wonder why anyone would go to such trouble and expense of leaving cut flowers in such withering heat that they're sure to die directly. Since Al is retired navy, the family is familiar with the concept of Memorial Day but are surprised that we do not differentiate between war dead and all other dead. Before we take them to decorate the graves of our common grandparents, Grandma Emmy and Grandpa Lige, we must drive a mile past the home place up the Right Fork of Greasy to pay a visit to Billie Edyth Ward, her sister Elna Ward Buster, and niece Marlene Wells. Billie Edyth, who has lived her whole life about a mile above the Lige Mollette home place, has been researching and writing about Johnson County families for the past thirty years. She is still living in the house where she was born, she knew every member of Grandma Emmy's family, and she taught at Three Forks of Greasy School with my aunt Stella, during the years after Aunt Stella was widowed and living with Grandma Emmy. If anyone alive has heard of Uncle Fred's daughter, Barbara, it is Billie Edyth Ward. She has indeed known of Barbara and says Aunt Stella used to speak occasionally of Leon's sister, who had gone to live with her mother's family. She agrees that Barbara bears strong resemblance to the Mollettes, especially Momma. She tries to recall stories of Uncle Fred, but since Billie Edyth was born after Uncle Fred left the home place, she remembers him only as a grown man. We spend some time discussing Uncle Fred and wondering what other choices he might have made when he abandoned both his children.

Then it's on down the Right Fork of Greasy to introduce Barbara and her family to what's left of her paternal grandparents. Barbara is near enough to my age I would bet she was born within a mile or two of the Lige Mollette home place, if not on this very site. All of Lige and Emmy's children were born here, as was I. We point out where the old house used to sit, then take the path out to the tiny gravesite, where Sister and

I remove the remains of the last flowers we brought here and put new ones in their place. This graveyard requires a little more work than the one on Bob's Branch, because the Bob's Branch graveyard is visited often, while I believe we are the only visitors to this one. Only two of Grandma Emmy's children are buried here, little Jake and Aunt Gladys, neither of whom left any heirs, so there are no children to tend to the graves. We explain to Barbara that right up through the year they died, Momma and Daddy tended these graves. Though we brought flowers and came with them on Decoration Day—most years at Christmas, too— we only helped. Since 1994, when our parents died, responsibility for tending the graves has fallen on Sister and me.

I cannot help but think how different this cousin's life might have been had Uncle Fred brought her here to his mother rather than leaving her with her mother Alma's people. However good to her Grandma Emmy might have been, it is hard to picture her being able to provide a better scenario for the young girl. Grandma Emmy loved Leon, but she was not able to give him anything but a life of hard work and little companionship with folks his own age. For Barbara, had she landed on Greasy Creek the choices might have been slimmer still.

The fact that Uncle Fred gave Barbara to her aunt is not so surprising; Alma had died and he was desperate. That he never made any attempt to see her again is far more disappointing, for it flies in the face of everything I have believed about my family. Yes, I knew Momma's brothers were sorry in that periodically they would be out of a job, but I attributed that to their propensity for strong drink. I always assumed that allowing for their lapses due to alcohol, they took care of their wives and children as best they could. Indeed, of the three Mollette boys, I always thought of Uncle Fred—who married Laura and supported their son, Donnie, and her two boys—as the best family man. And I certainly thought I knew all my first cousins.

In attempting to trace her mother's heritage, however, Barbara's daughter, Diana, not only uncovered evidence of Leon (10/2/26–4/12/66), but also two other children of Uncle Fred and Alma. Though in a March 1943 letter, Momma alludes to "Stella Mae" having died of typhoid fever, I had no idea who Stella Mae (6/30/24–4/6/40) was until Diana obtained her death certificate stating she died of typhoid fever and toxemia. And Uncle Fred's trail doesn't end there. In addition to Stella Mae, apparently Alma gave birth to at least one other child, because Barbara's birth certificate states that Alma had four live births.

We know Stella Mae is buried in Offutt, ostensibly in the old Ward cemetery, where Alma is supposed to be buried. We know Leon is buried in the Mollette cemetery around on Buttermilk. We decide to save the trip to the graves at Offutt and Buttermilk for maybe next Decoration Day, and we vow to make inquiries about Barbara's other sibling, living or dead. Barbara says this experience of family-finding leaves her head swirling— so much all at once—and I think about how much Momma would enjoy this visit with her niece, like looking into a mirror.

Momma loved to visit with family, no matter what their circumstances were. Momma's cousin, Joanne Clement, was born out of wedlock in the late forties—no, I won't give particulars—and her father's parents took her off to Alabama to raise. Every five years or so, the Clements would visit Johnson County. Once Joanne got old enough to drive, she would slip off and come see Momma and other members of the family. Though illegitimacy in those days was considered shameful, Momma loved that girl as much as if everybody had owned up to everything, and she always lamented the fact that contact with Joanne was limited. I know in reason Momma would have been thrilled to see Barbara any time during her growing-up years had she known how to get in touch with her. Since circumstances conspired to delay that meeting until now, Sister and I are left to bring Momma back for Barbara. However many stories we share with our newly discovered cousin, the two of us together are not a patch on our luminous mother.

We are at a loss to explain why Momma would not have chosen to be buried here in the bosom of her own family rather than Daddy's. For a time after Daddy bought this home place, he and Momma talked of being buried here, but ultimately Daddy wanted to rest on Bob's Branch with his parents, maternal grandparents, and five brothers and sisters. If Momma's brothers and sisters—especially Uncle Burns—had been buried here at Three Forks, Momma might have wanted to bring us all here. When her siblings were buried in various locations, however, Momma chose to be with Daddy, Sister, me, and our husbands and children, who also plan to be buried on Bob's Branch. All this we discuss with Barbara and her family as we are picking up the grounds and shuffling among cars to head back to Two-Mile to another Decoration Day tradition—the family and the Holbrook reunion.

I pull into Gwen's crowded driveway, and in trying to avoid blocking half a dozen cars I promptly get stuck in the ditch. No problem though, Gwen's husband, Wallace, brings several strapping Wards to lift my car back to dry ground, and we head into the hug fest that's a natural part of the scene. Every family reunion is a testimony to the power of DNA, and we spend most of the day at Gwen's sighting the familiar Ward mouth, nose, or eyes mixed in a stew of Holbrooks, Prestons, Daniels, or Lord knows how many other families. No matter what has happened in the year before, the Holbrook reunion is always a highlight of my year, and Sister's, too.

Over the past forty years, I have shown up at the reunion reflecting my own mode of the moment—in full-out counterculture manner, freshly divorced, or with a new husband, stepchildren, and step-grandchildren. None of the aforementioned states of being are acceptable to many of the attendees, and all of us know it. For that one day, however, there is a moratorium on telling me I'll go through hell on a holler log for my worldly ways. I know the ones who are thinking that. What's more, they know that I know they are thinking that, but that is not at all what's important here. These are people who continue to love me despite the fact that in the opinion of some I am well on my way to Satan's big roaster. They love me—and will continue to love me—though not all of them necessarily agree with my politics, appreciate my use of certain language, counsel my occasional consumption of alcohol, or indeed approve of the way I choose to live out my life. Let me say again, *none of that matters*. For this day, they just accept me, play catch-up with me, kid around with me, and insist that I eat more food than any one human should be eating in a given week. Whatever problems we have had the rest of the year—even with each other—we're all here, and we're all welcome.

While the amount of food is staggering, the quality begs mention here, too. It is consistently extraordinary. Over the years, a significant number of my friends from away have encouraged me to consider myself quite the dumpling maker, but Kathleen Holbrook Daniel's dumplings make me reluctant to stew another chicken. Kat's dumplings are plump, light, soft, and palest yellow, unlike those pure white bread scraps that restaurants try to pass off as dumplings. And the desserts . . . mercy, the desserts! There is never enough room to try all the confections that weigh down the sweets table. We were late getting back on the road Saturday evening, because Sister was so busy copying yet another recipe—fruit pizza, I believe it was. Let me just say right now that if she-who-shall-remain-nameless does not send me the promised specifications for punchbowl cake, I plan to expose her as one who is stingy with same.

As splendid as the food may be, however, reunions are about more than food. They are a time of coming together in community, of tracing our individual paths from *was* to *is*. Reunions are also a time of rebirth, as we seek to rescue those long dead from the darkness and the distance of the past so that we may introduce them to the youngest ones. We pass along well-told tales from the last generation to the next as a way of reminding ourselves how much of what we have become took root right in this special ground. And so, each year we return from all over and gather together, within sight of the ghosts of our past, to mark the spot once more. Families are, after all, the mirror of our memories, for we alone can testify to our common experience. In the midst of all the sharing of food and facts and more than a little foolishness, we come to recognize that however many forks there may have been in the road leading from Two-Mile to wherever, the mutuality of our journey has never been in question.

In a Different Voice

It is spring in eastern Kentucky, and Gwen and I sit on her front porch, looking across the road beyond the creek bed at the doublewide that rests on Daddy and Momma's old house seat. The land where our home place stood looks flatter and smaller than I remember it, and the sycamore grove that once sheltered it is all but gone. Gwen and I agree that the boy who bought the place has done a lot to clear the land and bring it back to where it was some years ago. The house Daddy built in '56 burned more than ten years ago, and the yellow brick shell just sat there till the weeds about took it. Clearly, though, this latest owner has some pride in him, and Gwen and I agree that Pop Pop and Daddy would approve of what this new resident has done with the place. He has a young wife and baby, though Gwen's not sure where they came from or who their people are.

I ask Gwen if she recalls how proud we were of that new house Daddy built the summer after our sophomore year in high school. Both of us remember even the smallest details of that house. Everything in it was the best the four members of my family could pick out and Daddy could buy. It was the first place I'd ever lived in that didn't have linoleum on every floor in the house and no traffic pattern through the bedrooms. Momma, Daddy, Sister, and I had chosen each article that went into that house. All of us agreed on the shape of the faucets, the color of the bathroom fixtures (pink), right down to the shade of stain Daddy laid on the hardwood floors (blond), and the color of shag throw rugs and draperies to go in each room. The choice we were most proud of, though, was the color of the exterior asbestos shingles—they were pink, with the palest gray stripe in them. They cost a little more than plain white, but we thought they were worth it. Daddy would have broken his back to give us what we wanted, and my whole family loved pink, no denying that. In my remaining two years of high school, I would proudly tell people I met that my house was the only pink house between Paintsville and Inez.

Not much remains of the Two-Mile that was there when I lived in the only pink house between Paintsville and Inez. By the time I left that little pink house to go off to college in 1958, things had already begun to change. Gwen and I talk about how our mothers continued to grow vegetables and can them for two more decades, but neither of us can recall going to a bean-stringing after we went to high school. By the sixties, then, all of us were more likely to buy a blanket than make a quilt, and we hardly knew anybody who raised hogs or kept a milk cow. I'll bet the boy who owns that tasteful charcoal gray doublewide sitting on Daddy's house seat likely never lived in a house without a TV, and his young wife wouldn't know what to do with shuck beans if she had them. It would be interesting to talk with the two of them about their notions of bringing up their kids on Two-Mile. A friend my age who teaches in a junior high school back home tells me that his students never hoed corn, never slopped hogs, never pickled kraut, never milked a cow, never raked hay, never used a pitchfork, never plowed with a mule—never, never, never. I think that's sad . . . for them. If a person never learns what it feels like to do a necessary job, he also misses the joy of finishing. That makes it tough for such folks to see themselves as competent, contributing members of their family or community. I do not think it is an overstatement to say that I hated every second I spent doing physical work. I never felt, however, that I was assigned those tasks unfairly. I did not expect to enjoy my work, and since I was female, I never expected to work for pay. I grew up knowing, however, that for all of my life my days would be filled with tasks that had to be done, and I would be expected to do my share of them. I do not believe anybody who lived on Two-Mile when I did could have made any other meaning from our experience.

Gwen and I agree that one of the beliefs we passed from our parents to our children was the value of keeping close to family. Our generation didn't have much choice about that. Since a seemingly endless list of chores greeted us every morning, we lightened the load by working together and earned respect by doing a good job. As we swap stories of our children, we try to recall the last time we picked sallet and doubt whether either of us ever actually picked and cooked it for our families. We ponder whether any of our kids, nieces, or nephews would know purple dock from poke—then we question whether or not *we* would.

So, as Gwen and I enjoy her sweet iced tea and porch on this spring day, the trees are greening up along the river, and the Mountain Parkway is lined with blooming redbud trees. Before too long, Momma's lilacs will be blossoming in front of the gray doublewide there on the banks of what's left of Two-Mile Creek. They've logged the hillside, and the weeds have taken Pop Pop's strawberry patch. I think I'm lucky, in a way, to have my home all locked away, safe in my memories and not have to wade around in the reality of what's become of it every day.

Meanwhile, Momma and Daddy's last house, close to town, belongs to Sister and me. But it's not home and never has been. I feel most at home on the porch of Gwen's cabin up the hollow or on the Bob's Branch graveyard, up there with Daddy and Momma and other family members who loved me and gave me a "comin' home" feeling for the hills that I can't seem to rid myself of. Then again, that "comin' home" feeling is one more thing that my generation has passed along to our children.

When Momma and Daddy died, Sister and I did not set a tombstone above their graves; we put in a stone bench. Though we engraved the vital statistics of their births and deaths on that bench, we could not begin to put on there what we wanted to say—what we thought folks who'd never met them should know about our parents. As it was with most members of my family, I was a babe in arms my first visit to that Bob's Branch graveyard, as was my baby sister. Each time we open the gate on the top of that ridge, Sister and I tease each other that we were carried there on our first visit and we'll be carried there on our last. We decided to mark Momma's and Daddy's graves with a bench rather than a headstone, because we wanted folks visiting the graveyard to be able to sit and look out over that river bottom valley. They can even sit there and read a little of their Bible if they're of a mind to. Mostly, however, we hope folks will stop and rest for a moment to recall some long-ago Decoration Day and the stories told them by those no longer able to tell the tales.

I can recall days when our car couldn't make it all the way up that steep bank, so we'd drive as far as we could. Then, with Daddy, Momma, and Pop Pop carrying the heavy flowers while I hefted an armload of smaller ones, Grandma Emmy would hold Sister's hand as we made our way up the hill. As our laughter rang out across that valley, we were hardly ever the only family on the way to pay our respects. Usually we'd meet somebody coming down the hill; still others would greet us at the top. Sometimes somebody would even sing a song. We were at home among our people, listening as stories of those resting there brought them back to us, still vibrant and alive.

Whether we want to or not, most of us pass along our values to our children as surely as we pass along our DNA. Heredity or environment, who cares? I inherited my mother's concern for cleanliness, love of books, and tendency toward hypochondria as certainly as I got her green eyes. And my "family first" feeling? Well, that's there, too, though I may not be able to specify the chromosome it rode in on. Momma and Daddy—Life and Grace—did not leave a big footprint on this earth, not in terms of pure protoplasm, they didn't. They only produced me and then Sister. Sister has a boy and a girl and I have one son, so you could pretty much wipe out all physical evidence of us in a minute. Still, it's not all about DNA, this passing-along business.

My boy is a bright, good-looking—just outstanding in every way—thirty-something lawyer in Washington, D.C. Okay, I'm his mother, so maybe I'm a little over-the-top here, but all those descriptives have added up to a lifestyle that is just about as busy as any other successful, city-dwelling, twenty-first-century bachelor. In addition to girlfriends, soft-ball teams, volunteer work, and house restoration, Brett Preston Scott regularly works sixty- to eighty-hour weeks at his job. Because of all those commitments, he doesn't get to Kentucky nearly as often as any of our family would like. Oh, he's always at my place in Montana along with Sister and her family at Thanksgiving, and we still gather in Kentucky at Christmastime, but other than that he only gets back to Kentucky every couple of months. It's a ten-hour drive, which means he tries to make it in eight.

In the early morning, Brett loads his duffel bag, CDs, golf clubs, and a cooler filled with Pepsi into the green Saab convertible that his Grandma Preston thought was so sharp because the hardtop automatically tucks into the trunk. He negotiates pre-rush hour D.C. traffic and takes to the highway, hoping to stop only for gasoline and restroom breaks in the

West Virginia mountains so he can get to central Kentucky before dark. That wouldn't be much of a problem—interstate all the way—except Brett has a couple of obligatory stops to make.

Once he maneuvers the Saab through Charleston and crosses the Kanawha River, he is on the lookout for the Value City exit some thirty miles down I-64. When his grandparents, both Preston and Scott, were still alive, he would stop at Value City and buy them new lawn chairs, or he'd pick up some good-looking rose bushes or geraniums to take to each of his grandmothers. Before all his grandparents died, he'd take a couple of those hydrangeas or whatever to Momma, plant them in her yard about fifty winding, hill-country miles south of I-64, and stay for supper with her and his grandpa. After supper he'd drive through the mountains another fifty miles to Pikeville and spend the night with his grandmother Scott. The next morning he'd plant the flowers he brought while his grandma fried up sausage and apples and made him some saw-mill gravy and biscuits before he left for Frankfort. His visits with hill-country grandparents yielded at least one distinct advantage: I'll bet my boy makes the best sawmill gravy and biscuits of any bachelor in the District—better than mine even.

Brett Preston Scott was lucky to have had grandparents who were around until his adulthood, who lived to see him succeed in college and law school and become self-supporting. Though his grandma Scott—a fervent Church of Christ member—was concerned about the Bible's statement condemning lawyers (Luke 11:45-52, "Woe unto you lawyers," is interpreted by strict fundamentalists to mean that lawyers cannot enter the kingdom of God), all four grandparents could not have been prouder of their grandson, and he was close to each of them until they died—so close, in fact, that his commitment to them did not end when they went to rest on top of the ridges of eastern Kentucky.

Though Mallie and Opal Scott died in '86 and '91 and he lost both Preston grandparents in '94, Brett Preston Scott's trip to central Kentucky continues to be interrupted. Just west of Huntington, he turns off the interstate onto U.S. 23 and winds southward through the hills to just west of Paintsville, where he turns onto KY 40. Then he steers the Saab through the back streets of Paintsville, crosses the Big Sandy River, and continues through the River Narrows, until just before "Grandpa's place" he cuts left off the main road toward Bob's Branch. A couple of miles down the road, he passes the rehab center on the left and all the fine houses that have gone up in his lifetime—some even built by Grandpa Preston. Then it's up over the railroad track, and he pulls off the road on the right and gets out to lift the heavy chain off the hook, open the gate, drive through it, then back to rehook the chain before heading up the steep bank to visit his grandparents one more time. In the floor behind the passenger seat rest several hydrangeas or lilies, some of which will be left here. Others are destined for Pike County and the grandparents Scott.

I had no idea that my son made this pilgrimage alone until I spent the year just past in eastern Kentucky and was surprised one day to find fresh flowers on Momma's and Daddy's graves. I knew that Sister and I made random spontaneous visits to the Bob's Branch graveyard, but I had no idea our children did.

My son spent his childhood in central Kentucky, lived for three or four years each in Massachusetts, Mississippi, Idaho, and Montana, and has worked in Washington, D.C., since 1988. Technically, he has no ties to eastern Kentucky—just the most important connection of all. No matter where we legally reside, this family lives and dies in eastern Kentucky . . . in Bob's Branch, and Greasy, and Two-Mile. We are family—first, last, and always. And we don't just go back nearly two hundred years in eastern Kentucky, we also carry forward our beliefs and our stories, wherever we may scatter.

Just as Life's and Grace's history did not begin on their dates of birth, neither did it end when the breath went out of them. Indeed the history of this family is extended every Christmas and Decoration Day—and all the times in between—when Sister and I and our children trek to the top of that ridge in Bob's Branch to pay our respects. First we clean the graves, replacing the flowers left from our last visit with fresh ones, sometimes putting in a new rosebush or some iris or lily bulbs. Then we linger a while on the stone bench inscribed PRESTON that marks Life's and Grace's last address on this earth. I think it is significant that my son visits that graveyard more often than some of my friends' children visit their living grandparents. The next generation's graveyard trips indicate to me that this family not only knows where we came from, we know where we're going to end up—right there next to Life and Grace.